Five Woodbines for Dad

A Memoir

Doreen Steadman

ISBN: 9798566532448

Cover design by: Art Painter
Library of Congress Control Number: 2018675309
Printed in the United States of America

Dedicated to my Dad.

Contents

Joan And Doreen

Part One

Prologue

'**O**f course, I come from North London originally', I find myself asserting yet again as prelude to the mantra-like recital about to follow; 'Yes, from Kentish Town, then we lived in Edmonton for a while before moving to Hackney. I only came to live here after I was married...not that I wanted to, 'I add, by way of denial, having it seems moved reluctantly from North to East London and beyond, by degree.

Since my confidant is often a fellow senior citizen, someone who almost without exception hails from the East End 'proper' i.e. Bethnal Green, Canning Town, Strafford or Bow. There's little doubt (if I'm honest), that disclosure of my own North London roots simply amounts to a subtle form of post code 'one-upmanship'. And, (almost by default), it also serves as an introduction to that which I have laboured over long and, with much relief, finally completed, one of those trips down memory lane; commonly referred to as a 'memoir'. A link with the past, which although it covers seventy-five years (and has its moments), it is in effect the memoir of a nobody.

Roots

O nce upon a time and on a certain day in 1933 was when it all began, not when I was born in April 1930, but when I was going on 3 years old and standing beside my mother on the steps of a big house. A cold day, a winters afternoon perhaps for the sky is streaked with red; then a vague recollection of the coalman coming into view with his horse and cart, whose arrival, no doubt, we had been waiting for. Another early memory, only this time I'm sitting at the bottom of the basement stairs while my mother is speaking to another lady (this would have been our landlady Mrs Main). Sitting beside me is a big dog and I have my arm around his neck, which he doesn't seem to mind. Later I try to wash his face (or muzzle) with a flannel of sorts (and have lived to tell the tale). A very vague recollection...that's of sitting in a wooden go-cart while a boy gives me a ride...round and round the garden.

Before we moved to Edmonton my only other 'awareness of being' concerns a bus journey...of the time we went to Croydon to see my mother's sister Aunt Mary. 'How many miles to Babylon? three score and ten. Shall I get there by candlelight? Yes, and back again'. Maybe there had been other nursery rhymes read aloud to me by my mother during the night time bus journey from Kentish Town to Croydon; for some inexplicable reason however, the bright lights on the bus, the darkness outside, together with the rhyme itself, are all that the memory has retained. Nothing at all recalled about my little sister although she must have made up the trio of those night-time travellers.

In Aunt Mary's house there is a big kitchen with lots of pots and pans, it seems very untidy. One day we went on a visit to the airport, no detail of it remains whatsoever. The reason for my mother's sudden 'takes off' to her sister's house that night? More than likely a domestic flare-up.

Less than an hour's journey by over ground train and a ten-minute walk from Gospel Oak Station brings me into Queens Crescent. Number twenty-eight is the house I'm looking for, so I keep to the left-hand side of the street. How typically London are these tall Victorian houses. Soon I will be standing before one and reviving my very first memories. But where is it? Number twenty-eight appears to be missing...in fact there is a sizeable gap in the long row of dwelling on this side. On closer inspection, it appears that the apparent gap has in fact been filled. Standing several yards back from the traditional houses, as if hardly daring to intrude, a block of three storeyed modern flats.

I learnt later, from a local resident, that the old block of houses had been demolished during the mid-seventies. Perhaps the 'old timers' had been damaged during the war.

As I walked back through the market end of Queens crescent and towards the station, I remember thinking; 'This is where my mother did her shopping all those years ago. Butchers, bakers, greengrocers; here she would have pushed her pram with my little sister and I cosily tucked up within (for Mum was a great wrapper-up) ...I'm walking in her footsteps now. It was as though I'd come full circle and the thought was somehow comforting.

For my mother; Bridget Mary Fitzgerald, accessing her early roots, had she ever been given the opportunity, would have entailed crossing the Irish Sea and journeying back to Cashel, County Tipperary; the place where she was born on the First of August 1900. Bridget, known as Biddy to her friends and acquaintances, Mum to Joan and me but always Cherie to my father, was the second eldest of four children. To begin with the children's lives had been comparatively carefree. My mother often spoke of their wandering all around the green fields of County Cashel. Of the times when a kindly farmer's wife would supply them with warm milk and freshly baked bread to see them on their way...the best of times for Bridget Mary and her siblings. In the winter of 1913, their mother died of pneumonia, thus leaving four children orphaned. John Fitzgerald, their father had died of lung disease some years earlier. They were now in the care of their Uncle Jim who lived in the same household.

I'm not sure if this had been the Uncle who had fallen foul of the IRA after enlisting in the British Army during the First World War. 'They came to get him' said my mother, 'but my sister Lena went for them with a broom and they went away'. Over the years, my sister and I came to hear of what had caused the IRA's anger, including the Irish Potato famine and the apparent persecution of the Southern Irish throughout history-especially of the Fitzgerald's, one-time Earls of Munster. Later, we heard of the Dublin uprising and of the notorious Black and Tans.

So, all in all there hadn't been much love lost between my mother and the English. However, with the outbreak of the Second world war came extenuating circumstances. After 'doing her bit' working in a Munitions Factory, enduring the Blitz of 1940/41, bearing the absence of her children for four years due to evacuation; mum would almost have been at one with the English, for a time anyway, and forgiven them just a little.

One of my mother's first employments, when she had come to England in 1918 after the conclusion of the First World war, had been at Boarding School for Young ladies in Broadstairs, Kent. The strictness of the rule, with regard to the pupils table manners, had been particularly noted at the time. This included the use of cutlery and the correct way in which to consume soup; 'always drink your soup from the side of the spoon, don't put it in your mouth and remember to ask permission before leaving the table', my sister and I were frequently reminded. My father was equally strict about table manners.

My parents had both met while both were working at one of the smaller hotels in Park Lane. I believe that this had been in the early twenties. My mother was a chambermaid at the time and my father Head valet. Prior to their meeting, however, it would have been her sister Mary who had kept mum company from time to time, especially when it came to sight-seeing up in town. There had been one occasion, apparently, when the London Underground's unfamiliar and rather complex system had the sisters literally going around in circles and wondering why there appeared to be so many underground stations with the same names.

Aunt Mary, my mother's sister, was employed as Resident Housekeeper to a Gentleman who lived in Croydon. The house in St. Saviour's Road was also home to one of those musical instruments quite popular during the twenties, or thereabouts, called a pianola. 'When biddy came to visit', Aunt Mary had told Joan and I, though many years after mum's death (sadly the sisters had been estranged for several years), 'she would choose a piece of classical music and 'ghost play' it, as if in a world of her own'. Maybe the long-term rift between the sisters had something to do with that late-night bus ride to Croydon way back in 1933; a first and last trip to see Aunt Mary.

My mother, I believe, was a frustrated artist of sorts. She had the most beautiful long, tapering fingers; delicate hands that had never been designed for rough work, now worn and lined by the household chores (which she always hated). In other words, and perhaps partly due to her Irishness, mum was a romantic.

Her brother Jimmy, who came over to England in the early thirties to seek work, had the same long tapering fingers. I don't remember Uncle Jimmy, although he stayed with us for a time when we lived in Kentish Town. However, there's an old sepia photograph that shows him seated in a studio chair, one hand resting on his knee, the other on the chair's arm. He has the hands of a gentleman, the looks of a young James Joyce. He was neither of course and the only work obtainable in those depression years, would have been that of labouring. Even so, it appears that Uncle Jimmy had energy enough for more pleasurable pursuits. 'He loved dancing', my mother told me once. 'If there was any dance music on the wireless, he'd pick you up, hold you high in the air and go dancing all around the room'. Jimmy also went out dancing occasionally, which no doubt had infuriated my father, who had no time for 'dancing men'. For Dad was a no-nonsense ex-soldier. A down to earth, practical type of person. A born organiser.

My mother and father's contrasting personalities might well have been complimentary to each other. Unfortunately, this was not the case. Dad wanted everything spick and span around the house, but Mum was not at all enthusiastic with regard to household chores. This lark of spit and polish would often lead to open nit-picking, which, in turn, resulted in angry words on both sides. Pre-war recollections surface here: my mother's bitter reaction at her task master's call to duty. The tearing up of old photographs before throwing them on the fire. Later, perhaps the next day, the sound of my mother singing, comforting herself with a medley of wistful Irish songs as she set about scrubbing, dusting and polishing with a vengeance.

Edward Charles Tompkins, commonly known as Ted, was born on the 13th of September 1893, the second eldest of five children. He would have been about ten years old when his father took off with another woman, leaving his wife and family destitute. My grandmother now left to raise five children single-handed and as best she could, an Edwardian single parent without any Social Security back up. A bleak prospect made even more so by the local constabulary when she had gone to report her husband as 'missing'...'well then, you'd better run along to the workhouse, hadn't you?' had been there kindly advice; instead of which, my grandmother had gone out to work as a domestic help and taken in other people's washing as a side-line.

Not that my father had ever spoken to my sister and I about

his father's desertion and his mother's sore plight, instead we had been regaled with tales about his boyhood. He'd learned to swim on being thrown into the local canal by his friends. He didn't like going to school, so when his mother deposited him at the main school gate, he'd make his escape by another. What he hadn't thought to mention though, was how upset his poor mother had been every time she went to visit him at the boy's remand home, where he'd been sent as punishment for bunking off school once too often.

Such detail and other family information had been revealed by his elder sister, our Aunt Bett, thirteen years old when she had been allowed to leave school in order to help her mother with the youngest children, the baby only months old. Elizabeth would have had good cause to remember the circumstances which had resulted in that sudden leap from childhood and into the adult world. For my father, however, it could have been a different matter. For any instances of hardship relating to his boyhood and early youth would have paled into insignificance when set against the horrors and hardships, which he and countless other young men of his generation, had encountered while fighting for king and Country in the First World war of 1914-1918.

Such fraught experiences would not have been at all suitable for the ears of two little girls...a somewhat filtered version of my father's service with the royal horse Artillery presented instead, together with many of those famous war songs. Dad knew them all. When it came to stories about the war, there was one in particular that appealed to Joan and I. The one about the wolves 'with their eyes gleaming in the darkness as they ran alongside the horse drawn convoy of gun carriages on the forest pathway one night. This had been in Salonika ...or was it Macedonia? Since my father had been an Outrider as well as a Gunner, this could well have been a rather unnerving experience at the time!

It was only later that we had come to learn of what else had happened to the rider and his horse, during the Battle of the Somme I believe. Both had fallen into a large shell hole and, for a time, half buried in all the mud. Now and then my father's equestrian past was apt to come to the fore. This was when my mother had washed our hair and then rough dried it. At this point Dad would take over the proceedings. Standing a few feet away, he would flap the towel briskly up and down, so as to create an efficient breeze. A method which had no doubt been used in order to cool down sweat-drenched horses, both animal and rider having been fortunate enough to have survived the day's awful combat.

The war had left my father with various health problems. Every year without fail he went down with a short bout of Malaria; many of his comrades had died of the disease. Dad's time as a Gunner had left him completely deaf in one ear...'walk on the other side' he would say, after we'd been chatting away without any response. A good character reference on leaving the Army had no doubt assisted him to obtain employment...once as waiter at the Athenaeum Club. With his upright bearing, polished shoes and trilby hat, not to mention his no-nonsense approach to life in general, it might well be said of my father; 'He was an old soldier par excellence'.

I have no idea at all of why we left Kentish Town and went to live at my Uncle's house in Edmonton. A most unwise decision on my father's part as it so turned out, although he must have had his reasons at the time.

Uncle Albert was my father's youngest brother, a skilled cabinet maker by trade. He and his wife (Aunt Emmy) were childless, so their orderly home had never been subjected to the wear and tear of family. Our imminent arrival must have caused Aunt Emmy a considerable amount of concern. Private lodgers were another matter and the upper part of the house, situated in a quiet back turning at the rear of the North Middlesex Hospital, was often let out to nurses. The lesser deal for the new arrivals was a medium sized, downstairs room; a lounge which had been hastily converted to a bed-sit, now occupied by a large brass railed double bed, a convertible armchair (which also doubled as a single bed) and somehow or other, squeezed into a corner, a small dining table and two chairs. Lastly, there was the doubtful pleasure for my mother of sharing a very small kitchen with her brother-in-law's wife, who happened to be an exceedingly house-proud Yorkshire Wife. Aunt Emmy was a cook, employed I believe by a North London college or similar establishment and therefore absent for several hours during the day, remaining blissfully unaware of the antics which her little nieces-in-law got up to occasionally. The very first of these having taken place a few days after their arrival.

Having noticed, almost at once, the lovely thick carpet on Aunt Emmy 's staircase and how, very easily, a large wooden tray of hers slid down over it, from top to bottom. It would seem that the idea was to give my little sister a ride and as she was still at crawling stage, it hadn't taken much effort to place her in 'take-off' position at the head of the stairs. More than likely, it had been the lovely thick carpet itself that lessened my little sister's bruises on having parted company with her makeshift sledge. Time has mercifully blotted out her yells and the well-deserved smack I'd no doubt received from my mother. It must have been about late 1933 when we commenced our stay as family lodgers at 3, Parkston Avenue, Edmonton. Late 1934 or early 1935 when we left.

'Odds and ends' go to make up my recollections of those 12 (?) months. A jumble of people, places, small things and brown leather gaiters that buttoned up the sides, right up to my knees. Dolly Mixtures, marzipan, Easter Eggs from the corner shop, which came apart to reveal a magic ring, a jewel of coloured glass and the yo yo which rolled under Aunt Emmy's kitchen cabinet and was never seen again.

One day my mother and Aunt Emmy took me too see Susanah of the Mounties at a big cinema in Edmonton High Street-one of Shirley Temple's early films. But I didn't like sitting in the dark... I wanted to go home...a temper tantrum later which, no doubt, put paid to any further film going.

Aunt Emmy's lodgers came and went during our stay. Once there had been a little boy whose parents were renting upstairs. Sometimes he came down and played in the garden with Joan and myself. By mutual consent on one occasion, he and I decided to swap clothes, but after I donned his dungarees and handed over my cotton frock, boy lodger had changed his mind and decided to go on an impulsive streak around the garden path instead...causing a degree of consternation within the grown-up ranks. I had probably been admonished for disclosing my vest and knickers. The boy from upstairs for disclosing everything.

Uncle Albert's shed at the bottom of the garden, home to the lawn mower and other household heavy tools, also provided a parking place for the large double-seated pushchair Mum used when we accompanied her on shopping trips to the High Street, a fair distance away and tiring for small legs. And what a boon it was, that particular pushchair with the wide hood, enabling two small people seated side by side and well hidden, to enjoy a private picnic: a lump of cheese and several slices of ham: which had been meant for their Daddy's supper that evening. Had the instigator of that small crime received a smack or merely a scolding? But memory proves a blank here.

Though 'little sister' was only accessory after the crime... follower of 'bossy boots' big sister, now and then Joanie did her own thing.

Worms seemed to have a certain fascination for my little sister when she was at toddler stage. Fortunately, there had been no intention to consume but a compulsion to try and put them through Aunt Emmy's wooden clothes mangle, with little success it has to be admitted. Many a worm's life had been spared by Joanie's inability to turn the heavy wooden rollers.

Only one other misdemeanour to tell tale on and this concerns an episode relating to the gradual disappearance of Aunt

Emmy's silver Apostle teaspoons. The mystery came to be solved in due course when I'd witnessed my little sister depositing a couple of Apostles in the drain hole by the kitchen door. 'You probably put me up to it' says the accused, 'definitely not' say I. This had been a piece of solo initiative on her part which left big sister blame free for once. Putting spoons down drains, even by proxy, wouldn't have appealed to me as 'adventure' at the advanced age of four years old.

There must have been times when Aunt longed for the restoration of her childless well-orientated household. That she and my mother finally 'fell out' is really not surprising...a blunt outspoken Northerner on the one hand and an easily offended, quick tempered Irishwoman on the other. A disaster waiting to happen.

1934-1935: The pinnacle perhaps of those 'depression' thirties years, entailing mass employment for many workers through no fault of their own. For a short time, my father had come within this category. A situation which would have involved having to apply for dole money; even the term itself bears connotations of begging...perhaps my father had decided to postpone the humiliating prospect for as long as possible.

Whatever the reason, it was my mother who made the initial visit to our local Relief Office, of that I'm quite sure because she took me with her. Of that which took place at the time I remember also...

There was a man seated behind a desk or table. For a time, he and my mother were talking, and she was crying. I'd never seen her crying before, maybe I wanted to cry with her, perhaps I did, though I have no clear recollection of my own reactions then. Later though, many years later, when as a teenager I had gradually become aware of the political world and its social history, only then did I come to recall that particular incident with clarity. The memory of my mother's tears and the shouting official who'd caused them. A prime example of injustice...the oppression of the weak by the powerful. Not a tale told by the

victim but a very personal recollection by the witness herself...
a first impression of the kind unlikely to be forgotten, even by
a four-year-old. Deep enough to have put in place the chip o n
my shoulder that has never quite disappeared. And, I have to
say, a recollection not entirely without it's advantages when I
became involved in political arguments with my Westminster
office colleague's way back in the late forties' as a bolshie type
eighteen-year-old standing my ground, the only Red amongst
the Blues who were castigating Nye Bevan, meanwhile extolling
the virtues of the pre-war status quo as various instances were
fondly recalled; about how lovely everything had been before
the war. At which point, my own less than lovely memory of
the shouting official and my mother's tears proved a valuable
trump card, which I'd no hesitation in playing. It's a wonder I
didn't get the sack.

When we left Parkstone Avenue, either in late 1934 or early
1935, one thing for certain, our exodus took place not with a
whimper but a rather loud bang; the culmination, no doubt, of
all the pent-up antipathy between my mother and Aunt Emmy.
A one-off drama staged in the hallway at the point of our departure; a brief episode of screaming, shouting and hair pulling by
the ladies and the strange sight of my father jumping on to his
brother's back...it was here that the fracas, as far as I'm able to
recall, came to an end, more than likely because of my childish
distress.

New Beginnings

Hackney 1935. Even though it meant having a cooker on the landing, the fairly spacious flat in Graham Road must have been a pleasant change for my mother, no longer being obliged to share a tiny kitchen, endure cramped living conditions, or for that matter, face a long trek to the High Street in order to do the family shopping. Our new surroundings were a world away from Parkstone Avenue; that quiet back street in Edmonton we'd grown accustom to. Adding to the interest of our new environment here on a busy main road, were the comings and goings of the number 77 trams, which came clattering along at intervals throughout the day and late into the evening. Fleeting recollections here, of laying in the in the darkness, drifting in and out of sleep, the rumblings of passing tram, reflections of its lights on the ceiling.

'Trams like these once ran on special rails in the middle of the road', I went at length to explain while on a recent visit to the Transport Museum in Covent Garden, accompanied by one of my grandsons, meanwhile quite forgetting that this young man had often travelled abroad with his parents by the latest in air travel. His eyes glazed over briefly, after which he resumed his pre-lecture activities by running around the museum looking for even more buttons to press.

Not long after our arrival in Hackney that year (1935), a Royal celebration was about to take place: The Silver Jubilee of their Majesties King George and Queen Mary. Union Jacks and bunting were to be seen everywhere. Apart from which, the only happening that I'm able to remember, with regard to the Silver Jubilee, concerns my father and a golden cardboard crown; leaning from our upstairs window at what looked to be a rather dangerous angle, determined to fix it to the wall outside no matter what, the loyal subject himself having opted for this somewhat challenging task rather than the mere suspension of a Union Jack from the window sill itself

The reason for our move to Hackney had been because of my father's new job, which was as manager/assistant in a working men's café, situated in Morning Lane. This very lucky break for my father had come via the 'family grapevine'. Aunt Bette, already employed, herself, by the café's owner (as a domestic help I believe), on hearing of the vacancy, had lost no time in putting a good word in for her brother, prior to which he'd been unemployed for several weeks. Due to a fire at the Engineer's Club in Coventry Street where my father had been employed as a porter cum valet, the premises had been badly damaged, the residents no longer in situ and all staff now out of work.

As far as my mother had been concerned, I'm sure that there must have been times when her husband's latest job had been seen as yet another step down in status, after all, he'd once been Head Valet at a hotel in Park Lane. But regardless of status or location, in actual fact, my father was ideally suited to his new occupation; one which required organisational skills: being up with the lark every morning, absolute honesty and the ability to carve slices from a leg of ham with the utmost finesse, causing my mother, when she'd been helping him out at the café occasionally, to accuse him of being a 'Boss Man'. 'Give the poor devils a thicker slice' she would say, her concern being for the 'down and out' looking clientele.

'I want to talk politics, not play darts, had been my father's response when my mother had once suggested that he join the Labour Party, which at the time had been conveniently situated a short distance away in Graham Road. But it was here, in this working men's café, with its sturdy marbled topped tables and captive diners, where my father would have been in his element. If, by chance, his political observations came to be challenged during these discussions there was always a trump card available (Dad always related this with a twinkle in his eye); 'Ah' he would enquire of the cheeky customer 'but have you read Hansard?)

In 1935, there had been yet another cause for celebtion, if not for myself or nationally, then for my mother. In   the April of that year and shortly after my fifth birthday I started school at Wilton Road Infant, which   occasion there had no doubt been a few tears shed...the same anxieties felt as those of my fellow 'first timers', What takes precedence, however, as far as memory is concerned, is an incident which occurred enroute to school a school a few days later, leaving a painful egg-sized lump on my forehead. Dawdling along behind my mother and sister, either in a dream or having had my attention temporarily diverted, I collided face first with a lamp-post. The uproar which had then ensued, I can only imagine now. A hysterical five-year-old wondering 'what hit me?' being taken along by her school afterwards remains a void. Such an unexpected jolt to the upper visage having been 'sufficient the day itself' apparently. Once I had settled into school and after I had come to the realisation that Mum's ongoing threats of 'I'm going to tell your teacher', when I'd been particularly naughty at home, were but empty ones. I believe that on the whole I quite enjoyed the experience. Anyway, I really liked the idea of having my very own writing slate and coloured chalks, also, my own box of various shaped building bricks of shiny wood; especially appealing; the small tin of brightly coloured beads and threading cord. That was in the infant's reception. However, the next class up meant having to do horrible sums for the first time and a stricter teacher...the humiliating experience of being called to task, standing out front by the blackboard correcting the letter or digit I had written in reverse. The kindest teacher, in a subsequent class, had been Miss Watson. Every Friday a special treat for her pupils, several boxes of assorted jam tarts to be shared amongst the class. I recall this classroom for another reason; being given a lesson in left and right-left hand nearest the wall by my desk. A mental image of this being the only way I'm able to remember which is which should I be called upon to do so at short notice.

Certain recollections about Graham Road, the family in the basement, Mr and Mrs Bradley and their two daughters...school-girls, one dark haired and the other fair. Mrs Bradley; slightly built, grey haired well before her time, no doubt, due to fam-ily circumstances. Mr Bradley himself; a stoutish, rather jolly bed bound gentleman. He had a wind-up gramophone on a table near his bed. Sometimes he would play one of his Music Hall type records for our entertainment: 'On Ilkley Moore B'tat, 'Two Lovely Black Eyes' and 'Ain't it Grand to be Bloomin' well Dead?' My sister didn't like Mr Bradley and only remem-bers that he had a bald head. I thought that he was quite nice though, possibly because he was a 'show-off' like myself. The two middle floors of the house were unoccupied when we first moved in. On one occasion this had been to my advantage. This was when my mother happened to be chasing me through the house, wielding a wooden coat hanger and in a great temper after I'd given her some 'cheek'. Having reached the ground floor well ahead of her, I dashed into the nearest room, diving im-mediately under a large dining table, I now found myself com-pletely in the dark.

The room was heavily curtained and now I couldn't see a thing. 'I know you're in there', I heard my mother saying, reminding me that 'darkness' was my friend, the enemy, outside in the hallway. However scary my bolt-hole under the table, I stayed quiet as a mouse, scarcely daring to breath until I heard Mum's footsteps as she returned to the top of the house. I decided to stay out for a while though, knowing full well that by the time I'd given myself up, my mother's fiery temper would have com-pletely fizzled out.

Jealousy and sibling's rivalry had no doubt been due, in part, to my attention seeking behaviour. My little sister having been seriously ill and taken to hospital with severe Bronchitis and then with Scarlet Fever, I would have needed much reassurance from both parents on her return home. Parents at that time, only allowed weekend visiting.

There would come a time when big sister, herself, became the recipient of much attention; rather more than she'd expected, or indeed, welcomed.

During the thirties, most elementary schools, in response to a much-needed programme of child welfare, came to receive annual visits from the school Doctor and Dentist. 'Nitty Norah', of course, came more frequently. There were also lessons on hygiene from time to time when I attended Wilton Road Infant School. We were encouraged to cut out pictures of toothpaste advertisements from various magazines. These, no doubt, would have been given us by our teacher. Later, we were all presented with free samples of Gibbs toothpaste and a brand-new toothbrush. Lovely pink toothpaste, in a round tin. It had a nice spearmint flavour...almost good enough to eat.

The only real recollections that I have of 'Nitty Norah' visits, seems to be after I started school at St John's in Mare Street Hackney. And when Joan and I had been transferred from Wilton Road infants...I'd never seen the actual results of 'Nitty Norah's' victims, until then. I felt quite sorry, for those unfortunate ones who'd been required to have heads almost shaven or cut very short indeed.

Their remaining locks doused in Lysol at the cleansing station, also, the smell hung around for ages. Being one of those irritating species of children who, despite their adult piers attempts at keeping the little ones in the dark, possible to allay their fears, can always sense that there's something going on, something being kept secret. If only my mother or even my teacher had mentioned what was about to take place that afternoon, during my first term at Wilton Road; namely a visit from the school doctor. On passing one of the classrooms on the way to the lavatory during the morning, I'd noticed that several desks had been removed and the space taken up by a few screened cubicles. There was a big white enamel bowl and a jug on one of the desks. And I felt sick with apprehension. What was it all for? What were they going to do to us? I wanted to go home. 'I've got a headache; can I go home?' I asked my teacher, 'Certainly not! Go and sit down,' said Miss Morgan. I may well have wondered 'what are they going to do to us?', as a result of being examined by the school doctor, accompanied of course by my mother, who was probably just as worried as her nervous offspring. It appeared that I was under-nourished and anaemic (no blood tests), diagnosis possibly due to my pale colouring. I was also short-sighted, furthermore I would need to have my tonsils removed, as they were enlarged. Tonsils removal was the cure for all ills, in the early thirties, if you were unlucky: adenoids as well.

For my apparent anaemia, I was prescribed iron medicine which came in a very large bottle, had the appearance of urine and tasted vile. A sweet immediately after swallowing it was scant consolation. I didn't mind the odd spoonful of jelly-like glucose though, that wasn't too bad at all. When my mother dispensed with both iron and glucose eventually and purchased a big jar of Cod Liver Oil and Malt instead, taking medicine was no problem. As to my awful wire-framed glasses, they didn't last long either. After a visit to Moorfields Eye Hospital to have my eyes thoroughly tested, the verdict was that I wasn't short-sighted after all. My enlarged tonsils though, that was another matter; a date set for their removal. But I wouldn't have to travel far; the German hospital was only five minutes away. In fact, you could see it quite clearly from our back garden in Graham Road.

Carrying an attaché case, which contained my new pyjamas, face flannel and toothbrush, feeling a bit sick in my tummy, being assured by Mum that I had nothing to worry about, I held her hand and tried to be brave. 'You'll be getting some lovely ice cream afterwards', which was something to look forward to.

27

When all the drama was over (there had been some concern because for days after I refused to speak; having been sick and noticed blood, I decided to keep my mouth shut in case more came out), I was escorted home by Mum and taken downstairs to see Mr and Mrs Bradley who made a great fuss of me.

The following year we moved yet again. Due to complaints from the new tenants who moved into the empty flat below. They could hear our footsteps overhead. Since most of the floors were carpet-less, this would have been unavoidable. Rather than have us all creeping around, my father chose the most practical way of dealing with the matter, rather too hastily perhaps.

After our roomy upstairs living quarters, the basement flat in Greenwood Road, just around the corner, must have been yet another disappointment for my mother, added to which, there had been the non-arrival of our beds by late evening. The mattresses turned up eventually enabling us to sleep on the floor that night but the row which erupted beforehand was almost inevitable. They always scared me as a child; these domestic upheavals. All the shouting between my parents. On my mother's side there would no doubt have been much in the way of bitter invective with regard to her husband's shortcomings; brief storms which blew themselves out before long. Not that these would have bothered my little sister at all, or so she tells me, which is probably true.

During the 'Little Blitz' which commenced in late January 1944, when the cacophony as we took shelter in our landlady's basement sitting-room...ack ack gunfire and nearby exploding bombs; enough to shake the house on it's very foundations, and I, shaking in my very shoes, Joan often slept through it all on Mrs Green's Victorian chaise-lounge, having the enviable gift of being able to switch-off in the face of chaos.

In 1936 of course, there was much going on in the world at large, rendering domestic confrontations of little importance in the scheme of things. Abroad: the ongoing rise of Nazism in Germany: burning of books and the increasing persecution of the Jews. In Spain, the outbreak of the Civil War. On the home front, much unrest: mass unemployment in Wales and the North of England. A hunger march and a miner's strike. Not to mention the Fascist gathering of Oswald Mosley's followers in Ridley Road. Such goings on in general, no doubt, evoking much in the way of political discourse at the café in Morning Lane.

But we as children then would have been living safely in our own little world. Various popular songs of the thirties seem to have been written with us in mind: The Teddy Bears Picnic, Three Little Fishes, Little Drummer Boy, My Little Lady Make Belief. On the wireless there was Children's Hour with its presenter Uncle Mac, who always sounded so kind; 'Goodnight children everywhere'. Lovely stories too: Worzel Gummidge (not forgetting Earthy Mangold), Toytown with Mr Mayor, Dennis the Dachshund and Larry the Lamb. As for comics we were almost spoilt for choice. Three for a start spring to mind: Dandy, The Beano and Radio Fun. Quite enough light reading matter to have kept even an adventurous child like myself well engrossed and out of mischief for a while.

And when it came to domestic upheavals, even within the Royal Family there were private skirmishes, though a rather more serious nature than those of their loyal subjects. Although my sister and I would have come to hear about King Edward's Abdication on the wireless, I don't suppose that it would have really meant much to us at all. All school children were presented with commemorative china mugs embossed with pictures of the new King George and his wife Queen Elizabeth. On the day itself, Joan and I wore new red, white and blue cotton dresses, Aunt Nell had made them, all in the latest fashion with large, puffed sleeves. She also presented us with a special book the following Christmas, entitled: The Princesses and their Dogs. It was full of photographs showing Elizabeth and her little sister playing with their pets.

How patriotic we all were then. A few years later my sister and I came to be living in the countryside, when we'd heard a parodied version of the National Anthem: 'God Save our old tom cat, feed him on bread and fat, long may he reign'. We were deeply shocked... you shouldn't make fun of the Royal family. We refused to laugh but weren't quite brave enough to have said anything at the time.

Although my mother wasn't a practising Roman Catholic; obviously, she'd considered herself as 'ex-communicated' having married my father in a Registry Office instead of a 'proper' church. My sister and myself had been baptised as Roman Catholics; news of which had somehow reached the ears of Priest-in-Charge at St John the Baptist R.C. Church and School in Mare Street, Hackney. And, in due course, Mum had been paid several visits both by Father O'Sullivan himself and Nuns of the Diocese. So, reluctant as Mum had been to remove Joan and I from Wilton Road School; and no doubt feeling the traditional Catholic guilt about her own secret lapsed state, she finally relented.

School was no longer just around the corner but a fair distance away. At the latter end of Mare Street; further into the East End and almost bordering on Bethnal Green. Going to school involved almost half an hours walk, right up to the end of Greenwood Road, into the London Fields and a turn left into Mare Street.

One of the Sunday treats that Joan and I were obliged to forgo now; our usual visits with Dad to Victoria Park, culminating in a visit to Nanny Tompkins on our way home; where, if we were lucky enough, Uncle Alf might be heard playing the piano. The latest tunes rendered, in what might be described as a 'rollicking' manner, the echoes of which, I can almost hear still. Echo's which accompany photographic recollections of highly polished, red, Turkish linoleum, the smell of roast beef cooking in preparation for Sunday Dinner; about to be enjoyed by Aunt Nell, Uncle Alf and Nanny. Now, as practising Catholics, we were obliged to attend Sunday Mass under pain of Mortal Sin. After a short time, Sundays became even worse. We now had to attend school in the afternoon followed by Benediction Service. We'd been provided with a special lady escort, a member of the church, who wore a Nazi badge on the lapel of her coat; obviously an admirer of a certain black-moustached German Dictator about to cause havoc; not only in Europe but eventually throughout the world...

During the summer months of my first term at St John's, what I had found rather odd, was the sight of certain children running about the playground barefoot. Only a few but there had been nothing like this in our former school. In Mare Street it seems that the nuns from the nearby Hospice in Mare Street had set up a Boot Club in aid of the poorer children, who were presented with footwear from time to time. In my mother's opinion; these went to 'scroungers'; an unkind conjecture on her part, considering my father had a job and there were only two children to clothe and feed (no doubt due to his common sense). These shoeless ones usually come from very large families where there would have been a fair amount of hardship anyway; unemployment being rife during the Thirties and birth control frowned upon by the Catholic Church.

Not long after I had been at my new school, the time came for my first Confession and Holy Communion. The latter turned out to have been quite a pleasant occasion; since having received Holy Communion and Mass now over, we were treated to a very special breakfast which had been laid out for the Communicants, (who'd had to fast for several hours previously) in the school hall. After which, there had been much running around and showing off, clad in white dresses and long veils; although, I doubt that at seven or eight-year olds we'd have altogether appreciated the Spiritual significance of just having received The Blessed Sacrament. For my own part, I'm sure that I enjoyed being the centre of attention for my mother; by means other than incurring her wrath.

All throughout my childhood, it was the thought of 'going to Confession' that I really dreaded; always worried that I'd accidently left out a sin. In which case, should I receive the Holy Communion without being in 'a State of Grace', and happen to die shortly afterwards, I'd be going straight to Hell! My own over-stringent interpretation of the rules, no doubt...Domini no sum dignus_' Lord I am not worthy'.

At my old school there had been a large assembly hall where we gathered each day for morning prayers. These always concluded with a hymn which more often than not turned out to be that most rousing of hymns: To be a Pilgrim. I have always tended to associate this with my time at Wilton Road School.

Not that the children at St John the Baptist's school lacked the opportunity to exercise their lungs. Apart from the Latin Mass on Sundays and Holy Days of Obligation, there had always been a special concluding hymn: A Faith of our Fathers; a stirring attestation of the Catholic Faith which, by today's reckoning, might well be considered as 'too partisan'.

At Wilton Road school, when May Day came around, we children danced around a Maypole in the main hall; weaving in and out with the gaily coloured streamers in order to form a pattern, un-weaving it again in time to jolly tunes played on the piano. Followed by the crowning of a May Queen. A less secular celebration at St John's during the month of May, when we walked behind a banner and effigy of Our Lady. One of the children carrying a basket full of rose petals, scattering them along the way, as we sang 'Oh Mary we crown thee with blossom today, Queen of the angels and Queen of the May'.

'Now girls', I heard Miss Doyle saying to some senior girls, one home time; 'I'm going out to dinner this evening. If you stay for a while, you'll see me in my evening dress'. Miss Doyle was our music teacher. She was young, petite and pretty., and, she told us, engaged to a French composer whose name was Francis Chargrin. Miss composer Doyle had taught us to harmonise with a section of part songs: 'London's Burning', Frere Jacque,' etc. We also sang other French songs during our weekly music lesson. How fortunate we were then to have enjoyed the luxury of music as part of our school curriculum and how sad that music, as a subject is no longer part of today's.

A few years after the war, when I happened to be glancing through the Radio Times, I came across the details of a symphony concert shortly to be broadcast on the Third Programme (now known as Radio Three). One of the works listed was by a French Composer: One Francis Chagrin. Could this have been Miss Doyle's ex-fiancé, now husband? More than likely, I imagine, as the saying goes: 'Truth is often stranger than fiction'.

It stands to reason, of course, that matters of religion will always feature to a large extent on the agenda of any faith school and St John the Baptist's was no exception to the rule. I have to say; however, that there had always been ample quality time allotted to other aspects of our education.

During the summer of 1939, our class of nine- and ten-year olds had already begun the reading of King Lear. 'Now, now Cordelia, mend your speech a little lest it may mar your fortune'. As far as I'm able to remember; the dialogue between King Lear and his youngest daughter, was the point at which the reading came to a halt. War became inevitable to the country. In time of course, we would come to read more of the Bard's works: 'The Merchant of Venice and 'Julius Caesar'. But we never managed to get back to the poor King Lear and his dysfunctional family.

Tricks, Treats and Perilous Pursuits

U ntil we were able to read well ourselves, Mum often read aloud to us from the usual children's story books. Dad, on the other hand, preferred to relate them himself. The trouble was that when he was halfway through a Fairy tale, he fell asleep. After we prodded him awake, 'Goldilocks and the Tree Bears' had now become 'Red Riding Hood'. Very occasionally, just to amuse us, Dad would give a display of walking across the floor on his hands, much to our admiration of course; though probably, to my mother's irritation at this rather extreme piece of showing off.

It was quite unfair, of course. Mum was the bearer of daytime naughtiness, (usually mine), and the doler out of dire threats of punishment. My father, always the bringer of gifts for Joan and myself. After his Saturday morning trip to Kingsland Waste, or even as far afield as the Caledonian Road, there would always be a 'lucky dip' for both of us. Interesting looking packages wrapped in newspaper and secured with an elastic band, the treasures within consisting of small trinkets: glittery junk that soon fell apart but to us they were jewellery.

On Friday evenings, sometimes there would be other parcels wrapped in newspaper; our evening meal which Dad had purchased on his way home from work: fish and chips, or better still savoloys, pease pudding and faggots. Lovely succulent savoloys of days gone by. A world away from today's glorious technicolour offerings full of E additives.

But the very best in 'treasure' that Dad brought in for us were carrier bags full of second-hand books, more bargains from Kingsland Waste. Many classics: Palgrave's Golden Treasury of Verse, Lambs Tales from Shakespeare. My own personal favourites; though, were schoolgirl adventure stories. I loved reading all about those lucky boarding-school girls who had midnight feasts in the dorm and rich uncles who sent them £5 notes for their birthdays.

Somewhere around Christmastime in 1936 or 1937, my mother took Joan and I to the Hackney Empire in order to see the current pantomime. By the time it had ended (and speaking on behalf of my seven-year-old self), I had reached two conclusions. The first being that life as I knew it then, seemed very unfair. All throughout the show and suspended almost immediately above our heads at ceiling level, there had been an enormous net of brightly coloured balloons; however, when they came to be released, my sister and I never got a look in. By the time we'd reached the stalls from our gallery seats, there wasn't a single balloon to be had. The other conclusion had been of a more positive nature, to begin with anyway, there was no doubt about it; I wanted to be a dancer; just like those young tappers and ballet dancers who had come on the stage between each act. The very first time that I'd seen and heard this kind of music, and dancing, I was badly smitten and afterwards continually pleaded with my father for some Tap and Ballet shoes. 'When you're older', He would say; rather than begin the useless task of trying to explain to a seven-year-old that his carefully managed budget would not extend to include dancing shoes of any description, let alone dancing lessons.

To assuage my ongoing urge to dance, I sometimes roped my little sister into displays on indoor footwork; 'Let's be fairies', I would say, trying hard to go up on my points, having stuffed the ends of my slippers with bits of rags. I had even tried to turn my outdoor shoes into ones that tapped; having saved a few discarded milk-bottle tops for the purpose, a futile exercise took place, even the bevelled edges couldn't be pushed into the soles.

Perhaps this lack of an outlet for creativity had been part of the reason for my being such a 'difficult' child. Returning home from school one afternoon a shocking sight met my eyes. There was a CANE hanging from a hook on the picture rail. I did in fact, but only on one occasion, come to receive a switch on the legs with it, after which the cane disappeared. Several years later and during the war when Joan and I were absent, my father, much to his amusement it seems, found it buried in the garden.

Situated about halfway along the market in Ridley Road, was the cinder toffee stall with its sculpture like mounds of honey-comb confection. This, no doubt, would have been our first pes-ter point when Joan and I accompanied Mum on her Saturday trips to Kingsland High Street. If successful, a small bag each of that delicious 'melt-in-the-mouth' golden toffee became our first, and possibly only, trophy. This would have depended on the amount of spare cash available when Mum had done her weekend shopping...not a lot, I imagine. However, my mother was generous by nature, as we well knew, so it was always worth a try, especially in Woolworths.

This Aladdin's Cave of earthly delights; a toy counter which had on display just about everything to enthral a child of the Thirties, pre-school and beyond: whips and wooden spinning tops, skipping ropes with brightly painted handles, packets of colourful glarnies and even larger glass marbles. Here too were Nursery Rhyme and Fairy Tale books whose shiny covers de-picting a red-cloaked Red Riding Hood or a trio of glossy pink pigs, were enough to make one want to pursue the inside story or to have it read to them. I was about eight years old when I read Hans Anderson's The Little Match girl for the first time; the saddest Fairy Tale I'd ever come across; the Little match girl, of course, had frozen to death in the snow after striking her last match. The ultimate in desirability came in the form of a bird on a wire (or length of cord); this was attached to a short-wooded rod and when whirled about rapidly, these luridly painted birds of paradise gave forth a series of sweet shrill notes; due to a cunningly placed tin whistle on their papier-Mache undersides...magic! They could sing! At least until the whistle finally gave out. This unique psychedelic Oriental bird was then callously cast aside, no doubt in favour of some other passing fancy from the 'cheap and cheerful' toy stall in Ridley Market.

Holidays, as such, were out of the question but we sometimes went on family days out, usually on Bank Holidays, when we either went for a picnic in Epping Forest or visited the big fun fair in Walthamstow. Once a year though a very special day out; by excursion train to Southend-on-Sea. For this event Joan and I wore our best frocks, straw sun bonnets and the inevitable white shoes and socks. The former newly whitened the day before and placed on the windowsill to dry. As usual, it was my father who did all the organising and prepared the sandwiches in good time, no last-minute rush, there was a particular train to catch. Whenever I've come across one of those wire egg slicers, either in a Charity shop box of household cutlery or on the shelf of a hardware shop; I'm immediately transported back in time to Dad's egg and cress sandwiches, our once a year Pre-War trips to Southend-on-Sea.

One of the best things about those excursions were the big ice-cream cornets from Rossi's kiosk just around the corner from Southend Central Station. Two of the worst; that crowded, noisy excursion train and the usual sound of bickering between my parents on the way home. Possibly, because Dad had dozed off on the beach leaving Mum to take Joan and I paddling and to look for cockle shells to take home. All in the future of course, that within a couple of years or so, that sandy beach, even the sea wall itself, would be encircled with barbed wire and 'out of bounds' to everyone, that England would be under threat of invasion by an enemy. It would be six years then, before any of our Island's vulnerable beaches became accessible once more.

Both in Europe and here in Britain then, other disturbances

were taking place: Oswald Moseley and his followers going about their special business in those pre-war years-1936 on-wards. Though obviously old history now. There were Fascist meetings in Ridley road and black-shirted marchers who came along Dalston Lane one day, all wearing Swastika armbands. Some bearing aloft the Swastika flag, and there was a big drum too! It all looked very exciting at the time!

My father was much given to aphorisma: 'Cut your coat accord-ing to your cloth'; a piece of advice that stood me in good stead during the years to come. Another axion quoted when I was growing up and had expressed annoyance when some plan had gone wrong: 'Life my dear is full of disappointments'. True of course but of little comfort to the complainant at the time.

My mother; however, would have had no need for such advice, having no doubt already been aware of the fact. Now and then Mum gave voice to her disappointments: 'When I first met your father, he was so smart, now look at him' (This would have been when my father was Head Valet at the hotel in Park Lane); 'He could run down the stairs balancing a tray of drinks on one hand', (a feat which had obviously impressed my mother at the time).

Dad's suits were always second-hand now and, out of necessity, but he was always smart, so this comparison was a trifle unfair. Bur there was more to follow: 'He once had a chance to go and work in Canada, but he wouldn't take it'. This would have been when my father was working as a valet to Tom Arnold, the Im-presario, and may well have been when my parents had become engaged. Being a romantic, Mum might not have considered the likelihood of her being left behind; or that Dad, having had enough 'foreign adventure' during the first world war, had merely wanted to settle down to family life in his own country now. Maybe she had seen the possibility of Head Valet leading on to greater 'in service' heights. But life in the Thirties tended, on the whole, to be no respecter of dreams; to have a steady job, even on a low wage, meant that you were very fortunate. In other parts of the country at that time, especially in the North, any dreams might have been the nightmare of unemployment and hunger.

By working class standards, we didn't do so badly. No luxuries but we never went hungry and there was always roast beef for Sunday dinner; Dad carved the beef and mashed the potatoes with milk and a little butter until they were white and creamy...Not that this managerial takeover would have annoyed my mother, carving the Sunday joint quite usual for the 'Head of the Household'. My mother was a wonderful cook, steak and kidney pies one of her specialities though quite wasted on me at the time it seems. 'She's a poor eater', my mother would inform the listener within my hearing: 'All she eats is a banana and a little pot of cream'. It appears that I was also very 'highly strung'. I'm sure that due to my latent creative skills, I managed to live up to my rather dramatic reputation.

My sister and I were always well clothed; our dresses either run up by Mum or Aunt Nell, who also made our coats. Very special items though came by post. One item that had delighted me no end when I tried it on for size, had been a shiny black oilskin Mackintosh and matching Sowester hat, complete with elastic under the chin. At the first opportunity, clad head to foot in my water-proof gear, Wellingtons included, I made my public debut. Having first asked for permission, I went to buy myself some sweets in Mrs Goldshaft's shop just around the corner. After which, I went and stood with several members of the public who were sheltering from the very heavy downpour of rain under the stripped canopy of the baker's shop a few doors away. After a while, and for my encore, I joined a small group of people who were also taking shelter from the rain, only this time under a large lime tree in front of the house. I stood with them for a few minutes then made my 'exit': in at the gate, down the basement steps and 'back stage' indoors; no doubt satisfied that I'd made an impression; even if there had been no applause!

I believe for all my 'naughtiness' as a 'wayward type of child' who often led her little sister into mischief, and was frequently quite disobedient, there had perhaps been one consolation for my mother. This was my almost platinum blond hair, which, after being washed and then rinsed in camomile liquid and dried, had been wound in pipe-cleaner curlers overnight, un-coiled the next morning and brushed out, all ready for the dis-play...

Skipping along in my bouncy plimsoles, wearing my best green dress and with my flaxen frizz aglow, I must have felt that I was the bee's knees on that sunny Saturday morning. I was on my way to Mr Horder's shop, on an errand; five Woodbines for Dad and a ha'pporth each of sweets for Joan and myself. For some reason that particular 'moment in time' has remained clearly in my special store of happy childhood memories, almost as though I'd automatically put it to one side like a favourite snap-shot; a cherished 'magic moment' for future contemplation.

Unfortunately, I was a separate entity from my 'delicate blonde' semblance, a rather over-active, self-willed tomboy in fact. The good fairy had not altogether forgotten me it seems. One of my saving graces being that, when all things considered, I happened to be quite kind-hearted really, but even this tendency was to have its negative repercussions in due course.

Given that seven is generally given to be 'the age of reason' for a child, there is no denying that what I'd contemplated and then carried out one day: I knew to be wrong. Just the same, acting on impulse, I went ahead with my plan. On either side of the man-tle-piece were our red tin moneyboxes. Both tins when I picked them up rattled promisingly. Mum had popped down to Ridley Road, knowing that Mrs Baldringer on the ground floor could be called upon in the unlikely event of an emergency occurring within half an hour or so. Using a broad-bladed knife I emptied both tins and could see at once that there was more than enough to buy ice-cream cornets for all my playmates who were wait-ing outside in the street. I replaced the pilfered coins with some buttons from Mum's button tin, then, together with my ill-got-ten wealth took my friend into Mrs Goldshaft's shop for the grand distribution; news of which was given shortly afterwards to my mother by Mrs G herself.

Being a light-weight skinny child, it wasn't too difficult to turn me upside down and administer several hard slaps to my rear end. A short, sharp, shock. More likely to have instilled in the subconscious of a seven-year-old the never to be forgotten reminder of the Seventh Commandment: 'Thou Shalt not Steal'... rather than 'Go in peace and for your penance say one Our Father and three Hail Marys'. Luckily for me; however, my temporary 'fall from grace' had occurred sometime before I had my first confession, thus never having reached the ears of Father O'Sullivan or Father Kelly.

Those long hot summers of my pre-war childhood...were they so? But that is how I have come to recall them; warm sunny days, and in the height of summer, days when I could feel the heat from the pavements almost burning through the soles of my shoes. Long before the advent of trainers, the sturdy casual footwear of today's youngsters, it would have been plimsoles or gym shoes that bore the brunt of our playing in the street during the summer months; their bouncy rubber-soled lightness being ideal when it came to running, jumping and skipping games. 'Bumps' in particular, when it was necessary to spring-jump as high as possible during the double-speed whirring of the skipping rope. The more bumps attained before falling foul of the rope making one winner of the contest.

There was little to disturb or interrupt our various street game then, apart from the occasional cyclist or the baker's or milkman's horse-drawn vehicle. On rare occasions; though, it was the sighting of a certain person, somebody who lived a short distance away in Fasset Square, whose stripped woollen hat, brown wrinkled stockings and unfeminine growth of grey facial hair that sent us scurrying down the basement steps to hide in the area. There we crouched as low as possible, determined to remain out of sight until the lady in question had passed by-just in case she put a spell on us.

At regular intervals during our street games, there would come the realisation that we were in need of sustenance: 'Mum, can we have some bread and marg and sugar?' 'Mum, can we have another ha'penny for some sweets?' But push my mother too far with our continual pestering...why then the result might prove to be more than we'd bargained for. A whole loaf of bread or even her purse would come flying through the air in our direction; 'there take the lot.'

My mother wasn't the only adult whose patience came to be sorely tried during the summer months, occasionally. On one such day Miss Skinner, a spinster lady who lived in the top floor flat; no doubt driven to extremes by the clamour down below, had opened her window and emptied a bowl of water over our little heads. Although, of course, it may not have been water at all, but the contents of her chamber pot. Dad had been very angry with Miss Skinner and went upstairs later that day in order to protest at the earlier unexpected downpour. It had certainly proved effective, there were no more noisy gatherings in the target area that summer.

Every so often, and in the midst of our street games, a certain dumpy little person came from just across the road to join us. Not to play; however, but to complain about her mother. Bessie was an aggrieved individual who wanted our sympathy, and her lips were always set in a pout. Petulant would be a good way in which to describe Bessie; some thirty years old but going on twelve. A day came around eventually when Bessie's grievance managed to attract more than their usual attention because the complainant was about to jump from the window of her mother's ground floor flat. Drawn to the spot by all the ongoing commotion, a group of us looked on, (a little callously perhaps) as Bessie put her plan into operation, placing a short stocking-clad leg over the wide sill and disclosing a fair amount of knee-length bloomers. Slightly disappointed perhaps, we could see that this was as far as the drama went, Bessie's long-suffering elderly mother having managed to haul her wayward daughter back into the room.

I'm not sure whether it was in late 1937 or early 1938 when a new family came to live in the vacant flat upstairs. There was just the three of them, a widow and her two sons, Reggie being the younger of the two by five years or so. I was slightly in awe of that big brother of his, who went to the local Grammar School and rode a 'grown-up' bicycle which had curved handlebars; a most superior being altogether was Leonard. Reggie; however, was quite different. An adventurous type of boy. An ideal friend and playmate for someone like myself. I'd never really enjoyed playing with girls; especially those like my sister and her friend Olive, who always seemed to be playing with dolls. Such had been my reputation for spoiling their 'dolly games', that in the end, I'd been refused entry into Olive's house by the pair of them.

Reggie was almost two years my senior. Almost like a big brother in fact, so I was now allowed to go out and about more. I often accompanied him when he went on errands for his mother. Sometimes we played in the garden; Reggie taught me how to play cricket, after a fashion of course. Due to the ball's annoying habit of disappearing over the wall into Mrs Green's jungle-like garden, our cricket sessions were rather short-lived. Neither of us brave enough to risk Mrs Green's annoyance by asking for our ball back or trying to retrieve it for ourselves, by a swift foray over the garden wall and into enemy territory. Her eagle eyes would have spotted us at once; she was an elderly lady, next door's house-owner, with a reputation of being somewhat ill-disposed towards 'pesky' children in general.

Being at a loss for something to do one day and feeling suitably chastened after Manny Cohen had recently emerged from his shop in order to give us both a good telling off (for having sent young David, who lived in the ground floor flat, to ask for two pennyworth of pigeon's milk), Reggie and I decided to venture further afield in search of adventure.

Via the back turnings, we emerged just opposite the Savoy Cinema in Kingsland Road. There's an interesting looking window on the side wall of the cinema: so, we cross the main road in order to investigate further. The window; however, is too high up for either of us to see in from ground level; which is quite disappointing...but Reggie had an idea. By standing on Reggie's back and clinging on to the wall, I was able to report, from my unsteady perch, that I could see the 'pictures'. I must have been more or less looking over the projectionist's shoulder. So, by following the diagonal beam of light, I had a bird's-eye view of the cinema screen below. Swiftly moving silent images that really made little sense; but actually, seeing the pictures for nothing would have evoked the childish enjoyment of having done something daring or forbidden.

Another of our daring feats, even though it had proved unsuccessful, had been in endeavouring to prize an extra half bar of chocolate from the vending machine in Dalston Lane. After we'd duly deposited our two pennies (or tuppence) in the coin slot and extracted our bar of Nestles 'paid for' chocolate, Reggie had assured me that it was possible to obtain an extra half for free. I forget the means we had employed for this Bonnie and Clyde enterprise.

It wouldn't have occurred to me at the time, I imagine, that trying to 'nick' an unpaid for, half bar of chocolate from a vending machine was stealing. If it had, I would have been obliged to confess it, to report our failed plan to Father O'Sullivan the next time I went to Confession. Such perilous pursuits would have been a sort of adventure...a lark in the face of our usual enemy: the grown-ups, who were always ready to spoil our fun. Especially Mum; who'd threaten me so often with The Girl's Borstal, that being naughty had by now just become part of my stock in trade.

1938: As we walked along Dalston Lane that afternoon in early November, I could sense that Reggie was bursting to disclose some important piece of news. Suddenly, and in a conversational manner, he announced; 'I know where babies come from.' Receiving no immediate response, he continued; 'they cut the lady's belly open and a baby comes out.' 'No, they don't,' I protested indignantly; because I knew for sure that this just wasn't true!' Mum had already told Joan and I how we came to be born...an Angel had brought us down from Heaven in a carrier bag. Apart from which, I somehow sensed, even at the age of eight and a half, that this was a forbidden subject. 'I don't want to talk about it,' I said to my friend abruptly. Thus, putting paid to any further conversation to do with babies.

However, Reggie's other piece of news was far more interesting because his mother knew of a lady in Sandringham Road who had an old mattress to dispose of; just what we needed, some more stuff to use for our bonfire tomorrow night.

She stood in the basement doorway looking on, the tiny elderly lady who had answered Reggie's knock on her door the following afternoon. Regarding us both a little anxiously as we hauled her old flock mattress off between us, tugging it up the narrow flight of steps and out onto the street.

'You're not bringing that dirty old mattress through my hallway,' said my mother, on our triumphant arrival home, 'it'll be full of bugs.' But, after some persuasion, she relented. After all, having dragged our trophy home via Sandringham Road, Cecilia Road and Dalston Lane, my friend and I could hardly have been expected to haul it back to its' original home. So, later that evening, as Dad set the Catherine Wheels spinning and we made whirling arcs with our hand-held sparklers; old Guy Fawkes, perched high on a magnificent funeral pyre, was having his final moment of glory!

This was to be our very last Guy Fawkes night celebration in the back garden of 99. Greenwood Road. By November, the fifth 1939, my sister and I wouldn't be living here with our parents either; but with another family, somewhere in the countryside and over a hundred miles away from London. Neither would Reggie and I be going in search of bonfire material; for, by then, we would have gone our separate ways forever.

The last time I saw Reggie, was on Friday the First of September 1939. Our evacuation train was about to depart from Liverpool Street Station, when, I happened to catch sight of him from the carriage window. One of a long line of schoolboys who were making their way along the platform and towards yet another evacuation train. Reggie was looking straight ahead and wouldn't have noticed me unless I called out. But children didn't do that sort of thing then, especially when their teachers were present. A few years later, when I got around to reading Richmal Crompton's Just William Books, both the illustrations and the actual character of William himself, reminded me very much of Reggie. During the war, his family moved away from Greenwood Road. I often wonder what happened to him though; my very best pre-war childhood friend, fellow adventurer and partner in crime.

Part Two

Prelude

1939: Ever since the beginning of that year, there had been talk of war. Certain conversations overheard by children now and then which, perhaps, caused vague misgivings. On the whole; however, these rumours of war would have had very little meaning within a child's domain., leaving only the adults uneasily aware of its looming shadow.

As the year progressed and various preparations for a possible war began to take place; rather than causing we children alarm, if my memory serves me right, such goings on had merely added to the interest of our everyday activities.

To begin with, there had been the sudden appearance of a huge silver-coloured balloon, floating on high over Hackney Downs. This barrage balloon soon became the focus of studied observation; any indication of its gradual descent was enough to send us scurrying through the side-streets, eager to watch this whale-like monster hauled to earth. As to its purpose? I doubt if any of us would have been at all bold enough to have made enquiries at that particular point in time.

Even the deep trenches that were being dug in London Fields (potential air raid shelters), would have caused we children little concern. In fact, rather than the danger, they suggested immediate adventure: those great mounds of excavated earth and wooden planking. Making sure that nobody was around; there had been the odd occasion when we'd climbed over the low railings in order to investigate. Whether or not we had tried any plank-balancing, I really can't remember. There probably hadn't been time, for at the first sighting of a grown-up, the war-zone would have been vacated immediately; our home journey recommended at double-quick speed.

It was Manny Cohen, oddly enough, who'd quite by chance managed to put things in perspective for me- a carefree nine-year-old, until I happened to be walking past his shop that day. He was standing in the doorway of his shop and engaged in conversation with another gentleman. Manny's words enough for me to grasp their meaning. So there really was going to be war after all! I suddenly felt a surge of anxiety: for the first time I began to feel afraid.

We were prepared for it of course, my sister and I: prepared for the evacuation. Even if bombing hadn't been mentioned, we quite accepted the reason given for our being sent away from London. It was for our own safety. The gas-masks we'd been issued with recently had been necessary also. The Germans had used gas in the First World War: on our soldiers. Dad himself had been gassed- he said that it had left him with an enlarged spleen, but we didn't know what this meant.In order that children might become accustomed to wearing their gas-masks, should an emergency occur in the future, gas-mask practice would no doubt have been carried out by most London schools, in the run-up to the war. The idea being, of course, that lessons could proceed even during an actual gas attack by the enemy: with us all wearing the necessary equipment.

In the event; needless to say, the Germans had never resorted to this form of warfare, which is just as well. Our education would have suffered a great deal if doing our lessons whilst wearing our masks had been adhered to. Not that we children minded our practice lessons, for even if the vision section became steamed up after a while and we couldn't see a thing, there were certain compensations. If we breathed extra heavily the snout-like ends made lovely snorting noises; a slight lifting of the rubber face piece whilst doing this emitted an even sharper and more suggestive rasp. This was apt to cause an outbreak of covert tittering. If our teacher happened to be absent from the class during this experiment: a burst of loud laughter.

Although my sister and I had gradually become used to the idea of 'going away,' we had no idea at all of our destination, neither had our parents. 'Just think,' said Mum; 'you could be going to stay in a grand house with servants.' My father, meanwhile, ever the practical, cut out cloth covers for our gas-mask cases and ran them up on Mum's sewing machine. My mother's suggestion of a 'grand house' really appealed to me and lessened my anxiety, which had no doubt been her intention. I began looking forward to this new adventure.

Redgate Farm

September the First, 1939. It had been a long journey: Liverpool Street to Thetford by train. Then somewhere in a big hall with grown-ups handing out mugs of water, hands reaching out eagerly. We were all so hot and thirsty because the train had been crowded and the day very warm. Afterwards, another journey, this time by coach, which seemed to take forever. Now another hall: in the village school. And there we waited, feeling very tired, and perhaps, a little scared; as people came and went, taking with them those whom they'd selected from the waiting children. My sister and I, together with two other evacuees, were among the last to leave.

When the little Austin Seven, driven by a stout lady in W.V.S. uniform, finally deposited us at the entrance to Redgate Farm, on that mellow, late, summer evening: complete with our small suitcases, gas-masks and wearing out identity labels- we must have presented a pathetic sight. This was later confirmed by Uncle Fred, who was overheard to remark; 'When I saw them thar' poor little beggers', I went up to that thar' field piped my eye.' (Cried).

The front door of the farmhouse stood open and down the short flight of steps came a tall elderly lady with thick grey hair, which she wore in two short plaits. On her feet were sturdy leather sandals- not a grand lady but a hard-working farmer's wife. She really seemed very kind though. 'Come you in and set you down,' said the kind lady whom we came to know as Aunt May, leading us up the steps and into the homely looking farmhouse parlour. 'Come on in and set you down.'

We unpacked our suitcases, handed over the carrier bag with our emergency rations (a tin of corned beef and a large slab of chocolate), wrote our new address on the pre-stamped post-cards that Dad had given us, had something to eat and, finally, fell exhausted into a large feather matressed brass bedstead upstairs.

Unexpected though it had been, because the idea of a farm had never come up, even in Mum's imagination, and much better than a Grand House, which was really just as well, because Redgate Farm was to be our home for the next four years.

Once we had overcome our initial fear of the farmyard chickens, our surprise at the absence of electricity and piped water, not to mention a flush less lavatory which was situated a fair distance from the house (quite discreetly in a secluded alcove behind an ivy-covered fence). When we had learned how to draw a bucket of water up from the well instead of turning on a tap, grown used to the soft glow of oil-lamps on winter evenings, it was as if we'd lived on the farm and known Aunt May and Uncle Fred all our lives.

Aunt May and Uncle Fred (as we came to know them), would have been either in their late fifties or early sixties. Two of their three daughters were married but there were no grandchildren. Perhaps my sister and I served as surrogates for that reason, and therefore all the more welcome.

Uncle Fred was the archetypal farmer of that decade. On market days he wore breeches and buskins (stiff leather gaiters), and always a flat cap; for he was completely bald...well, almost so. I liked Uncle Fred and we always got on well. He insisted on calling me Flip instead of my real name. Probably because I was inclined to flip (or climb) over every gate rather than open it and walk through; forever in a rush to get somewhere or other. He was a real character whom I remember with affection. Uncle

Fred had his own way at looking at things. Arriving home from school one day and eager to impart my newly acquired knowledge of the universe, I asked him; 'Uncle Fred, did you know that the sun doesn't move, it is the earth that moves around the sun?' He was most indignant: 'You aren't a-going to tell me that thar' sun don't move... how is it that thar' sun's over thar (indicating east), in the mornin' and over thar (pointing west) in the evening?' he simply wouldn't have it.

There were two other children billeted with us on the farm: Joey, a little boy of seven-years-old and his thirteen-year-old big sister. Joey remained on the farm for a time, but his sister went to another billet in the village itself, as a result of many arguments with Aunt May (to do with boys mainly). Coping with a teenager, even way back in 1939, no doubt had it's hard to deal with situations...

Christmas 1939: Our first Christmas away from home. There is a party taking place down in the village hall; a special party for evacuees kindly provided by the villagers. On the stage a fair-haired girl in a red dress sings a song; a poignant war-time melody written with the evacuees in mind: 'Goodnight children everywhere, your Mummy thinks of you tonight...lay your head upon the pillow...don't be a kid, or a weeping willow.' Its pathos lost on most of us; apparently, as we tuck in cheerfully to fish paste sandwiches, brightly coloured jellies and iced buns. Afterwards, we wait in line as Father Christmas gives out exciting looking packages from a big sack. Mine turns out to be a beautiful glass bottle of eau-de-cologne. I keep its contents going for aged by topping it up with water at regular intervals.

Even after all these years, Christmas Day at Redgate Farm is something special to remember: roast goose with all the trimmings, a Christmas tree up to the ceiling (courtesy of the local plantation and Harold the farm hand) and usually, a visit from Mum. In the run-up to Christmas, various acquaintances dropped in; possibly just to sample Aunt May's seasonal mulled ale. Always welcome at the farm, our ever-cheerful Percy the postman; who, despite his club foot, rode his bicycle through all weathers delivering our letters and small parcels from home; together with fictitious verbal messages from our teachers, now billeted at Necton Hall Lodge. 'That Miss Thomas, she says to me, I love that Doreen to a cinder;' which we of course knew wasn't really true, but it made us laugh just the same.

We were showered with presents that first Christmas because all and sundry felt sorry for us. Then Mum arrived bringing yet more. Mr. Woodgate, a family friend, dressed up as Father Christmas, though recognised at once by little Joey: 'I know it's Mr. Woodgate because of his big ears.' Sad to relate that Christmas 1939 had been the first and last time he'd dressed up as Santa Claus for us. During the following year, Mr. Woodgate's only son, a member of the Royal Air Force, was posted as 'missing, presumed killed'...

Winter 1940: One of the coldest winters of the war years-a veritable mini ice age. We children had never felt such bitter cold and bitter winds; had never previously experienced walking along a country road between high snow drifts. At home in London, what snow we remembered hadn't been very deep and in cold weather, Joan and I had been gloved -up, scarved and wrapped-up by Mum. Our long scarves crossed at the back and secured with a pin- 'to protect our kidneys, she told us.'

But now we were at the mercy of the weather. Feet cold in our leather school shoes because our Wellingtons hadn't arrived from home.

I had chilblains on both heels which itched and hurt. I was so cold and miserable on the way home from school one afternoon that I just sat down by the roadside and wept. After which, I probably pulled myself together and continued home to the farm, where Aunt May had some hot soup waiting for us. During the horrendous winter, there would be a township evacuee faced with the shock of having to endure an 'Artic' countryside winter for the first time in their lives...or having to walk to school no matter how icy the roads or high the snowdrifts.

Eventually, our Wellington Boots arrived, as well as the inevitable new vests and liberty bodices. Especially welcome: our new velvet ankle-strapped slippers.

Whilst our parents were no doubt worrying themselves back home about their two precious little girls, in all the dreadful weather; the girls were busy out on the frozen pond and streams, sliding on the ice in their new slippers, the soles of which, were ideal for the purpose. We carried our slippers 'skate wise'-our Wellingtons necessary wear across the snow-deep surrounding fields.

On Uncle Fred's advice, we always tested the safety of our makeshift skating rinks by throwing as large a piece of rock or stone onto the ice, but in those war-time winters, most of the field-ponds had been frozen to well over twelve inches in depth. We could see this just by looking.

Redgate Farm was a long 'L'-shaped brick building; the shorter section being the flag-stoned sunken dairy. This was the storage place for all the household's perishable food. Taking up a sizeable area of the floor space were several large Aladdin-type, tall, earthenware storage vessels. These were used to store cuts and joints of pickled pork. This was a pig farm and boiled bacon; together with all its side products, contributed in no small way to our being well fed, in a time of food rationing. In fact, living in the countryside had cured me of all my former 'finicky' eating habits.

Running around the farm, climbing the odd tree and helping with the farm work in season, not to mention the long walk to and from school each day, had awoken my appetite with a vengeance. Good plain meals including: boiled bacon with plenty of fresh vegetables and sometimes a bowl of rabbit stew on our arrival home from school in the winter, were now something to look forward to.

On observing Aunt May preparing a comestible, which we had only previously seen as slices on the cold meats counter in Dalston's Sainsbury's, just at first, we had been not only fascinated but slightly repelled. The pig's head, having had its whiskers shaved off and its eyes removed, was then put into a large pot of water to simmer: it's jaw bones later removed when the mixture had cooled down, prior to setting in the process of becoming Brawn. All that served as an occasional reminder of its origins when the tasty slices were about to be consumed, accompanied by lettuce and tomatoes from the kitchen garden: a tiny black bristle.

In time we grew blasé with regard to farmyard husbandry; though. I never grew quite accustomed to the sight of dead chickens strung upside down to bleed, before being plucked and prepared for sale to various meat-rationed customers, from time to time. Later during the war when we came to be surrounded by American Air Bases, the odd chicken would come to be in much demand from local farmers.

At the rear of the farmhouse stood the deep brick-lined well. After a time, we became quite adept at hauling up a bucket of water, when necessary, from its moss lined depths, but this was only for drinking and cooking purposes.

This ice-cold spring water was not to be wasted on daily ablutions the contents of a large water-butt immediately to the right of the back door had to suffice. The quantity and quality of which depended on each season's rainfall. During the winter months, gaining access to it's contents often required making a dent in the thin layer of ice which lay on top. One of the pure luxuries which my sister recalls after we had returned to London in late 1943: was of obtaining water from a tap once more. However, I have to say, that in due course, such temporary inconveniences merely became part and parcel of our life in the countryside.

Just beyond the well and adjourning the vegetable garden; there ran a long narrow pathway and beyond that the orchard. During the height of summer: a time when all stinging nettles are at their most lethal and bare legs the most vulnerable; I soon discovered that the only means of gaining access to the orchard was by way of 'running the gauntlet' as swiftly as I could. This involved a sudden dash followed by a series of hops, skips and jumps... the higher the better!

One of my special secrets lay up there in the orchard, but only in springtime; hidden away, shyly, in the long grass and underneath a rose bush: a cluster of sweetly scented white violets... only I knew where to find them. Rather oddly perhaps, since there were four apple trees and at least one plum tree in the vicinity: whose blossoms must have been quite beautiful to behold at that time of year, it's only those tiny white violets which I've unconsciously stored away in memory.

Another of my special 'secrets' lay elsewhere in springtime, though somewhat later, perhaps in early May: a whole bank of Bluebells to view, if I walked as far as the third field and climbed through a gap in the hedge, when on one of my solitary expeditions.

But again, it's the orchard where a very special event took place during the spring...supervised by Uncle Fred himself.

Even though we children had seen it all before; there was at least one day each spring where we walked in procession along the orchard pathway, following Uncle Fred as he proceeded at snail's pace, anxious not to spill the deep bowl of warm water he was carrying so carefully. For this, after all, was the main requirement for what was about to take place. First, the selected eggs: those ready to be hatched, were carefully placed, two or three at a time into the water; bobbing about for a short while until a few hairline cracks appeared, followed by larger ones, then a break as each bird in turn pecked its way into the world. In due course, there would be at least a dozen newly hatched birds ready to be brought indoors and set down to 'fluff-out' in a shallow cardboard tray by the parlour fire. If the new arrivals happened to be chicks, this would soon empty. It's former occupants now settling in the soft black fur of the old mother cat, slumbering away at the hearthrug.

Rather reluctantly, perhaps, since I would have preferred to

57

dwell on my 'pretty water colour memories' for a little longer, due to an unfortunate jog to the memory; an association of ideas or words i.e. 'Old mother cat' and 'the parlour'. I am obliged to recall one of those stories without a happy ending; this being the unforeseen but inevitable demise of a baby rabbit which I'd managed to rescue from the jaws of one of the younger farmhouse cats one day. She'd probably meant it as an 'offering' anyway when she brought it into the parlour. Having wrapped the little creature in an old woollen scarf, I took it up to the orchard and placed it in a disused ferret hut which I'd lined with straw. Even though the weather was very cold, I was sure that the baby rabbit would be safe and warm during the night. It wasn't of course, overnight there was a heavy frost. Much to my dismay, I arrived in the orchard nest morning only to find my dear little 'rescued rabbit' frozen stiff, still wrapped in the woollen scarf...

There was only one other adult who lived on the farm and this was Harold, the resident farm-hand. He was about thirty-five years old. A bachelor who'd been jilted by his fiancée several years earlier. That's what Aunt May had told us anyway. I don't recall Harold ever mentioning her himself. One day, when rummaging through a box of old photographs that we'd come across in the spare room chest of drawers, there had come to light one of Harold's ex-beloved. A studio photo of a young lady with coiled hair and wearing an old-fashioned ruffled blouse; trailing a rose in her fingers, she gazed dreamily at the camera: a soulful look. Rather unkindly, perhaps, we decided that Harold's ex-fiancée was 'cross-eyed,' however, we kept this to ourselves.

As well as being Uncle Fred's right-hand help, Harold was our special hero. He cut our hair, even if a little crookedly at times, mended our shoes, teased us occasionally and, much to our delight, had a large repertoire of dubious rhyming ditties, which we took trouble to learn by heart.

When my mother came to visit us, usually every few months, these were often proudly presented for her entertainment on the long walk back to Redgate Farm from the Three Tuns cross-roads. Fortunately, due to our tender years, most of the ditties had been watered-down. Besides which, Mum being of an unsophisticated disposition, wouldn't have got the joke: which was perhaps just as well. Our favourite was the one about the 'Brave old Scotsman of the Battle of Waterloo... the wind blew up his petticoat,' etc. etc., sung to the tune of 'the British Grenadiers'. Even today, whenever this stirring march is played during a radio broad cast or when a special military event is shown on television...automatically and involuntarily it is Harold's version that springs to mind. Harold's father had apparently been a lay-preacher; maybe too much of being preached at as a child and youth had inspired Harold's latter-day deviation from the paths of righteousness.

Because Uncle Fred, himself, suffered from some form of physical handicap, making it necessary for him to walk with a stick, it was Harold who did almost all the heavy work on and about the farm; ploughing and drilling according to season with the aid of Boxer and Smiler. Belying their huge size these farm horses were gentle creatures. I was never afraid of them and thought nothing of ducking under the belly of one or the other in order to fasten the girth strap; although, the very thought of my 'child-self' doing this is apt to be a little worrying at this moment in time. My sister, on the other hand, has less complacent recollections of being in close contact with Boxer and Smiler on occasions. This would have been when Harold took the horses down to the village Blacksmith's to be re-shod. For a seven-year-old, it must have been quite terrifying to have found herself perched so high-up and on such a very large and unfamiliar creature; hanging on for dear life alongside Harold, as the horses plodded their unhurried way. With Harold to keep an eye on her, Joan would have been quite safe. Just the same, proof if ever there was that one's childhood memories of 'life on a farm', and life in general, for that matter, are purely subjective: not all of the 'rose-coloured' variety for others.

But what stalwarts we formally cossetted girls had turned out to be. During our four years as 'farm children,' we learnt to hoe mangolds and sugar beet efficiently in late Spring and were able to use a bill hook quite safely when the mature mud-ladened beet needed trimming after they'd been ploughed up in late November. A real finger-numbing task in wet weather, even with gloves on. But this was wartime, even children were expected to 'do-their-bit' for the war effort. Farm hands, due to conscription, in short supply; and we were always proud to do so: 'stooking' the corn at harvest time and, on occasion, mucking out the horse stable or pigsty. 'What can we do today Uncle Fred?' we'd ask when at a loose end on Saturday mornings. In the Autumn we went collecting acorns for the pigs to eat. Uncle Fred paid us 2/6d each for every half sack full or carrying load. I sometimes wonder what todays youngsters would do if required to muck out a pigsty...call Childline probably!

With its log fire and soft lamplight, the farmhouse parlour was a very cosy place on those cold, Norfolk, winter evenings. During the week, Joan and I would sit at the large dining table to do our allotted homework and write our weekly letter home. Most Saturday evenings; however, would find us engaged in activities of a more relaxed nature.

Out would come the playing cards, and all present, with the exception of Uncle Fred, indulged in a simple form of gambling. Newmarket was the name of the game, but since the stake money consisted of ha'pennies only, in real terms, winning or losing was of little consequence. Nonetheless, playing Newmarket was an entertaining and enjoyable way of passing a long winter's evening. Uncle Fred; meanwhile, sitting patiently by, peeling and coring an apple for himself as he waited for the nine o'clock news to begin.

Once the strokes of Big Ben had sounded and finally died away, all throughout the broadcast 'complete silence' was the rule, until the all-important war news was over. This meant that it was now our bedtime, a procedure we were always reluctant to face. The cold and almost pitch-black stairway, even with the light of a flickering candle, was most uninviting to say the least; especially if our journey had been given some momentum by Harold, when he happened to be in one of his teasing moods. 'Look out, here comes Owld Skinner!' he would say loudly, just as we were halfway up the stairs. With little shrieks and cries of alarm, we would stumble hastily up the remaining flight and make for the sanctuary of our bedroom. From below would come the sound of Harold's laugher and the admonishing of Aunt May. 'Owld Skinner,' according to rumour, had been a former tenant of Redgate Farm and hanged himself on the premises. Once we'd snuggled down under the bedclothes and said our night-time prayers, I doubt very much if Owld Skinner's ghost had kept us awake for long.

The very mention of bed-time prayers brings to mind our fellow evacuee: little Joey; one of 'them thar poor little beggars' who'd set foot for the first time on Redgate Farm at the beginning of September in 1939.

Being new to life on a farm, little Joey, just like Joan and myself, was much taken with the various livestock: pigs, chickens, ducks and geese, not to mention the two large working horses in the stable. However, it was the farmyard geese who seemed to hold a special fascination for Joey. Standing as close to them as he dared, Joey would then proceed to make loud hissing noises in their direction. For a time, the geese seemed quite impervious to his earnest attempts at communication; there came the day; however, when it became obvious that there'd been one hiss too many.

'They'll hev the arse outa his trousers one O' these days,' said Uncle Fred, standing aside to make way for Joey, as he came hurtling through the farmyard one morning. At his heels, hissing, screeching and cackling: came an entire flock of vengeful geese. Just as it seemed likely that Uncle Fred's forecast was about to take place, Joey, with great presence of mind: no doubt born of sheer terror, did a sudden left turn by the dairy and made for the back door; leaving the pursuing flock bereft of their quarry. If Joey is still around after all these years, I imagine that his once narrow escape from the angry beaks of those Norfolk geese will not have been entirely forgotten.

It was good to have Joey around though, he was always chirpy and cheerful. A regular little comedian who often made us laugh, sometimes at inappropriate moments.

Because there was no Catholic Church locally, here in the village, on some Sunday mornings, one of the priests from the Roman Catholic Church in Swaffham, came to say Mass for the evacuees and their teachers. On special occasions Necton village itself; ever friendly, he always came and stood next to Joan and I when Mass was being said on Sunday mornings. The local vicar kindly made the Necton Village Church available for us. Mostly; however, Mass was said in a temporarily converted local village hall. Even though Joey had been long gone from Redgate Farm by late 1942 and now lived in Necton village itself, ever friendly, he always came and stood next to Joan and I when Mass was being said on Sunday mornings.

Joey's proximity at solemn moments; though, was apt to make us nervous, and this particular Sunday was no exception. Mass was always sung in the Latin then: 'Ora pro nobis,' chanted the priest; 'All pick yer noses,' sang little Joey, echoing the chant in perfect tune, but only just loud enough for our ears. How difficult it had been not to laugh; though even to be caught giggling at Mass would have meant really big trouble.

In the future, as he went through life, Joey's wit, pleasant disposition and ready sense of humour, would doubtless turn to stand him in good stead. But when he lived at Redgate Farm, it was being 'little Joey,' his lack of inches, that sometimes proved to be his most valuable asset. Had he been a few inches taller, Joey wouldn't have aroused our protective instincts towards him, and what is more, he would never have been granted the privilege of having his bedtime prayers said for him, (my sister's recollection this time). 'I'm tired, 'Joey would plead, 'can you say my prayers for me?'...so how could we have refused? After all, his own big sister was no longer around to look after him (she lived in another billet), and he was so little and so very tired. His bedtime prayers were either included with ours or said as an 'extra': a task probably given to my sister.

Not that our own prayers were really lengthy, just the usual 'Mathew, Mark, Luke and John,' plus an 'Our Father' or 'Hail Mary.' It was the God bless list that prolonged our intercessions-beginning with 'God bless Mummy and Daddy.' (With real emphasis when we'd heard on the news that there'd been yet another air raid on London). Then a request for The Almighty to bless: Aunt Bett, Aunt Nell and Uncle Alf, Aunt Emmy and Uncle Albert, (who was in the Royal Air Force... but only as ground staff, because of his age), cousin Dan and his wife Rose. Then followed the second list: beginning with Aunt May and Uncle Fred, their daughters Violet, Lily and Freda (plus their spouses). Last but not least: Harold the farmhand, plus any other deserving grown-up we could think of. We never thought to inquire if Joey had a God Bless list also, for by then he'd be fast asleep.

Necton Village

The ease with which we had settled down to our new way of life, apart from the novelty of life on a farm, had been due to our on-going link with home.

Every week there would be a letter, every few weeks a parcel with sweets or small articles of clothing; mainly socks and vests. Mum always had a thing about vests; at one time we had about twenty between us. Larger parcels arrived every so often, either at Easter or Christmas, with our new outfits. My mother, akin to all women over the age of 'call-up' during the war, was required to be employed in essential 'war-works.' She worked in a munitions factory in Enfield and travelled there every morning from Liverpool Street Station. At one time during the war, Mum told us, the passengers ended up lying flat on the floor as an enemy plane swooped down and began machine gunning the carriages. A fair amount of my mother's wages must have gone towards our new clothes; they were always of good quality, always identical. People must have thought Joan and I were twins!

Our teachers from St John's had been evacuated with us, although we had hardly any Catechism now; there being no priest at hand to put us through our paces... for which, I'm sure, we were all quite thankful! Our lessons were much the same as before with the emphasis on English and Grammar. I loved anything to do with English and Composition but dreaded Arithmetic lessons; this subject was my Achilles Heel. Decimals and Fractions left me all at sea, and there was no concealing my ineptitude from the rest of the class. 'Hands up those with eight right'...and so on, my hand remaining down until the disgraceful: 'those with two right.' Our schooling had been part-time to begin with because we had to share the village school with the local children. Lessons in the morning and a nature walk in the afternoon, or vice versa. We didn't share a playground with the local children or mix with them at all; although eventually, we were invited to take part in 'stool ball' games on the field... a form of rounders. Later, we were allocated our own section of the school and lessons became full-time. Having had his quiet village school disrupted by an influx of London evacuees, his own school children consequently obliged to receive reduced teaching time, in order to accommodate the newcomers, that the headmaster wasn't inclined to regard us with favour is not at all surprising.

He certainly wasn't one to mess with, as a schoolfriend and I discovered one lunchtime. Taking advantage of our teacher's temporary absence, Harold and I were endeavouring to play a duet version of 'Chopsticks' on the classroom piano. We were having a great time and didn't hear Mr. Birtwhistle enter...at first that is. 'Get out,' he roared at us, his face livid with rage. We needed no second bidding as we were hustled out and ordered to stand outside by the cloakroom wall. 'You're not to move,' we were told. Being virtually scared stiff by our berator, we stayed put for the rest of the lunch hour; during which time, both of us dreading what next might be about to befall us, should our bout of unruly behaviour reach the ears of Miss Ladd, our headmistress; a keen exponent of 'one stroke on the palm of the hand,' which brought the tears to one's eyes and left a thick weal on the target area. I'd once been caned for being late for school...and it didn't half hurt! Luckily for my friend and I, the misdeed had gone unreported, but thenceforth, I kept my distance from the piano keyboard and resisted the urge to 'have-a-go' on it.

Mischief is to adults what adventure seems to children. A tendency I'd been prone to from way back. Naturally, I'd been one of the small group, who, from time to time, indulged in this pastime: a rather tame mischief when compared with that of the present.

Our lunchtime was over an hour long; sometimes we drifted off around to the village Windmill Bakery, which stood opposite the village pond. The baker often sold us lovely jam puffs for a few pence each. In the autumn, Mrs Bell, who lived in the little thatched cottage next to the school, sold off her surplus pears at 2d for a large bagful. But at a certain venue, there would be a form of 'edibles' for free...

We had discovered the sweet chestnut trees quite by chance when on one of our lunch-time explorations of the local area. Having followed a tree-lined driveway; we found ourselves in the vicarage grounds. It probably hadn't occurred to we adventure seekers that we were trespassing, even if it had, this would no doubt have simply added to our enjoyment of the situation. There had followed the usual ploy of stick throwing in an effort to dislodge a few chestnuts from the overhead branches, soon bought to conclusion by the sound of a violent rapping on one of the Vicarage windows, which had us all running at full pelt back up the long drive and minus any chestnuts.

A mere successful foray into unknown territory took place one lunchtime when my desk-mate, Kitty and I went on an apple-scrumping expedition to a local orchard. Even though the owners had given Kitty the assurance that we: 'could take as much fallen fruit as we liked,' she thought it best that we keep our heads down whilst crawling about in the long orchard grass.

'Kitty and Doreen, what are you giggling about?' asked Miss Davis sharply that afternoon; quite unaware, of course, that two of her pupils had been up to no good that lunch (even with the owner's permission) and were doing their best to avoid disclosing the contraband box of ripe apples beneath their desk.

Most of the evacuees had been billeted in or near Necton Village itself. A few; however, including Joan and myself, had been allocated to out-lying farms, well over a mile distant in some cases. During the spring, summer and autumn months, our long walks home from school were pleasant enough. Sometimes, we stopped by the blacksmith's to watch Mr Lloyd at his work or clambered over the meadow gate to pick wildflowers and, during the autumn months, there were always conkers to add to our collection or blackberries to pick.

WINTER...however, those war-time arctic winters were a different matter. Our morning wash became a mere cats-lick with icy water from the butt by the back door. We then set off for school with our pyjamas legs rolled up under our coats to keep our legs warm till we got to school, removing them before going into class and stowing them away in our shoe-bags.

On such cold and slippery mornings, the rare sound of a car engine was like music to our cold ears, because, we knew that the car's owner: Mr Lyons, would be stopping in order to give us a lift into the village...not that we ever spoke to him, except to say, 'thank you.' I think we were too shy and, perhaps, just a little in awe of him because he was 'posh'. Mr Lyons was a Gentleman Dairy Farmer, whose premises were situated half a mile or so from Redgate Farm.

We automatically dealt him the same respect we accorded to the seasonal Fox-Hunters on their horses; for whom, we gladly opened the gate in the lane so as to let them through-in spite of Uncle Fred's indignation at the hunters' disregard for his crops when in full Tally-Ho!

Apart from our much-appreciated lifts to the village occasionally; another of the blessings we should have been grateful for were the thick, long, pale green stockings (kept up by elastic garters), that had been especially knitted for us one winter. Mrs Ayres, a friend of the family, who visited the farm now and then, always seemed to be knitting up something or other on her four needles...though at the time, we'd little suspected that the pale green wool was being used for our benefit. I absolutely hated mine and felt self-conscious when wearing them for school. Even though they kept my legs warm, they came in for a great deal of comment. Fortunately, due to their pastel shade, frequent need of washing and eventual shrinkage, they soon became unwearable. My sister didn't appear to mind wearing her pale stockings; however, going to school one morning, one of her anchoring garters snapped- a rather more distressing event which she still remembers. And I even have a vague memory of this myself, but not the outcome. I can only hope that the problem wasn't solved by one of my 'sudden ideas.'

Tucked well away in the heart of the Norfolk countryside for a couple of years, at least there had been very little to remind us of the war itself. Except through the wireless broadcasts. In due course; however, a couple of incidents had occurred which served to remind us of its realities.

My sister and I were strolling home from school one afternoon and were about half a mile from the farm. Suddenly, as if from nowhere, there had come the roaring sound of an air-craft engine immediately overhead! 'Enemy machine-gunner' had been my first reaction and shoved my sister into the roadside ditch, throwing myself down behind her. But, as the plane flew overhead it became obvious that it wasn't one of the enemy's: no black German cross on its under-wings, instead the 'star' markings of an American fighter Bomber. By 1942, America had entered the war and now there were American Airforce bases situated in various parts of the East Anglian countryside. The 'low-flyer' must have been a pilot practising a bit of 'hedge-hopping.' Some months later I had seen one of those fighter-bombers coming down in flames; no doubt, having been 'limping home' after a bombing mission, the pilot hadn't quite made it back to base. I didn't know what to do and in a blind panic dashed into the village phone box with a vague idea of reporting it to someone, although the incident had been some distance away. Nothing to do; continue on my way to school (or home?). I can't remember which.

In April 1942 there had been two consecutive air-raid on Norwich. We could hear the wail of the siren, the muffled sound of the bombing and anti-aircraft guns, even though the city was some twenty miles or so distant. Flares lit up the night sky incessantly. At the siren's first wall that evening, everybody left the farmhouse and went to stand in a dry ditch beyond the orchard: a safety-first procedure I suppose and our observation post until we heard the sound of the All Clear at last.

When the siren's wailing had reached our ears the following night and yet again, we heard the muffled sounds of yet another air-raid, the reaction had been less immediate. This time there had been no mass exodus, no trailing to the orchard or standing in the ditch beyond. Instead, all of us watched the distant night sky being illuminated by enemy flares, and the searchlights criss-crossing in the background, from just outside the back door.

Having anticipated further episodes of standing around in an orchard ditch observation post: that very morning I'd gone out of my way to be prepared for such an event. Taking two large Witney blankets from the bedding chest on the landing, I placed them on a chair next to our bed; at the same time, issuing my sister with a certain amount of 'what to do' if there was another air-raid. 'What you be a' doing with my best blankets?' Aunt May had enquired on discovering them later. When I explained that they were to keep us warm in the ditch, she was not impressed! Reluctantly, I placed those lovely white 'warmers' back in their rightful place, at the same time, wondering at the lack of Aunt May's appreciation with regard to my 'special plan.' I found it very hard to understand grown-ups sometimes.

Footnote: Quote from Norfolk in the Second World War by Frank Meayes.

'The greatest damage to the City of Norfolk was done in two Baedeker raids on the nights of 27/28 and 29/30 April. Ordered by Hitler in revenge for the British raids on Rostock and Lubeck. Of all

the people killed in air-raids on the City during the war, 60% died on those two nights: 162 people were killed in the first attack and 69 in the second.'

Apart from the local country busses which ran at intervals between the market towns, the odd army lorry or speeding motor bike of a despatch rider, there was very little traffic on the narrow road which ran past the farm. Petrol was rationed, and motor cars were something of a rarity. In fact, there was nothing of interest that would have caught our attention whilst working in the fields nearby or playing in the meadow adjacent to the road itself.

There had been one particular day; however, when whatever game we'd been playing suddenly lost its interest. For, as far as the eye could see, there were army lorries; a seemingly endless convoy winding its way along the road and gradually slowing it's pace. Finally coming to a complete halt with one of the lorries now stationary beside the meadow gate. Curiosity having overcome our shyness; Joan and I made our way over to where it stood. There were several soldiers seated in the back and before long there had probably been mention of our London roots. In the course of our somewhat tentative chatting with the soldiers one of them had enquired jokingly if (seeing that this was a farm), we had anything for them to eat...

They had struck gold! It was Autumn and the season for apples and in the orchard, there were four apple trees of different varieties. Seizing the moment and quite forgetting the adult censure which usually followed such moments of inspiration, I volunteered to fetch the hungry soldiers some fruHaving, with my sister's help, struggled across the field with a sizeable basket full of apples, which had been much appreciated; I was on my way back for another load when my Lady Bountiful operation had been brought to a halt by the sudden appearance of Aunt May. I was quite disappointed: my generosity with other people's goods new no bounds. Left to my own devices, the whole convoy might have been supplied with that year's entire apple harvest!

And Further Afield

Even though I must have been a really annoying sort of child, what with my schemes and sudden ideas, I remember that Aunt may was always very kind to me: when I had expressed a keen desire to own a bicycle, she had kept my wish in mind. One Friday afternoon, much to my surprise and delight, Aunt May returned from her market day trip to Swaffham with the very object of my desire; Whether she had ridden it all the way home or persuaded the local driver to make room for it on his bus, I've no recollection of at all, but there it was! Not a new bicycle of course. Aunt May had put in a bid for it at the market auction and acquired it for two pounds, ten shillings. This bike, with the saddle lowered was just the right size for me, not a toy but a real means of countryside transport.

Learning to ride a bicycle for the first time proved to be more difficult than I'd anticipated; event though I had taken myself off to a quiet spot in the lane to do this in private. Having mounted and fallen off time after time; eventually, and after what seemed like hours of pure frustration...I took off! perspiring, flushed but breathlessly triumphant! I could ride a bike! What possibilities presented themselves now. An opportunity to 'go off' on my bike occurred sooner than I had expected; not by myself (as I would have preferred) but with two of our teachers and about half a dozen of my classmates: an educational excursion to Castle Acre.

Until the Reformation, Castle Acre had been a Roman Catholic Abbey, but now, there were only the ruins that Cromwell 'knocked about a bit.' A guided tour with plenty of history for we children to take note of and digest. I doubt very much if any of us did though. What had taken our fancy at once was the steep grass slope surrounding the castle. At the first opportunity: up we climbed, down, down we rolled, then toiled to the top again to repeat the process. A wonderful feeling of reckless abandonment at each descent, a joyous awareness of being, frozen in time.

Soon after acquiring my bicycle, and probably at Aunt May's suggestion, I began visiting Mrs Woodgate occasionally, usually on a Sunday afternoon. It had been some time now, about a year I think, since she and Mr Woodgate had come to receive the sad news that their son, who had been serving with the Royal Airforce, had been posted as 'missing, presumed killed.' Quite probably he'd come to share the fate of the many aircrew shot down over enemy territory.

Mrs Woodgate's little cottage, which was situated about a mile or so distance from Great Fransham and down a narrow side-lane, had been difficult to find on my first visit. All local signposts had been removed in anticipation of enemy invasion at any time in the near future, and large coils of barbed wire were placed at intervals all along the roadside. Not that I would have paid their sudden appearance much attention.

Although, at a guess, Mrs Woodgate would have been in her early fifties, she appeared much older, mainly due to her slightly eccentric appearance: She always wore a long skirt and a tweed jacket that had seen better days, and, on her head, she wore a small black velvet cap. Mrs Woodgate spoke in an 'educated' accent with no trace of a Norfolk dialect. All during our fireside chats she had never mentioned her son.

If, at the time, I had thought that she was a 'bit odd,' it would have been due to my perspective as a child. I wouldn't therefore have been at all aware of the effects of grief nor the depths of a mother's sorrow at the loss of her only son.

*Footnote: Quote from 'Norfolk in the Second
World War' by Frank Meeres:*

*'Practical measures were taken in the face of the new
threat. By October 1940: 1,697 miles of barbed wire,
73 miles of anti-tank mines and 440 miles of anti-
tank obstacles had been set up in the area. Germany
had invaded Holland: Britain stood alone. Invasion
was a real possibility and Norfolk one of the most likely
locations where the enemy might land.' (end of quote.)*

Hence the 'nasty looking' barbed wire.

When I'd first heard of Aunt May's plan to cycle all the way
over to Syderstone in order to visit her widowed sister-in-law
Blanch, I was, as per usual, eager to take part in what I perceived
as yet another adventure. To my acute disappointment, Aunt
May had nipped my enthusiasm in the bud almost at once. It
seemed that I was too young to undertake such a long cycle ride.
'But I'm over eleven years old' I'd protested...but Aunt May was
adamant.

I can only guess at the intensity of my indignation on learning
that Aunt May was to be accompanied over to her sister-in-law's
by Walter; our latest temporary evacuee, who often helped out
on the farm, being a sturdy 'almost fourteen-year-old lad.' Furthermore, as I was soon to discover, Walter, not possessing a bicycle himself, was to borrow mine. MY bicycle!!

Aunt May must have gone to some trouble in order to borrow
young Dorothy Clarke's Bicycle on my behalf. And so, it was, on
a bright Saturday morning in midsummer, wearing my favourite Harlequin pattern dress and feeling unaccountably happy
(no doubt had having got my own way), I set forth with Aunt
May and Walter; bearing him no ill-will, even though he hap-

pened to be riding my personal bike.

Although Aunt May knew all the short cuts, Necton to Syder-stone was quite a number of miles; she was right, it was a long ride for an eleven-year-old. Not that I intended to admit it how-ever much my legs ached. Soon, I wasn't just tired but very wet also. We had just passed through Sculthorpe and on our final lap, when the storm, which had been brewing ever since we'd reached Fakenham, now broke without warning. In next to no time the three of us were drenched to the skin. Shortly after-wards Aunt May has knocked on the door of a roadside cottage, asking permission for three bedraggled cyclists to enter for a while and dry off. In true country style, we were made most welcome and allowed to dry our hair and warm up a little be-fore a large kitchen range, by which time, the storm had passed, and we were able to resume our journey.

Had Walter and I been awestruck, I wonder, on discovering that Aunt May's sister-in-law lived in such a big house? More than likely we had been just a little surprised and consequently on our best behaviour.

From the window of a large flag-stoned kitchen, where we are now being plied with refreshments by Aunt Blanch (it was polite to address all grown-ups by either Aunt or Uncle then); we have a close up view of a very large walled garden. 'What were those things growing up wires?' we wondered. 'Peaches,' Aunt Blanch informs us!

Later we are all shown upstairs to a long dining room where we probably had lunch. I've no recollection of the meal whatso-ever, only that of a large, colourful painting on one of the walls: fruit, or flowers perhaps? A polished black grand piano stands at the far end of the dining room, the lid of which is open. How inviting the keyboard looks: I would love to try it but never dream of asking permission to do so. That would indeed be tak-ing liberties.

Now comes the long ride home in the heat of the late afternoon. Thirsty work and tiring on the leg muscles. I'm glad when we stop at a village pub, somewhere and Aunt May buys me a big glass of fizzy lemonade. When she had asked me what I would like to drink, that is what I requested; careful not to make the same mistake as I once did by saying airily 'I'll have a pint.' On that occasion, when I had been accompanying Aunt Lily and Aunt May to the little village pub in Fransham one evening (we'd been in the private side -room, not the bar itself), Aunt Lilly, ever one for a joke, had called my bluff and set 'a pint' before me. I took a couple of sips and it was really horrible!

This afternoon Aunt May had a glass of Ale, and Walter, being a big lad, is probably allowed a Shandy.

Being a summer's evening, it is still light when we reach the Three Tuns cross-roads in Necton: nearly home now, only about three quarters of a mile to go. Soon the road begins to incline slightly; all uphill now until we get to Clarke's Cottages. Although Aunt May must be all of sixty years old, she has taken the lead. Walter struggles on a few yards behind her with my saddle-sore self, bringing up the rear.

The sound of a heavy vehicle approaching obliges us to pull in quickly to the side of the narrow road, the inevitable army lorry passes us, there are several soldiers seated in the back. We remount our bicycles and resume the journey home.

The sight of all those young soldiers seems to have inspired Aunt May: She begins to sing, not loudly, but quite merrily, a popular war-time song; 'Oh Johnny, Oh Johnny, Heavens above. Oh Johnny, Oh Johnny how you can love. You make my sad heart jump for joy. And when you're near, I just can't sit still a minute'...and so Aunt May sings on. We've just passed Clarkes' Cottages and are now on the home straight. It's been a pleasant day all round: we've been to a large house that had running water and electricity, a beautiful dining room to, which contained both a lovely painting and a grand piano. Just the same, it's good to be home again.

And it's back to earth for Aunt May also. For as a farmer's wife she has much to keep her busy. Apart from the usual household tasks of cooking and cleaning, which includes all the household washing with only the aid of a large wood-fired boiler and wooden mangle. There are the seasonal jobs of fruit bottling and jam making, and, of course, the half-yearly duty of preserving (or pickling) of pork. After Christmas there will always be goose feathers or duck down available for the filling of home-made pillowcases. Nothing was ever wasted. Old stockings were knitted up on very large wooden needles and turned into small, but presentable, bedside mats. As well as looking after the evacuees and doing the weekly shopping in Dereham, Aunt May, being the scholar of the two, did all Uncle Fred's book-keeping.

Was she appreciated? Like most of her kind and generation, not nearly enough, until it was too late. Aunt May smoked: a habit, which had no doubt, led to her final illness. She also liked a drink from time to time. Good luck to her! What she really deserved was a medal.

Odd how a few words or a certain paragraph in a newspaper or magazine immediately brings to mind 'remembrance of things past.' Even the phrase itself, bringing to mind a certain gastronomical delight. In my own case; however, it isn't the Proustian 'madeleines dipped in tea' but the rather more surreal recollection of hot toast with goose dripping which my sister and I ate for our supper, seated on the farmhouse door-step on a mellow summer's evening some sixty years ago.

I share this particular memory with my sister who is of a more practical turn of mind than myself, and; therefore, inclined to retain memories of the gastronomical rather than the pastoral. Considering the fact that I'd occasionally left her struggling to make her descent unaided from the odd tree-my own skill at this particular feat making me impatient and unsympathetic towards her plight-it stands to reason, that, her enthusiasm for the pastoral scenes of 'days gone by', doesn't quite match my own or that I'm sometimes reminded of my unsisterly past. But my apologies have been sincere, my sins now hopefully forgiven.

The advertisement in the holiday brochure reads: 'Refurbished holiday cottages, North Creek.' Aunt Lilly's old, whitewashed cottage perhaps?

Summer 1941, we are staying here for two weeks with Aunt Lily and Uncle Hector. Aunt Lilly is fat and jolly, she's probably offered to have us here to give her mother a break. Aunt Lilly cooks on a small Primus stove, there being no other means, even a kitchen range like Aunt May's. The Primus stove is fuelled by methylated spirits; even our chips have a hint of the strong smell, but we don't really care about such things.

There are no strict rules, we are free to roam the local woods. We really love staying here. Tonight, we are going to a whist-drive with Aunt Lily. This is to take place at the village hall.

Before each game commences, a loud male voice announces; 'hearts are trumps' or 'spades are trumps.' Little Joey echoes; 'large lumps, large lumps' and we do our best not to fall about laughing.

When the whist-drive is over, a three-piece band comes on to the stage and begins playing for the dancers. The saxophone wails out a waltz tune. We've heard it before on the wireless and even know the words; 'Who's taking you home tonight after the dance is through?' On the dance floor, young couples sway in time to the music; most of the young men are in uniform and probably on leave before shortly going into action. Being children, we do not appreciate this and any hint of romance or soppiness that we observe, regarded with silent scorn or smothered giggles.

Luckily, we have not had to stay until the end, and, across the street, the fish shop is still open. Aunt Lily buys us all fish and chips, which we are allowed to eat on the way home: cooked in dripping and they taste lovely.

During that holiday, Aunt Lily let me borrow her bicycle, which was much better than my own. It had low handlebars and was much easier to ride. One day I cycled into Burnham Thorpe to see 'Union Pacific', showing at the picture house there. I went with some friends whom I'd teamed up with during that fortnight; though I don't remember much about them now. The film starred Joel McCrea and Barbara Stanwick: a cowboy cum railroad epic. What seems really strange at this point in time, is the fact that we simply left our bikes outside the cinema: there being nothing remarkable at all that nobody had made off with them, they were still there when we emerged.

I recently read in a holiday brochure that; 'North Norfolk is a place of great natural beauty and ideal for cycling.' Well, I knew that didn't I?

Alas my cycling days are over and as for fish and chips cooked in dripping: strictly off the menu. Bad for the cholesterol. Likewise, toast with that goose dripping...our suppertime from long ago. Such epicurean delights only in our remembrance of things past.

When Aunt Lily and Uncle Hector came over from North Creek, it was invariably their means of transport: a very noisy motorbike and sidecar, which gave us news of their imminent arrival. Which in turn indicated that we were in for an entertaining evening, during which, Aunt Lily would be doing her very best to tune into Lord Haw Haw's propaganda broadcast from Germany. This of course was really the English Traitor: William Joyce.

Later that evening, just as we'd hoped, there was Aunt Lily twiddling the wireless knob in all directions, until finally, from across the English Channel, came the awaited pronouncement: 'Jarmany calling...Jarmany calling...this is the Reich Sende Hamburg.' Lord Haw Haw most certainly had it in for his ex-countrymen; much of the vitriolic rhetoric amounting to veiled threats should we fail to surrender as soon as possible. More than likely, it also hinted at the forthcoming invasion. Sometimes, the rhetoric would include a swear word or two, which Aunt Lily thought very funny. And so, did we!

Uncle Hector was as slightly built as aunt Lily was stout. One of the reasons that we always looked forward to these occasional visits included the possibility that Uncle Hector had remembered, at last, to bring with him the large slab of toffee he had once promised us. We were far too polite to have enquired as to the whereabouts of its non-appearances. However, after two years of its non-appearance, we could only assume that the big slab of toffee had been a figment of Uncle Hector's imagination, or, that Aunt Lily and he had eaten it themselves in a weak moment.

We Happy Few

By the end of 1941, many of the evacuees had returned to
London. Some of these having reached the school-leaving age of fourteen would have gone back home to seek
employment, or to become apprentices. Because there were
now so few children, our teachers had returned home also. Now,
the remaining children would be allocated a new teacher and
receive their schooling in a new location. No doubt much to the
relief of the Necton Village School Headmaster, whose well-run
establishment had been temporarily invaded by aliens.

Our new teacher was Mr Obendorf, who'd formerly taught in the
boy's section before the war commenced in 1939. His wife and
little girl came down from London with him. He had two other
children, much older than Rita, who must have been about nine
years old then. His son was in the Royal Airforce and I believe
that his elder daughter lived in occupied Holland. Sometimes
he read us part of her letters home, all of which had been heavily
censored by the occupying Germans.

He was an extremely good teacher, though we didn't appreciate
this at the time and regarded him as rather eccentric.

Our new school was to be Holme Hale Village Hall: two miles
distance from Necton. This entailed catching the school bus
every morning. If we happened to miss it, which we did a couple
of times, it involved quite a long walk. 'Wicked children, lose
five marks' said Mr Obendorf, as we made our sheepish entry an

hour late, losing five marks was quite a stiff penalty; especially, if we'd managed to accumulate several of these as reward for having clean fingernails and well-polished shoes each day and were in with a chance of receiving five shillings worth of saving stamps. Those unfortunate lads who were billeted at Sunder's Farm never got a look in: their boots were often muddy, but Joan and I always managed to avoid this by taking the short cut across our side field, then climbing over the gate and on to the main road.

The village hall had not been used as a school for some time, I imagine. There were no traditional flap-top desks, so we were obliged to make use of what were available. During our formal lessons, we sat at trestle tables: three pupils to each. At other times we sat on slope-backed wooden benches. These, of course, were normally used for various village meeting and events. When two of these benches were placed seat to seat, they made a realistic boat (or barge).

This came about because we were in the process of reading Tennyson's Morte Arthur and our teacher had, well ahead of his time, sought to enhance the poet's verses, to give the words meaning: by having the death of Arthur enacted by his pupils. Those who'd been selected for the main roles: the dying King Arthur and 'the Fairest Queen of all', more or less miming the action (or inaction), as he narrated the verses.

Prior to this, all of us had a turn at reading the lines, and the very first, as luck would have it, had fallen to the lot of little Joey; though not so little now, he must have been about ten years old. All went well until the lines; 'I am so deeply smitten through the helm, that without aid, I cannot last till dawn.' I think it must have been the 'smitten through the helm' bit that got to Joey. For the words were accompanied by a faint snuffling and snorting sound and the beginning of a grin. But a sharp glance from Mr Obendorf would have quickly put paid to any further loss of control. (My sister's recollection here).

Perhaps, luckily for all, and out of respect for Alfred Lord Tennyson, the role of King Arthur hadn't been given to Joey. Instead, it had fallen to the lot of Harry. A sturdy lad and one of those billeted at Saunders's Farm; not really cut out for a dying Arthur; who was required to lay prone in the barge whilst 'The Fairest Queen of all' wept bitter tears upon his brow. Playing the part with much seriousness, Mr Obendorf's little girl, Rita, who probably grew up to be an actress (very dramatic).

I'm sure that Harry would sooner have been anywhere else other than in the makeshift barge, but he bore it well. Had Joey; however, been called upon to play the part of Arthur, lying flat upon his back in 'dying' mode, especially on hearing he'd been 'smitten through the helm'; why, it would have been a different matter altogether. Even a sharp glance from the narrator himself, wouldn't have been enough to prevent the King's undignified revival.

In common with many schools during the period, even at elementary level, we children learned reams of English poetry by heart: Tennyson, Shelley, Keats, Masefield and Robert Browning. Shakespeare, we took in our stride. Even excerpts from Lord McCaukey's 'Chronicles of Rome' came within our remit in due course. 'How brave Horatio kept the bridge in the brave days of old.' One line we tended to await with added interest, subject to the 'daring' of the reader's emphasis: And the proud Umbrian's gilded arms clashed in the bloody dust.'

We had an excellent choir, and our repertoire was as varied as our reading matter. English, Welsh, Scottish and American folk songs (though no Irish for some reason). Then there were 'Sea Shanties' and 'Negro Spirituals.' Mr Obendorf was an exacting choirmaster and choir practice always occupied the whole of Friday mornings. We prepared to take part in the local village concert and perfection was required and invariably obtained. On Friday afternoons, when lunchtime was over, and we'd finished eating our sandwiches, Mr Obendorf would read us a story, or excerpts from a book he'd chosen, whilst we sat at our knitting. The 'knitters' were of course 'we girls', most of whom were able to knit socks or gloves. This was a skill that had been introduced as a matter of course, together with sewing lessons- a must for future wives and mothers. When it came to knitting, it would have been our elders at home who had provided extra help when needed. All sewing lessons came to be abandoned: those awful grubby bits of stitch practice cloth, sharp needles and pricked fingers.

Our introduction to classical music had been by way of wind-up gramophone. There were two records: John McCormack singing 'Who is Sylvia' (I remember his tenor voice quite clearly), and the other 'softly wake my heart' from Samson and Delilah (my sister always referred to this as 'Samson in the Lilac'). We were always encouraged to sing along during the final bars of this aria; perhaps to see if we ran out of breath before the contralto solo- ist...and we usually did! As well as singing, we occasionally got to dance, again, to the accompaniment of gramophone records. There were two only, I seem to recall. 'Gathering Peasecod's' had us dancing round in a circle, hands joined, first left then right, at intervals skipping in the centre and clapping high into the air. The other folk dancing tune was; 'Sir Roger de Coverly.' This was most fun and a good way to warm-up on a cold winter's day. Two lines of children facing, each couple, in turn, dancing down the middle in time to the music. I loved these sessions; I believe we all did then.

It couldn't be all fun of course. Much as we enjoyed our music and dancing, the day of reckoning arrived, with unavoidable regularity, and, to our ongoing dismay, it must be said. Except for my friend Beryl, who was good at doing sums (arithmetic). Betty, Beryl and myself were usually seated in the front row and more subject; therefore, to a certain amount of trepidation...we knew what to expect!

'What is the common denominator?'...'The lowest common de- nominator? 'our teacher would enquire of us each in turn, after having set down those horrible looking fraction sums on the blackboard. Which was propped up as usual and alarmingly close, on its wooden easel. If he received a 'blank', as he often did, his wrath could be fearsome. 'Stupid children' he would shout in frustration, slamming the blackboard down hard on the front table; causing we unlucky three to jump out our skins! He was entitled to be angry. As far as arithmetic went most of us were a dead loss.

Fortunately, there were no regular exams then, which would have exposed our lack of maths savvy. Though it must be said that we'd have done very well as far as English Literature was concerned, and, most likely have been contenders for Choir of the Year.

When we returned to London in late 1943 and began to attend our former school again, the advantage of being taught in a small classroom and without the interruption of air-raids was apparent. Our standard of learning being well in advance of those children who had remained in the city. We were really very fortunate: mainly due to our having had an exceptional teacher who'd always made our lessons interesting...even if a little hair-raising at times.

Part Three

The Return of the Natives

I n the summer of 1943 and during our school holidays, Joan and I came home to London for two weeks. There had been no air-raids for some time, so it was considered safe enough for us to pay a brief visit. My mother came along to collect us, and we caught the train from Kings Lynn, arriving at Liverpool Street late in the afternoon.

Everywhere was thick with smoke and steam: loud with the noise of departing trains. My sister took one look at the dirty smoke-caked surroundings, burst into tears and said she wanted to go back to Norfolk. After the peaceful countryside, Liverpool Street Station was like a shock to the senses. It was difficult to make our way along the platform, it's space being occupied by seated Italian Prisoners of War, recognisable at once by their brown uniforms. I'd seen Italian P.O.W. before; many of them had been sent to work in the surrounding farms near Necton. In fact, when I used to cycle through Frensham, they would often wave to me from across the distant fields.

Instead of the basement flat of no.99, we now lived next door in two flats. My father had been obliged to rent two more rooms now that Joan and I were four years older. No longer of an age where we could share a bedroom with our parents. I was almost thirteen and a half, my sister going on for twelve. It was nice to be home for a while, taken out and about by Dad, having been introduced to our landlady, Mrs Green, almost as though we were royalty. But, our London break, had turned out to be the beginning of the end of our Norfolk idyll. On returning there we had found it difficult to re-adapt and I became homesick for the first time ever; which no doubt had something to do with my having become a teenager.

We returned home to London for good about six weeks later, and in the October of 1943, the presumption was that the war would soon be over. It had gone on for more than four years now, surely the end was in sight? Everyone seemed to be of that opinion.

How strange it seems to me now, that just as my sister and I had almost effortless adapted to, and embraced, our new country-side surrounding. Our new lives on a farm, four years previously ... giving little thought to our poor bereft parents back in London. We now relinquished it with similar equanimity, being eager to return home to London and resume our lives there. That we had probably left a large gap in the lives of Aunt May and Uncle Fred, who had fostered us for four years, wouldn't have occurred to us then.

Although Aunt May had been in poor health for some time prior to our leaving, when Joan and I had waved goodbye to her from the window of our bus bound for Kings Lynn, on that October morning in 1943, leaving her standing at the farm gate. We could never had guessed that this would be our last sight of her; for we had promised to come and visit she and Uncle Fred the following summer. But when I'd written then, the reply to my letter had not been from Aunt May, but instead, from her eldest daughter; who informed us that her mother was very ill and in Coltishall Cottage Hospital. I wrote to Aunt May there and had brief reply...a few lines which had obviously been a struggle to write: 'The nurse is holding me up to write this.' A few weeks later, one of my old school friends, who still lived in Norfolk, wrote to me enclosing Aunt May's obituary notice from the Fakenham Times. Uncle Fred survived her by a year, or there-abouts.

Which was really very sad, because I would have liked to see them again when I was older; to have thanked them for taking us 'poor little beggars' under their respective wings. Harold too of course. Hardworking and kindly simple folk remembered by 'them thar' evacuees' with mush affection and gratitude.

When I revisited Necton a few years ago, passing Necton Church in the village, I was immediately reminded of Uncle Fred. Easter 1943, attired in his best breeches and buskins, standing by the alter waiting to give his daughter away on her wedding day.

A very jolly Uncle Fred, obviously intent on livening things up as the family guests embarked on the final wedding hymn in a somewhat faint-hearted manner. 'Come on, come on, sing up!' says Uncle Fred, turning to face the singers. Meanwhile giving his new checked cap a few encouraging whirls. Joan and I, acting as Freda's bridesmaids, feeling slightly taken aback at this unfamiliar lack of decorum during a church service, to begin with anyway. Then we managed to overcome our reservations and 'sang up' with the others. After such an earnest entreaty from Uncle Fred, what else could we have done?

A war-time wedding, with a war-time cake to match: no three-tiered offering with royal icing and beautifully decorated. Instead, a lovingly prepared, slightly lop-sided chocolate flavoured sandcastle, coated with soft icing and stuck all over, higgledy-piggledy with silver paper horseshoes. A cake that we could hardly wait to sample.

A comparatively brief period of our lives, those four years on a Norfolk Farm. Nonetheless, very special indeed. Being uprooted and then transplanted into a completely strange environment, had been the lot of all we war-time evacuees. For my sister and I, this had turned out to be an enjoyable and interesting experience...it could well have been otherwise.

Sometime, even now, I wonder what became of my pet ferret, Jackie, after we'd left so suddenly that October in 1943. Harold would have seen that he was fed and cleaned out I imagine. His regular carer no longer around. Joan have been slightly puzzled by what they came to discover in the deep side oven next to the kitchen range. There in his long-time resting place, a small ear-less teddy bear abandoned in time of war.

Shortly after returning home, we resumed our schooling at St John's in Mare Street. There were many new faces, and the classes were now mixed; before the war, all the boys had been taught in a separate part of the school. In fact, everything seemed alien to us now. The children here rougher and much nosier than our school friends in Norfolk. For our school din-ners we had to go along to another building in Mare Street. This was the Lady Hollis School; now given over to the business of providing mid-day meals for various of the local schools. It was often necessary to queue up for twenty minutes or so in order to wait for dinning places to become available. On eventually finding a couple of vacant places at one of the long dining tables, it was nothing out of the ordinary to find ourselves seated op-posite other diners who were using their spare moments to flick peas at each other. I'm unable to recall much about the food it-self; however, except that we consumed it as quickly as possible in order to escape. The general commotion not exactly condu-cive to the luxury of lingering over one's meal.

Nothing remarkable to recall about Christmas 1943, except that the weather was very cold. No roast goose for dinner this year. Hear in London meat was well and truly rationed: any kind of poultry more or less unobtainable. Our festive fare turned out to be a baked rabbit; which, given my mother's cook-ing skills, would have been quite delicious anyway.

It must have been an unusually quiet Christmas at Redgate Farm. For the last four Christmas days there had been children around. Unless, of course, Aunt May had been assigned another batch of refugees.

When I started back to school after the Christmas holidays, it was with the knowledge that this would only be for a few months: my fourteenth birthday was approaching. After the 5th of April I would have to leave school and then start work; whether I wanted to or not. I wasn't looking forward to leaving school; however, especially since I'd no idea at all of the work I might be required to do.

Mum was doing her best to be helpful and, as usual, her imagination was running riot. 'How would you like to work at painting pottery?' Considering the fact that in order to learn this skill, I would need to take up residence in the Staffordshire area. Her suggestion hadn't been taken seriously. Mum's suggestion would no doubt have been an involuntary expression of her own artistic leanings. Given half a chance, painting flowers and patterns on pottery, would have been her own choice, rather said that she might be able to get me a start in the tailoring trade. This idea didn't appeal to me at all. It sounded very boring and I hated anything to do with sewing anyway. Events took place towards the end of January, which put all thoughts of leaving school and starting work on hold. This was the commencement of what came to be known as 'The Little Blitz.'

Joan and I had been safely tucked away in the Norfolk countryside when London had been bombed for a period of seventy days and nights during the 'Big Blitz' of 1940/41. Our only experience of an air-raid viewed from a distance of some twenty miles: these had been the two air-raids on Norwich in April 1942. We were about to discover for ourselves what the word Blitz really meant.

The very first raid of the 'Little Blitz' took everyone by surprise since there hadn't been any air-raids for a considerable length of time. One evening in late January 1944, there had suddenly broken forth the loud blaring wail of an air-raid warning: that stomach churning undulating pitch of a siren. Up and down it went, up and down, causing one's stomach to do the same: a sickish roll of fear on hearing it at close quarters for the first time. Mrs Green called up from her basement and invited us all to come downstairs and sit in her parlour until the raid was over, rather than go outside in order to take cover in the damp Anderson Shelter. Although later that year, had we known it then, we were destined to spend many a night under its iron canopy.

Meanwhile, Mum, Dad, Joan and I cover in Mrs Green's cosy basement living room, all amidst the stout Victorian furniture: velvet curtains and flourishing aspidistras, as the grown-ups made polite conversation. And the mayhem took place outside: the deafening racket of anti-aircraft guns and nearby exploding bombs; when the whole house literally shook, ready to come down about our ears at any moment.

On that particular night, the 21st of January 1944... 268 tons of bombs fell on London.' (quote from 'London at War 1939-1945' by Philip Zieger).

So, not surprising, when all's said and done, that the ex-evacuee's introduction to 'being bombed' had been so ear-splitting.

In the weeks and months to come, there would be other air-raids on London, and at varying intervals. But life carried on as usual. Adults went to work, and most children went to school. People even went to the pictures-it wasn't all gloom and doom.

My sister and I had acquired American pen-friends. My pen-friends name was Margaret Roll, she lived in Trenton, New Jersey and was about to start the new term at Trenton High. In reply to her letter I mentioned that I was soon to leave school and start work, though I made no mention of the recent bombing raids here in London. It went without saying; as numerous posters in public places served to remind us all 'Careless talk costs lives.' It was common knowledge that there were enemy spies throughout the world, it wouldn't do to let any information as to the location or results of the random bombing raids that had recently taken place.

There were other posters also, just to remind we citizens of Great Britain of our duty in war-time: 'Is your journey really necessary?' 'Make do and mend.' 'Dig for Victory.'

There had been one poster in particular which, had given me

some concern, when I'd come across it in a public toilet for the first time. A poster that had been both perplexing and worrying to a raw teenager. (We were all pretty raw way back in the forties!)

Quite a large poster in fact, with the heading in unusually large print, right in front of me on the toilet door: 'VENERAL DISEASE.' A long list below the heading gave the curious 'spender of a penny' details of all the symptoms, followed by some advice to the sufferer: what to do, whom to contact. After diligently reading all the listed information, I came to the alarming conclusion that I'd somehow come to be suffering from V.D. myself! One of the listed symptoms only. Just the same it had me worried. Even if I knew nothing about the sexual relations as mentioned on the list, I could have caught the germ from a seat. Should I tell Mum? Somehow, I couldn't picture discussing such an obviously private matter with her. Best not to. After a time, I forgot all about my secret concerns with regard to V.D., having now found something else to worry about. Like how I was going to tell Mum when I started my periods? I'd known all about the matter since the age of ten or so, when one of my school friends had become very distressed after a visit to the toilet one playtime. This was when 'we girls' had all rallied round and after much whispering between us (in the presence of boys), made haste to report the dramatic occurrence to Miss Davis. It was then forgotten: only part and parcel of certain information gathered via the playground. However, such snippets were only part of our lives; no great deal at the time. Even when some of us came across the odd used condom along the country roads, we'd more interesting things going on in our lives as children to have given these discoveries much thought. The 'grown-ups': an odd lot anyway, nothing to do with us.

Our generation, though: out to work at the age of fourteen after the war, were still children, and, (unlike todays youngsters) under no pressure to abandon our childhood. For a 'late developer' like myself; obeying the house rules was, on the whole, no problem.

There was one rule; however, that Joan and I felt rather unfair. This was Dad's insistence on our going to bed, at what he called a 'reasonable time. 'Most of the interesting programmes on the wireless were often broadcast after half-past nine in the evening. Plays in particular, were of interest to us: especially those with an 'adult' theme. Sometimes we crept downstairs in our pyjamas and sat on the bottom stairs: which were only a few feet away from the living room door. By straining our ears, a little, we caught most of the dialogue; enabling us to get the 'gist' of the drama in question. Saturday evenings were special 'eavesdropping' forays to the bottom of the stairs. Although, if Dad happened to be on late night shift at the café in Morning Lane, Mum would let us keep her company whilst 'The Man in Black' was being broadcast. Background effects were often quite riveting: such as that of a heavy trunk being dragged stair by stair and down into the cellar...it's heavy 'thudding' leaving the listeners in no doubt as to the fate of the 'draggers' wife. At the conclusion of the drama, when all had come to be revealed, over the air came Valentine Dyall's throaty drawl: his sinister tones inviting us to 'listen again next week for yet another Mystery Murder Tale' (or words to that effect). At this Mum would switch off the wireless: all three of us then, not wishing to be 'last up', hastening upstairs to bed with more alacrity than usual.

There were quite a few entertaining radio broadcasts during the 'forties'. It was special, of course, and had been going on for some time during the war years. Tommy Handley's death came as quite a shock to the radio listening public, not least myself, when I'd overhead someone speaking of it as I was on my way home from work, via a number 38 bus from Victoria. What was classed as humour then would be considered 'corny' now: when the emphasis seems to be on a form of satire: but that of the cruellest sort. But as a fan of 'slapstick' (especially Charlie Chaplin), I would say that wouldn't I?

I was once admonished, when I was fifteen years old, for laughing too heartily at the antics of Abbot and Costello in a local cinema. 'Do sit still girl', the lady seated next to me said crossly; 'You're shaking us all up.

One of the 'corniest' wireless broadcasts about that time, was a weekly quiz, involving members of the older generation. At each individual interview, the Quiz-Master, Wilfred Pickles, would ask the preliminary question; 'And 'ow old are you Vera?' (Albert or Betty), Upon the amazing and unbelievable disclosure; 'I'm seventy-four Wilfred,' a thunderous applause would erupt from the similarly geriatric audience: whereupon would follow the simple quiz. At each inevitable correct answer- yet another burst of clapping. On the quiz masters directive; 'Give 'er the money Barney,' or 'Give 'im the money Barney'- even more tumultuous applause. Then would come the closing 'sing along': the signature tune 'Ave a go Joe, cum on and 'av a go,'), I've forgotten the rest of the chorus). The piano accompanist Violet Carson; who later became famous as the somewhat dour Ena Sharples of Coronation Street.

Wilfred Pickles had once enjoyed a brief spell as a BBC Newsreader, but, at a time when Public School type English was the requisite for broadcasters in general, Wilfred's underlying northern accent would not have been the ideal. Subsequently, he came to be allocated broadcasting of a less conventional kind: namely, 'Ave a Go' and later a special poetry reading half hour on a Sunday afternoon. On hearing Wilfred Pickle's presentation of A.E. Houseman's 'A Shropshire Lad,' his hint of a northern accent made the verses come alive for me, and, their sentiment clear. I immediately became hooked on A.E. Houseman and made for Hackney library, as usual, in order to search for a volume of his poetry, plus any other new reading matter I'd heard of and which might prove interesting. But, not quite all of my teenage reading matter was of a 'serious nature.'...

Occasionally, I bought a copy of the weekly woman's magazine that went by the name of Red Letter and cost 2d. After I'd left school in 1944 and when on my way home from work in Clerkenwell, I would sometimes catch sight of these seemingly 'daring' items displayed in a newsagent's shop. The front covers of which, often depicting a curvaceous looking female (usually in a tight red dress), sometimes relaxing in a hammock or low chair (a bed was nowhere to be seen), I had been tempted to find out more...But none of the stories within ever lived up to the front cover brashness. Just the same, I couldn't help feeling a little guilty about my Red Letter magazines and kept them well hidden from my mother. If, by chance, she'd come across that wicked lady in her tight red dress, I knew that my shameful reading matter would have been regarded with a certain amount of suspicion. To my mother's way of thinking, it would mean her daughter had shameful thoughts, typical of one, who, as a child, had been a prospective candidate for the girl's Borstal!

But redemption was fairly close at hand: namely Hackney Library. Within those hallowed walls, I eventually managed to discover the likes of: H.G. Wells, John Galsworthy, George Bernard Shaw and Warwick Deeping. Even HENRY James, whose 'prose' style took some getting used to at first. Since our literary grounding at school had involved some of the classics: 'Silas Marner,' 'A Christmas Carol,' plus plenty of Shakespeare, despite my early departure from formal education, the 'jump' to adult reading matter had not required much effort. The same applied to poetry. Having been already familiar with the English poets throughout my school days: when Keats, Shelley, Masefield and Tennyson had to be learned by 'rote', it hadn't required many stepping stones later en-route to A.E. Houseman and T.S. Elliot.

I had almost forgotten until now, that my initial 'stepping stone' had presented very much earlier in my life, especially when it came to poetry. I would have been about eight years old when I turned the pages of Palgrave's Golden Treasury of Verse. When I first read 'Tiger tiger burning bright, in the forest of the night' and 'My mother bore me in the southern wild,': William Blake having been made accessible to a little girl in Hackney via her 'bargain hunting' Dad and courtesy of a second-hand book-stall on Kingsland Waste.

As a bookworm-type teenager, post-war, I did a lot of second-hand bargain hunting; both for books, and (when I discovered classical music), for 78 Gramophone records. When it came to reading matter, Kingsland Waste, as well as Hackney library, played a valuable part in my acquisition of diverse literature. Alfred Lloyd Tennyson on one hand...Mickey Spillane on the other. The latter's detective story, with its potent mix of crime, romance and vaguely suggestive sexuality...had me glued to every page. I'm unable to recall the title of the book itself but the very last paragraph had concluded with the discovery of the murderer's latest victim. The punch-line that the dead lady, upon closer examination, was in fact... a MAN! Even if the author had used the term Transvestite, I wouldn't have had an inkling of what it implied. So, after having eagerly devoured the final chapter, the whole 'drama' of the detective's discovery had been completely lost on me. I had thought it disappointing and 'rather odd and creepy'...That was all.

Busy Days and Noisy Nights

I n the March of that year: 1944, my mother and I joined
evening classes for 'make do and mend.' This was a war-
time project; clothing was rationed, like everything else,
and on coupons. The idea was to make use of an old garment by
unpicking it, then turning it into another.

Quite by chance, and as a result of attending these sewing
classes, I'd been lucky enough to have obtained my first job. The
enrolment officer, who worked for the Civil Service, knew of a
current vacancy for a Junior Clerk. According to Miss Clarke, I
was a 'credit to my mother.' (she meant polite and well spoken):
a requisite when it came to presenting for an 'office job' at that
time. And so, it came about that I was given a letter of introduction to Head of Department, together with instructions of how
to reach The London Insurance Committee: an imposing block
of offices situated in a turning just of the Pentonville Road.

The whole set-up was extremely daunting: even if the lift at-
tendant wore an important looking liveried uniform; no doubt
rendering my mother, who'd accompanied me here, almost as
nervous as her offspring about to be interviewed by the Head
Clerk. Shortly after being ushered into the awesome presence
of the gentleman in question, my ordeal began to take place.
On being confronted with the question 'and what does your
father do?' I had immediately responded with: 'He works in a
caff'...'You mean café, 'the Head Clerk corrected me. My face
burned with embarrassment now. I wanted to go home. I hated
this horrible man and this big place. I didn't want to work

here either. However, it appeared that in spite of my linguistic ignorance, I'd passed muster. 'Now if Doreen stays here until she is sixty,' I overheard the Head Clerk's Secretary say to my mother...'She will be entitled to a special pension.'

Seated next to mum on the No. 30 bus, I was on the verge of tears: 'I'm not going to stay until I'm sixty,' I told her, feeling decidedly worried at the thought. We were on our way home to give Dad the good news that I had landed the prestigious 'office job' applied for. I wouldn't need to work in a factory after all. Just the same; however, and even though we really needed the money (as my father had emphasised), I wasn't at all ready to leave school. And I certainly didn't like the look of that London Insurance Committee!

The transition from school to work had been sudden. As far as I was concerned, too sudden. On Friday the 5th of April: my fourteenth birthday, I had been at school. Three days later I found myself in a completely strange environment and receiving instruction on how to sort and distribute the post throughout this large building. Not only to the various departments but also into a series of postal pigeonholes. I was totally confused, finding it difficult to remember the given instructions or to interpret what I'd jotted down in my notebook; mainly because I felt so nervous. I longed to be back at school again. My lack of confidence was made even worse by a very snooty girl (Anita was her name, I've never forgotten her), who informed me rather tersely, on my second day at work; 'You needn't think I'm going to show you how to do this anymore.'

In time, of course, I grew accustomed to the world of work, and, no doubt, felt quite virtuous as I handed over my share of the housekeeping budget every Friday. My starting wage was 25/- (twenty-five shillings). Dad said that I was to give Mum one pound (twenty shillings). I could keep the five shillings for my clothes and bus fare. Mum often helped me by taking out a Provident cheque (but not to tell Dad, who didn't believe in any form of debt), when I needed a new dress.

The only real angst that I'm able to recall with regard to my new world of work, was the trepidation I'd felt on approaching the hallowed precincts of the Secretarial Department with my trolley load of post; painfully aware on some damp mornings that my 'pageboy' was now mere 'rats tails,' my rolled fringe drooping 'shutter like' down over my eyes. 'Good morning Miss Tompkins,' came the lofty greeting of the supervisor before I could slink out unseen. The truth was that I simply hated my hair, which regardless of setting lotion or curlers, insisted on staying straight.

I also hated my knees which I thought were too fat. I was so concerned about them, that I wrote to the advice section of Home Notes. I also mentioned my hips when I wrote because I had similar concerns about these. I received a very helpful reply from Home Notes: the cure for fat knees was very simple. It involved sitting up in bed each morning and slapping each knee in turn for five minutes. More drastic measures were required in order to cure fat hips. This entailed lying down flat on the floor, clasping my knees (whilst bent), and rolling from side to side. This remedy was not only rather uncomfortable to put into practice: our bedroom floor consisting of linoleum and a couple of mats, but, resulted also in a fair amount of noise, including outbreaks of laughter. 'Now what's going on in there?' Dad would call out when my rolling from side to side had caused me to collide with certain of the bedroom furniture. I gave up in the end; however, since neither of these cures appeared to be having any immediate result.

Even though fairly gregarious by nature, when it came to being in the company of seniors at my place of work: my immediate office elders; it had the effect of rendering me almost completely tongue-tied. When I had completed my morning duties of delivering the office mail throughout, I shared a small room with three seniors and occupied my time by various kinds of 'pen-pushing.' Tasks involving index cards and other paraphernalia, neat hand writing being the only requisite for this slightly boring occupation. Thus, the morning the-break always came as a welcome interruption. Instead of tea; however, all the juniors under a certain age were entitled to a free cup of delicious National Cocoa. It's chocolate rich taste being a real treat when sweets and chocolate were rationed.

One of my immediate seniors was a youngish gentleman with a fair moustache. Possibly he'd been invalided out of the Services. 'You stick to your own style of writing Miss,' he said one day. Having intervened when my hand-writing had been remarked upon by a lady senior. Sadly, this made me so shy of him that if he happened to be standing at the same bus stop as myself, I would walk as far as the next in case he spoke to me.

As the weeks went by, the world of work became familiar and its surroundings less formidable. After three months, I was promoted to another department and awarded a salary rise of 2/6d a week. I had also managed to make friends with three other juniors; all recent school-leavers, like myself, now earning their keep.

During our lunchtime, the four of us would sometimes wander down Amwell Street and across Roseberry Avenue into Exmouth street. Here we did some window shopping before going into Woolworths, just to see if there was anything for sale in the way of combs, hairgrips or soap. This was usually in vain since toiletries of any description were in very short supply during the war...being classed as luxuries.

Later that year, my American pen-friend sent me a gift-box containing some highly coloured and strange tasting boiled sweets and two very large beautifully scented bars of soap. At Mum's suggestion I gave one of these to Aunt Nell.

This, of course, was the Aunt Nell who'd made some of our 'Prewar' coats and dresses and taken my sister and I out and about up to London a few times since our return from the country. The Aunt Nell who had never married (although once engaged): slightly scatty, always cheerful and a keen fan of the musical theatre. Especially The Olays of Ivor Novello. Throughout the war and despite the heavy air-raids, Aunt Nell had stayed put in her top floor flat in Navarino Mansions: trusting in providence, which had chosen to desert her in the end. Just before 'Victory in Europe' had been declared in May 1945, she had died in hospital of an in-operable brain tumour.

1944: in June of that year, after the Normandy Landings had taken place and things seemed to be on the upturn...there came a new series of air-raids, somewhat unexpected since there had been a fairly long period of respite, giving people the impression that the air-raids on London had finally ended.

'Cowards, English cowards,' called Mum after our retreating backs one evening, as Dad, Joan and I made yet another dash down to the garden air-raid shelter: covering the three flights of stairs and basement passage in record time. The blare of the siren had sounded yet again, when just half an hour previously the 'All-Clear' had us trooping back up-stairs. These alternating alarms and all-clears were quite unsettling. Mum had finally decided to stay put. Her Irish dander was up. She'd already been through the Big Blitz at the end of 1940. Now with the enemy's ability to have us all running up and down stairs all evening, Mum wasn't moving. Instead she decided to follow Aunt Nell's regular advice: 'Trust in providence Bid, trust in providence.'

But the air-raids now were of a different variety, though nobody had been aware of it at first. These raids turned out to be the first of the Doodle-Bugs: the V.I. Rockets, pointless planes, a weapon by any other name but just as lethal. These were very lethal and very frequent. Night and day over they came; a few at first, but then increasing in number and frequency: even Mum, in the end, was forced to take cover with the English cowards. When a raid was taking place and overhead came the drone of yet another Doodle-Bug, hands would go over ears as we heard the engine suddenly cut out: that meant it was now diving earthwards...'Please God don't let it be on us.' A few seconds of silence then a deafening explosion somewhere further on: other people dead, other homes demolished-then the all-clear siren.

It meant we were safe, for the time being anyway.

And; thus, we grew accustomed to sleeping overnight in the garden shelter, a chance to get a little sleep between raids. Mum and Dad slept on the two bottom bunks, Joan and I on the ones above. The candle, which, apart from our emergency torch, was the only means of light in the night-time shelter, often threw weird shadows on the corrugated iron walls. We both amused ourselves by laughing secretly at the elongated shapes of our parent's noses: especially Mum's nose, which was inclined to be tapering. I often think that's the only way in which to describe the average teenager during a certain period of their 'metamorphosis', is by the word obnoxious. The war-time variety being no exception it would seem.

When the dawn came after such shelter nights, it was always to find Dad 'long gone,' having been 'up with the lark' as usual, so as to get things going at the café before any hungry customer's, or, seekers after a nice cup of tea, arrived at breakfast time. Mum and I leaving later, after getting washed and dressed in the more comfortable surroundings of 'indoors' before going to work. My sister left to slumber on for a little longer before getting herself ready and setting off for school. All of us on such mornings, almost taking for granted our survival, after the night's heavy Doodle-Bug raid: when, by unlucky chance, the house, or even our 'dug-out' shelter, could have suffered a direct hit.

There had been one morning in particular during these Doodle-bug raids, when I saw at close hand the effect of such an occurrence; though, if my sister and I had been in London during The Blitz of 1940/41, the sight would have been only too familiar. As I alighted at my usual bus stop in Roseberry Avenue, just opposite Amwell Street, it was to find that the small block of corner houses was no longer there. Instead, a vast and awful mountain of rubble, rescue workers with stretchers climbing about on the fallen masonry and tangled mass of what had recently been the dwelling places of those Londoners. Families, who now lay dead, or, seriously injured beneath their ruins. At a single stroke of fate, one of those droning Doodle-Bugs, maybe one which had passed overhead as we'd lain, hands over ears, willing it on to 'somewhere else,' 'had shortly afterwards 'cut-out' and plunged to earth on this very spot...here, in Clerkenwell.

It was not a scene to stand and gape at, however, and I hurried up and along Amwell Street towards my place of work. Once back in the world of work, all thoughts of flying bombs took second place. True that there had been the odd trip down to the basement canteen when the sirens had sounded, because, yet another rogue V.1. had somehow managed to get through the anti-aircraft screen. But there were other diversions during the day: work in particular, though not difficult, it was required to be accurate and neat. Filling, collating and compiling new medical case notes. We juniors were also required to take a turn at 'waiting on tables' at lunch time. Waitresses would have been in short supply; women under a certain age now in the Armed Forces; engaged in essential work in munitions factories, even driving busses.

Not that we minded helping out anyway, even if we had to wait until all senior staff had been served with their meals before eating our own. By which time, most of the seniors would have returned to their various departments. We juniors could now sit together and have a good natter.

Our conversation wasn't anything to do with 'boys'...in fact, we rarely saw any boys our own age. In any case, they wouldn't have been of much interest to us because of their immaturity. No, our conversation was mainly to do with films and film-stars. Eileen, a slightly more sophisticated girl than we other three, had been to see Gone With the Wind. She said that it was daring in places. We were all agog and wondered if we'd ever get the chance to see this film ourselves. I'd been particularly interested at the time, since all matters concerning adult relationships: men, women, babies etc. appeared to be unmentionable. If a neighbour was 'expecting,' my mother would impart this to my father by whispering behind her hand. Having lived on the farm for four years, both my sister and I would have become well acquainted with the 'basics' of procreation anyway; complete ignorance of such matters when applied to human beings hadn't, therefore, been an issue. It was the forbidden aspect of grown-up relationships that made me keen to find out more. Hackney library, as usual, came to be the means of satisfying my 'satiable curiosity' to some extent when, I found myself leafing through one of Emile Zola's novels by the Z bookshelf. Unfortunately, the very page I'd lightened upon, featured the ill-starred female in the process of giving birth: hanging on to the bedrails and having a really bad time. No wonder Mum whispered about it. I abandoned Emile Zola and went back to P.G. Woodhouse instead; at least Bertie Wooster made me laugh.

By the Autumn of 1944, the flying bombs were easing off and it wasn't really necessary for us to spend so many nights in the garden shelter. In due course, we reverted to spending every night in our own beds.

Although I had seen at close hand, the effects of a Doodle-Bug raid, when on my way to work one morning during the summer, and had once run for cover when a low flying V.1 had passed overhead, after the siren had sounded (I had been walking along the Pentonville Road towards The Angel on that particular afternoon.) Being fortunate enough to have been living in the Croydon area round about that time, those ongoing rocket raids would have left a much deeper impression on the psyche of a fourteen-year-old: a couple of 'one-off' recollections bear no comparison.

Quote from London at War 1939-45 by Phillip Ziegler: 'The devastation wreaked by the V.1's had been fearful and repair work was only just getting into its swing. In Croydon, people were sleeping in undergrounds and shelters. Fifty-four thousand houses in the borough had been damaged. Many could be patched-

up, but the hundreds of building workers drafted in from other areas had to sleep somewhere. Those lucky enough to have habitable houses were urged to share them with the dispossessed.' (End of quote).

One of the last Doodle Bugs had landed on a garage in Mare Street, just opposite the John the Baptist School. Both school and church had been destroyed by the blast. Fortunately, this had been during the school holidays.

A very brief respite followed prior to the advent of yet another rocket, which came to be known as the V.2. This there would be no warning enabling one to take cover. These were long-range weapons fired from launching pads in Holland- high into the atmosphere, a 'bolt out of the blue'. Capable of blasting every-thing in the target area to 'Kingdom Come.'

Since the destruction of St. John's, my sister had been going to another school in Homerton. But this had been short lived. In late October she was rushed to hospital having produced a posi-tive swab for Diphtheria. Probably there had been a local epi-demic though, due to all the war news this wouldn't have been considered news-worthy.

Due to a late diagnosis by our family doctor, by the time she was admitted to hospital my sister's illness was in an advanced state. Until my father had insisted that I cancel my Saturday morning plans to meet up with my friends, in order to go roller skating; I'd been selfishly set on my original intentions. Feeling rather ashamed of myself when I'd been made aware of how very serious her condition; furthermore, since Diphtheria was a con-tagious disease, I would need to have a swab taken also. In the event, this proved positive.

Christmas Day 1944 saw both my sister and myself on the Junior Ward of the Homerton Isolation Hospital. Joan, having needed intensive care at first, placed in a separate ward. It was several weeks before she was transferred to the main one. As if Mum and Dad hadn't had enough to cope with during the earlier part of the war: what with the air-raids and their absent off-spring; on their Sunday afternoon visits to the hospital they now had to don white 'barrier-gowns', due to the contagious nature of our current illness.

Although I was virtually only a 'germ carrier' and hadn't any actual symptoms, apart from a sore throat, my treatment for the illness had been no different from that of any other Diphtheria patient. This entailed being absolutely bed-bound for six weeks and flat on one's back, since, the complications of the disease included a possible strain on the heart. Even our meals, during this period, had to be consumed in a more or less laying down position. Soup, which unfortunately often included leek soup, had to be supped from a spouted container- although what particular technique was needed for solid food, I fail to remember. The atmosphere on the ward was quite informal and the nursing staff obviously well used to dealing kindly with junior patients. Our ages varied.

Finally, the six weeks of being confined to bed came to an end; though having been thus positioned, when it came to walking again, there presented many difficulties.

First of all, there had been the inability to set foot to floor without sharp shooting pains through lately redundant leg muscles and the necessity to hang on to any available means of support, in order to avoid falling over. In addition to our unsteadiness, which didn't help matters at all for both myself and fellow 'walker': another very giggly fourteen-year-old, the almost impossible task of controlling our spontaneous laughter as each of us surveyed the other, shuffling along the ward in our hospital gear...long floral dresses, thick black woollen stockings and short lace-up boots. The latter obviously needed to support our weakened ankles. I returned home in late January, but it would be another month or so before my sister was able to do the same. On being discharged, she was sent to Bognor Regis for a fortnight's convalescence, courtesy of a Catholic charity.

'The winter of 1944 and the beginning of 1945 had been one of the coldest for fifty years.' (Quote from 'London at War-1939-45' by Phillip Ziegler).

It certainly had! Outside there were icy winds and slippery pavements, piles of frozen snow. Indoors, once the fire had died down, it was pretty chilly too. On one such evening, I think it would have been in early February, Mum and I had gone to bed early (it being the warmest place). Dad, meanwhile, preparing to leave for his night shift at the café. All of a sudden, there occurred the most terrifyingly loud explosion I had ever experienced. It seemed to be taking place all around us and the whole house shook on its foundations. Every scrap of glass had been blasted out of the window frames, the particles of which now lay buried in the top blankets of our beds. All throughout the house there now drifted a thick pall of acrid smoke in which floated the blackened shreds of our bedroom curtains. While across the end of my bed, resting at an angle, the toppled wardrobe blown forward by the blast of the V.2. rocket, until Dad came running up the stairs to move it. Apart from feeling a bit shaken, (possibly quite a lot), Mum and I were otherwise unharmed.

We were the lucky ones. Here at the Dalston end of Greenwood Road, up near London Fields, less than ten minutes' walk away and where the V.2. rocket had landed that night; there had been death and destruction.

One icy morning, Mum and I joined several other people who were waiting in a long line outside the Salvation Army Hall in Clapton; the issue point for docket holder's, (issued by the authorities), needing new blankets. We weren't the only ones who'd had their windows blasted and bedding ruined. In due course, temporary repairs were carried out; enough to withstand the continuing cold weather anyway.

A few years ago, I paid a return visit to Hackney and walked through to London Fields. No more little corner shop where we bought our 'pre-war' sweets: penny ice-blocks, bubble gum and long strings of red liquorice. Like all the surrounding Victorian type dwellings, the little shop had been blasted out of existence in February 1945. The usual low-rise post-war flats now in situ.

Intending to take a short cut through to Mare Street but wondering if this was still accessible; I made enquiries of a young lady who happened to be passing by, at the same time mentioning (as we 'I was in the war' oldies tend to), the V.2. rockets of 1945 and the one that had destroyed the former houses nearby. 'It must have been a big rocket,' she remarked. No doubt referring to those that bear relation to fireworks. But I didn't have the audacity to have recommended that she visit the Imperial War Museum and see for herself those floor to ceiling monsters. After all, it's old history. Just the same, I still have an aversion to sudden loud bangs on firework night: those modern rockets which sound like explosions. My cat; however, apart from a slight twitching of his ears, appears quite unruffled despite the noise. It's alright for him of course, he wasn't in the war.

What Now?

When Victory in Europe was proclaimed in May 1945, I was barely fifteen years old. Had I been an adult then, looking forward to the return of a son, husband or fiancée, my reactions to the almost unbelievable news that, at last, war was over, would have been those of elation and tremendous relief. But, at the age I'd been at the time, my own personal thoughts and feelings were, if anything, somewhat complex. A fleeting sense, almost, of anti-climax to begin with. For so long being used to hearing that reassuring phrase; 'When the war is over,' now that it had finally come about, and the prophecy fulfilled, my first reaction had been to wonder 'What now?'

I was, of course, at that awful 'in-between' stage: too young to have participated in grown-up celebrations, but, now I'd left school and out to work, decidedly too old to have joined in all the fun of our local street party. My sister, on the other hand, had just about scraped in at the age of thirteen. Standing at our front room window and looking down at the jolly scene below, not to mention the goodies laden long festive table, not only did I feel a little wistful but vaguely sorry for myself too. In fact, it wouldn't have occurred to me at all that I'd been lucky enough to have survived the war: 'lived to tell the tale,' and would probably do so in the years to come, every time the anniversaries of Victory in Europe came and went.

Yet another anniversary; the usual television old newsreel, May 1945, the cheering crowds, the King and Queen and the two princesses come out onto the balcony of Buckingham Palace. More cheers as the crowd surges forward. 'We were in the crowd,' I repeat to whoever happens to be present. Not strictly true; however, since my sister and I were only on the outer perimeter: on my father's orders. 'Stay here or you'll be crushed against the railings when that lot push forward.'

The journey home took ages; the bus crawling at a snail's pace, trying to make its way through the dancing, singing throngs along the way. Now we have reached the outskirts of the real East End, where a jolly crowd of ladies board our bus. 'Roll me over in the clover' they are singing. Dad laughs but I blush with embarrassment: a rude song in front of my father! I could hardly wait to get home.

Although the war was over, there was much to remind us all of its six-year duration: vacant lots, large spaces between diverse houses and buildings which had been created by both the bombing raids, flying bombs and latterly, as a lethal postscript, the V.2. rockets. Sometimes there was only half a house left standing, as though it had purposely cleft in two; it's inside construction now grotesquely exposed. A missing outer wall that had left a flight of stairs clinging desperately to its anchorage: the interior wall of an upstairs passageway perhaps. And weirder still, the sight of a lonely looking fireplace, minus a hearth and exposed to all the elements, high on a wall overlooking the street. But it is only in retrospect that those sad post-war ruins come to mind. As a typical teenager then, I would have been too busy going to work and getting out and about in my spare time (within the limits of a fifteen-year-old), to have been concerned about such matters.

Continuing shortages of various commodities meant there were still a certain amount of food rationing. My mother would still have had to join a queue occasionally for items in scarce supply. Not long after the war, she had managed to procure a large tin of fancy biscuits; including the chocolate variety, the like of which we hadn't seen for years.

The plan had been to save this treasure for Christmas. One evening; however, Mum opened the tin for just one each. Sad to say, the original plan was abandoned because within a few evenings we'd managed to polish off the lot between the three of us.

I was now working as Junior Clerk and Receptionist at a local builders merchants. No more worries about remaining at The London Insurance Committee until I was sixty.

On entering the supervisors office on my first day's return to work I had been greeted with the words: 'Good morning Miss Tompkins, I hope you haven't brought any of your germs back with you.' My mother had been furious and wrote to the Head Clerk informing him that her daughter would no longer be working at the L.I.C.; probably much to their relief. I daresay that Diphtheria wasn't at all acceptable or indeed a 'respectable' illness to have contracted when working for that particular branch of the Civil Service.

Sunday evenings just after the war usually meant Albert Sandler and the Palm Court Orchestra on the wireless: for one thing in common that my parents had, apart from Joan and I of course, was a love of music. Until we came to discover classical music for ourselves a year or so later, these Sunday evening sessions bored my sister and I rigid and we made ourselves as scarce as we possibly could; probably retreating into the front room until the broadcast is over; leaving Mum and Dad free to enjoy the music without any background mutterings from their teenage offspring.

Dad's favourite piece of music was the Barcarolle from 'The Tales of the Hoffman' and I am always reminded of my father whenever I hear it played. This is mainly due to a certain incident that took place shortly after the war, when Dad took Joan and I for a trip to Southend on Sea. Our very first visit since before the war and now that all the surrounding barbed wire barriers had been removed. For six years previously, sand and sea had been inaccessible.

Making good use of the newly available strand was a musical

entertainer: an accordionist. We sat on the sea wall with Dad, enjoying the summer sunshine and listening to the pleasant selection of popular melodies. Eventually, of course, the accordionist came around with his collecting bag. Ongoing to drop a few pennies within the proffered bag, Dad had accidently let slip a half-crown coin. Quite a sum of money for someone on a low wage. It was a very awkward situation for my father, who must have been tempted to plunge his hand into the bag so as to retrieve his half-crown piece. Instead Dad had nonchalantly waved the surprised musician away, though with a special request in lieu of such an unexpectedly large contribution. 'Tales of Hoffman' said Dad with just a hint of command. From the puzzled look on the accordionist's face; however, and his subsequent failure to include Dad's request in his musical melodies, it was quite obvious that he had no idea of what 'Tales of Hoffman' meant; even though it happened to be a popular classic. Perhaps Dad should have asked for his half-crown back...but as he had come to expect: really 'life was, indeed, full of disappointments.'

But the Palm Court Orchestra wasn't the only thing that bored Joan and I. Occasional Sunday visits to Edmonton for Aunt Emmy's 'high teas' were not something we looked forward to at all: even if the spread itself was something of a treat in those immediate post-war years. During these rather formal family gatherings, anything that cropped up in conversation was apt to set us off. In fact, it had been quite a strain for two 'apt to get the giggles' teenagers who had suddenly discovered that Uncle Albert; never missing a birthday and even during the war, often sent them small parcels of sweets or chocolate, had a slight speech impediment. Uncle Albert couldn't sound his R's...those at the start of a word or conjoined to certain consonants. A discovery which had now become a source of secret merriment.

To make matters worse, anything uttered by Uncle Albert: who was by nature 'a man of few words,' promised to be a special announcement. 'Course, I've always been a bit of a webel,' he had uttered on one occasion; somewhat of a surprise to Joan and I, but no actual grounds for mirth. At a subsequent family gathering; however, when for some reason or other the subject of cabinet making, (Uncle Albert's trade), was under discussion: we could see at once he was about to make a declaration. Taking his pipe from between his lips he announced slowly, 'Course dere's big dwars and little dwars, (referring to the drawers in a wooden cabinet). It was almost too much to bear! The gigglers, having at once translated the disclosure into 'big knickers and little knickers.' With my father seated just opposite me at the dining table, I had managed to turn my emerging splutter into a cough; meanwhile doing my best to avoid my sister's eye.

Most Saturday mornings saw Joan and I catching the number 30 bus in order to go up West: to Oxford Street usually. First of all, to the Marble Arch branch of C & A, where we tried on hats just for fun. Then, we went window shopping all along Oxford Street. Later, we went to have lunch either in Lyons Corner House or a Marks & Spencer cafeteria.

Occasionally we ended up at Foyle's Book Shop in Charing Cross Road, where there was always a good selection of second-hand books to rummage through on the stall outside.

At other times we went to the pictures: many good films were doing the rounds then. Our favourite was The Seventh Veil: this was because we had both taken a shine to James Mason. We cut out every magazine photo shot that we could lay hands on and stuck them all over the walls of our bedroom. We went to some trouble to even catch a glimpse of him in an old film: usually in some old 'flea pit' cinema in Hoxton or Homerton. With his dark handsome looks, together with his beautifully articulated speech, to us, James Mason was the ultimate in male perfection. We had never seen (nor were we likely too), any male to match him in and around the immediate Dalston area.

In the film, of course, there had been all that emotive classical music; music which I'd heard for the first time: Greig, Beethoven, Rachmaninoff. I was immediately captivated and set about exploring the world of classical music; pursuing the subject with the same youthful enthusiasm that had taken me into the world of literature: another voyage of discovery.

For my sixteenth birthday, my sister bought me the Decca recording of Eileen Joyce playing the Grieg Piano concerto in A Minor. This had been the main background music in The Seventh Veil. I spent many a moment listening to it, with my head stuck under the open lid of the gramophone cabinet; in an effort to drown in all those Norwegian waterfalls and tumbling mountain streams. I was completely lost to the world in: Arpeggios, Schertzos, Prestos and Allegro Vivaces. Fortunately, there were no stereo speakers available then: to have also drowned my next-door neighbours.

Not long after the war, one of the enterprises of the newly formed Arts Council, had been 'Culture for the masses.' There was ballet at Haringey Arena, with Alice Markovo and Anton Dolin as Soloists and the Hackney Empire received a visit from the Philharmonic orchestra, (I'm not sure if it was the London or Royal Philharmonic). The central hall in Mare Street became the venue for a piano recital by the illustrious Moisevivitch. On this occasion, I couldn't help noticing, with some embarrassment, that the famous pianist had been obliged to open up the heavy lid of the concert grand himself, before being able to commence his recital: a gaffe of the first order. Those in charge obviously not familiar with concert etiquette. Quite understandable really, for up until now, the Central Hall in Mare Street had only been host to the local Salvation Army Band.

In due course, Joan and I discovered the Henry Wood Promenade Concerts at the Royal Albert Hall. We usually went to these on a Saturday afternoon and joined the long queue, patiently waiting for opening time. As soon as the doors were open, and the tickets issued, there would be a rush for the best places in the promenade area: or a dash up several flights of stairs to the gallery. First-comers were sometimes lucky enough to find a chair by the balcony: though seats were in very short supply. I always preferred the gallery rather than the promenade. It gave a good view of the audience below; and, on the Last Night of the Proms, especially when Dapper Dan, (Sir Malcom Sergeant), was conducting the orchestra. He was very popular with the young audience: the Promenaders, (many of them music students I imagine): a jolly lot. Where are all the young people now? Glastonbury I expect: classical music no longer considered 'cool.'

The post-war years may have been a time of freedom for Joan and I, but there were certain rules that still applied. In by ten 'o' clock: which was no problem, because the only venues locally for under eighteens at the time were: evening classes, the cinema or a local youth club, which shut at 9.pm. anyway. Then of course there was a certain rule which went without saying: no make-up, i.e. lipstick, powder or rouge; though this didn't bother us because only 'flash' or 'forward' girls wore make-up: or Hollywood film stars.

We did have certain beauty aids; however, one of which was diluted Camp coffee- a horrid tasting drink at the time due to the amount of chicory it contained-applied and stroked carefully on to our white, stocking-less legs. During the summer months, it produced a life-like tanning effect; unless one had the ill-luck to be unexpectedly caught-out in a summer downpour of heavy rain: when the streaking result might prove a trifle unsightly.

Another of our cosmetic aids to beauty was an unwanted hair remover; a foul-smelling product which went by the name of Veet. This is still on sale, I believe, but would hope that it's original 'blocked drains' odour has come to be replaced with a slightly more pleasing fragrance. 'What's that smell? What's going on in there?' Dad would call out on the other side of our locked bedroom door: but modesty forbade us to enlighten him. Poor Dad! One teenager would have been enough to put up with, but a duo of the weird species must have been doubly mystifying and annoying.

However, trying we might have been then, as far as any parental worry with regard to potential boyfriends, there would have been absolutely nothing of concern because immature youths would have been of little interest to us. Besides which, we rarely came across boys of our own age, except for Peter, who lived next door and was 'a bit odd.' He spoke in a loud voice and veered about from side to side when walking, (the poor lad probably had hearing problems which affected his balance).

The fact was, that our romantic thoughts were always fixed on the older man: the glamorous sophisticated older man, who only existed, for us, in the remote world of the cinema screen.

There were quite a few of these delectable hero's at the time. Laurence Olivier in Henry the Fifth: 'Once more unto the breach dear friends, once more, or close the wall up with our English dead.' We'd learned this speech at school, though it hadn't registered with me until Olivier's beautifully precise, clipped tones, bought the words to life. Another of those suave gentleman actors had been Anton Walbrook. The hero of Dangerous Moonlight, who'd bravely continued playing his concerto as Warsaw, itself, was being bombarded by the enemy. Right up until the ceiling had caved in and when he'd been obliged to take cover under the grand piano: together with the beautiful heroine, Sally Gray, to keep him company. Clarke Gable was very handsome too, big ears or not. Our number one pin-up, though, was James Mason.

All the older men utterly unobtainable and consequently all the more adored. Nothing at all for my father to have been remotely concerned about; even if he'd been aware of our secret celluloid heroes.

What Dad was aware of though, was our weekly gadding about up to Oxford Street every Saturday morning, when we should have been helping Mum with some of the housework. She often had 'funny turns' but we didn't know what they were about: or really wanted to know: we were too selfishly intent on enjoying our newly found freedom.

Dad had attempted to explain Mum's problems; however, when he had approached us in a serious manner, just before we were about to take off one Saturday morning. We'd immediately gathered that we were in for one of Dad's lectures. 'Your mother' he said, 'is going through what is known as 'The Change of Life.'' To this he received but little response because we simply had no idea what he was talking about. What did he mean 'The Change of Life?' Our lack of reaction must have come across as unconcern, which was true to some extent I suppose. Anyway, it caused Dad to lose his temper with us; 'useless ruddy ornaments,' he said angrily. 'useless ornaments, you should be helping your mother with the housework.' Perhaps we tried a bit harder after that: for a while anyway, but like most youngsters of that age, empathy with the older generation was sadly lacking. Although, Joan and I were not the only 'useless ornaments' at no. 97...

At one time during the early twenties and before he met my mother, Dad had been valet to the then famous music hall comedian-cum-violinist, Stanelli. This was no doubt when my father would have acquired his fondness for violin music; which, he said, was far more expressive than the human voice.

Stanelli, according to Dad, was much given to writing poetry, usually after having taken a little wine; and on such occasions would walk up and down the room quoting verses from the Rubiyat of Omar Khayam. My father could quote verbatim one verse in particular: 'Ah love, could thou and I with fate, conspire to grasp this sorry scheme of things entire, would we not shatter it to bits and the remould it nearer to the heart's desire.' A verse, that perhaps, would have been of special appeal to Dad, (on the whole that is), since he disliked 'muddle' and was all for tidying things up. The trouble was; however, that he sometimes inadvertently added to any prevailing domestic disorder himself. This was due to his enthusiasm for bargains on the one hand and his lack of expertise with regard to household repairs, on the other.

One of the built-in cupboards in our front room was always full of Dad's past 'bargains': large china ornaments, various glass-

ware including vases, old gramophone records and enough cutlery for a veritable banquet. One of Dad's bargains in particular
deserves a mention here. It was an unforgettable snip: a wireless set obtained at a special price from that bargain hunter's
paradise known as Kingsland Waste. It was in perfect working
order and could be seen working- literally. That the wireless in
question lacked any form of outer covering had obviously been
noticed by its purchaser but still considered irresistible at its
knock-down price. And there it stood on a side table in our
living room, exposed to all and sundry in its shining metallic
glory. My mother was not impressed and at the time there had
been a few words on her part: not only at its stark appearance
but in protest at the wireless set's ability to deliver a brief but
sharp electric shock, should any member of the family be careless enough to brush against its innards.

Dad's innovative method of electrical wiring consisted of a series of loops across the ceiling. Given that the only wiring cable
available post-war was thick and fabric coated, the looping process, when completed, came to resemble an unsightly out of
season Christmas decoration. In fact, a rather sorry scheme of
my father's own making. There would come a time; however,
when this form of D.I.Y. creativity was to prove invaluable.

For a long time, I had been scouring the local papers in search
of a second-hand piano. I wanted to learn how to play: this had
been an ambition of mine for some time now. As a child I'd
often itched to have a go when in the rare vicinity of a piano
keyboard. The only time that I had managed to do this was
when I was about ten years old. That rather un-nerving episode
when the village school Headmaster had caught Harold and I
indulging in a 'Chopsticks' duet on the classroom piano one
lunchtime. An incident that had so grossly offended him, (almost to the point of apoplexy). The bare face audacity of these
London evacuees in daring to lay their sticky fingers on the village school's piano! But that was all in the past. I intended
to have my own piano soon and has been saving up for several

months with this in mind.

I finally came across just what I'd been looking for in the Musical Instruments for Sale column in the Hackney Gazette. 'Walnut piano in good condition £10.' I was exactly two pounds ten shillings short of the required some. Dad very kindly helped me out here; so, I went ahead, paid the vendor and arranged for my 'bargain' to be delivered. In my naivety, having taken the advertised 'good condition' simply for granted, instead of going along and trying the said instrument out myself. However, whilst in the process of endeavouring to play my exercise 'scales in contrary motion'; I discovered soon enough that the 'good condition' only applied up to a certain point: a maximum of about four and a half octaves; beyond which, the rest was silence. On removing the front panel, the reason for this became clear at once. The leather fabric, which should have been attached to the wooden hammers, in order to facilitate the striking of wires behind: had completely rotted away. But all was not lost. Help was at hand. After studying the Modus Operandi for a while, my father came up with a brilliant idea. In order to repair the faulty hammerheads and restore the instrument to full working order. The only materials required were: a length of narrow elastic, a packet of drawing pins and a stick of sealing wax.

Having cut the elastic into several carefully measured pieces, Dad set to work: using strategically placed drawing pins to secure the elastic replacements of the rotted fabric. I can't quite recall what the sealing wax was used for, but the hammerheads were now completely functional. The finished article made a colourful display though obscured from public gaze, once the polished walnut panel had been replaced.

A 'botch up job' it may have been, but it did the trick, and I was now able to play my scales in contrary motion, plus any other pieces of music I needed to practice. Dad himself, was now able to try out a few tunes by ear, occasionally. Not technically perfect; perhaps, but well worth eight out of ten for effort; especially since it was the violin that took preference when it came to musical instruments. As far as he was concerned anyway: much more expressive than even the human voice.

For some reason, possibly because of the odd 'not quite up to it' and straining for the top note; female voices one heard on the wireless now and then, my father had a strong aversion to sopranos. 'Bitch…bitch…cinder under a door,' he would say, as his eardrums were being assaulted. Choirs were another matter: The Russian Credo of the Orthodox Church happened to be one of my father's favourite pieces of music. Then, of course, there was Paul Robeson, whose pitch and timbre of voice brought nothing but pleasure to those with sensitive ears.

Once more, we were in for a very severe and prolonged winter: the discomfort made worse by a government directive. There was a crisis with regard to coal production. As a result, there was to be fuel rationing. Even electric fires required to be switched off at certain times during the day.

In my small receptionist's office at R. Wright and Sons, Builders Merchants, it was exceedingly cold at times. Even with the small electric fire, (when it was allowed on), was no proof against the icy draughts which blew in from time to time; as incoming victims of burst pipes arrived in order to report their misfortune and seek assistance. It was 1947 and my booking ledger abounded with the entry: 'to repairing burst pipe, 7/6d.' A paltry sum now but that was almost sixty years ago, when a tradesman's working wage would have been about five pounds or less. I knew of this because one of my tasks had been to check through all the time sheets of our carpenters and plumbers. Another of my duties entailed the typing-up of lengthy job specifications. At one time during that icy winter, I had actually tried to type with my gloves on because my fingers were almost numb with cold. A foolish idea of course, every time I went to type, I managed to hit two keys instead of one.

Although I'd learnt my basic office skills at this builders merchants, it was, on the whole, a decidedly unglamorous venue for a teenager. Once Molly, the secretary, left, after her husband had returned home from serving with the Royal Navy, I was the only female in a world of 'P' bends, 'S' bends, W.C. cisterns and Ball Valves. The replacement secretary now being a male, there was no lighter female chatter to alleviate the somewhat dull atmosphere. I began to feel very lonely.

Now and then, when leafing through one of those ego boosting horoscope booklets, I've often come across the observation that on the whole, those of us with an Aries birth sign, tend to be very lucky. I must say that I've found this to be true. After all, what else could it have been other than a huge stroke of luck to have found myself in the October of 1947, no longer sitting in a very draughty outer office in Stoke-Newington but before a large light-giving window, in a modern suite of offices, in Parliament Street S.W.1.? Not an 'S' or 'P' bend W.C. cistern in sight.

That the company for whom I now worked had been in need of an efficient clerk/typist: which I'd come to hear of through the 'who you know' grapevine, had of course been a contributary factor. Just the same, what a fortunate co-incidence that our landlady: Mrs Green, had a daughter with 'family connections' of a senior nature within the firm itself and knew that I'd been on the lookout for a new job.

My new employment; however, had come with certain stipulations...from my kind advocate that is: 'Now I know that your father is a Socialist but it's best not to discuss politics in the office.' How this good lady had acquired knowledge of Dad's left-wing leanings, I really don't know (but can only guess). She didn't live in her mother's house anyway. In any case, he wasn't given to singing the Internationale within its portals. Neither was he known to have lectured Mrs Green, herself, on the Chinese Revolution. True, that Dad bought the Daily Worker newspaper occasionally and enjoyed listening to the Russian Orthodox Choir's version of the 'Credo': not to mention Paul Robeson singing: 'The Song of the Volga Boatmen.' More than likely it had been my mother who'd 'blown the whistle' on Dad to Mrs Green: A True-Blue Conservative; maybe as a form of revenge: the aftermath of a domestic altercation. Thus; I'd been warned! In other words:' no Red Flag to be fluttered, come what may.' Since all my work colleagues were Conservatives, a piece of sound advice which I took heed of. Until...Nye Bevan's rhetoric in 1948: when his plans for a National Health Service were in danger of being scuppered by the opposition. Uproar in our office, during which I 'came out.' The only 'Red' in an office full of 'Blues'; but very nice ones just the same.

I had a much longer journey to work now which involved catching a number 581 bus as far as the Angel. A quick change onto a tram (when it finally made an appearance), and once seated, a silent prayer that my conveyance would get a move on. I didn't want to be late. A tram, of course, couldn't be hurried.

The old iron giant: a soon to be extinct relic of the thirties and forties, trundles along on its tracks in the middle of the road. Stopping every now and then to take on new boarders. Thus, it continues, at what seems to be, to the anxious passenger, at a snail's pace down along: Roseberry Avenue, Theobalds Road and left into Holborn; where, it clankety-clanks it's heavy way down the slope of Kingsway Subway and emerges from the darkness; after a short time; up and onto the Victoria Embankment. It picks up speed a little...good! For in the distance I can see the face of Big Ben: five minutes to the hour! Hurry up tram! Don't let there be any more stops for boarders to delay your progress (which is slow enough already). I've just caught another glimpse of Big Ben...three minutes to the hour now as I'm alighting at my tram stop: which is situated right opposite Scotland Yard. My short-cut. I might just make it. A dash through the Yard: quick, quick...turning left immediately into Parliament Street...a few yards along, then up the steps and along the hallway towards the lift...the chimes of nine 'o' clock are already beginning. I'm in luck...the lift is already down. As it rattles its way up to our suite of offices, the final chimes ring out, but before the very last: I've entered, shut the office door, removed my coat and presented ready for work...just in time!

A few years on and the old trams would have become redundant. After which, I travelled to work via the 76 bus from Dalston Junction to Waterloo Station. Then, walking, (or running), over Westminster Bridge. It was only after travelling by the 76-bus route, that I'd come to be aware of the devastation all around the area of St Paul's Cathedral. The ruins: a reminder of the all-out blitz on London during the war. But that would have been when Joan and I were far away in Norfolk, living our carefree lives in the countryside. We may as well have been on another planet It is not; however, the 76 bus route (through the City, over Blackfriars Bridge and via York Road to Waterloo Station), which figures in a certain recurring dream that I've had in recent years: But of my old journey from the Angel Islington to Westminster, in the course of which my connecting tram appears to be going on a de-tour, much to my concern, instead of keeping to its usual route. At one of these unfamiliar venues, I catch sight of a large clock: the hands show that it is fifteen minutes to the hour, and we are only halfway there! This is when I begin to feel anxious: I'm going to be very late for work now. When I awake, at this point, it's with great a feeling of great relief: thank goodness...it was only a dream!

This dream had often left me wondering, as to why my subconscious has carried me so far back in time, yet again! A distance of some fifty years. I've come to the conclusion that these dreams of 'long ago' are due to my age. Shades of 'The Old Man and the Sea' in fact: whose sub-conscious had a habit of hauling him back to the waves whenever he dropped off, just to remind him of his fishing days. Here the analogy ceases to be relevant. A slow tram ride from Islington to Westminster, however worrying, can hardly be compared with having a dead killer whale lashed to the side of your fishing boat. Only to discover on reaching shore, that the dead trophy now consists of skeleton only: due to it having been got at by various hungry creatures en-route! Nightmare or what? What a wasted journey...poor old chap. (That's all I can recall from the film version of Hemmingway's book).

But; perhaps, on the other hand, these nocturnal reminders of the past may have occurred as a result of a jog to the memory just beforehand. When, after one of my rare visits up to town: perhaps in order to attend Mass at Westminster Cathedral. Afterwards walking down Birdcage Walk and subsequently ending up in Whitehall; with the intention of catching an 11 bus through to Liverpool Street. This wait at the bus stop, would have inevitably caused me to glance across the road and up to a certain group of windows. Five of them, on the top floor of the building. Counting from left to right: Boardroom, Manager's Office and the main one. This is where we clerk/typists sat busily typing away; only pausing now and then for a little chat...'Come on girls get on with your work,' our supervisor reminds us. In the left-hand corner and facing the end window, there had been a switchboard. This box-like contraption: with its three rows of 'up' and 'down' hinged buttons, together with the 'wind up' side handles, a few whirls of which, together with, 'hold on I'm putting you through now,' connected both parties. It is more or less a museum piece now; though still glimpsed on rare occasions, should an old fifties or sixties movie turn up on the television screen. Likewise, those old-fashioned adding machines with pull down handles and rows of buttons; with whose assistance the company's ledgers had been balanced twice a year.

It also occurs to me, since I've touched on the subject of 'windows': those which overlooked Whitehall...that during those particular years:1947 to 1954, there had been much to observe in the way of pomp and circumstance. Almost a cavalcade of events: both joyous and sad. I'd only been in my new employment for a matter of weeks, way back in 1947, when the wedding of Princess Elizabeth was about to take place. Because the surrounding streets would be closed off very early on the day itself; all staff slept overnight in the office. Ladies in one room, gents in the other. We girls slept in our curlers, which must have been pretty uncomfortable, I imagine. In turn had come: the wedding of Princess Alexandra and Angus Ogilvy, the funeral corteges of King George the sixth and later, that of Queen Mary the Queen Mother. The State Opening of Parliament each year provided yet more spectacle. Interesting to look back on; although at the time, it was more than likely that a job with such exceptional 'perks' had simply been taken for granted: in other words, it went with the territory.

Part Four

Courtship

My sister met her husband-to-be when she was seventeen years old. He was about six years her senior: the dependable and much coveted 'older man.' By then, I was going on nineteen but a late starter in every way: flat chested (well almost), and painfully shy of the opposite sex. Nonetheless, I suddenly developed an excruciatingly painful crush on one of my colleagues at work. He was about eight years older than myself, and in any case, just as unattainable as all those romantic heroes of the cinema screen. He was married, my teenage crush, thus making it a guilty secret. What if my mother found out: or worse still any of my female colleagues, or heaven forbid, should the object of my worship: my teenage crush, come to suspect the reason for my tell-tale blushes should he enter the room where I happened to be working. No doubt, he'd been well aware of the reason for my odd behaviour. It had probably caused him some amusement at the time, though he gave no sign of it...my naïve torment. Naïve it certainly was because if he'd at all reciprocated: taken advantage of the situation, I would have been absolutely horrified! Not to say terrified! Fortunately for me, my hero happened to be a gentleman.

In time; of course, my misery abated and the following year, when Joan and I, together with our aunts and uncles, went on vacation to a holiday in Surrey; I developed yet another crush on one of the male campers: only a few years my senior. Although Joan and I went for a meal with both my cousin and his friend one evening, the object of my attraction, obviously puzzled by inexperience and gauche behaviour, lost interest immediately.

It was proving to be a long and winding road in the direction of maturity. My sister, on the other hand: being the uncomplicated one, happily involved in the process of traditional courtship. Having met Mr Right the first-time round, she was going steadily towards that ultimate in achievement for young women of our generation. What else, other than marriage?

I was just over twenty years old when I met my first boyfriend. No sudden 'falling in love' though... no 'chemistry': no doubt, due to the fact that matters relating to 'physical attraction' had not yet kicked in within my 'beginner's' remit...'full of Eastern promise!' I most certainly hadn't been sitting there all alone in my apartment: 'ice-maiden' blonde indifference; one evening at Freeman's Dance Academy; when my first ever boyfriend came over and sat beside me. He seemed very nice and it turned out that we had a lot in common. I allowed him to see me home. Perhaps I'd even let him give me a goodnight kiss; instead of merely saying 'thank you,' and dashing up the front steps. A tactic I'd employed a couple of times when an unsuspecting dancing partner had seen me home: thus, putting paid, immediately, to and budding romance. No wonder I'd been a late starter!

My incredulity at the time new no bounds. I couldn't believe it! I actually had a boyfriend at last! What's more, he had a motorbike: an AJS; which he liked to take apart and reassemble every Saturday morning. A ritual which I usually went along to observe and occasionally 'give a hand' to, down at a local garage in Chatsworth Road.

Now and then we went for a spin, 'put your head down, I'm going for a ton.' Clinging on for dear life as we zoomed along an outer London highway; feeling the numbing effect on my stockinged legs from the cold wind, I resolved to buy myself a pair of slacks or ladies trousers. The last time I'd been dropped off after one of our 'spins,' so numb had been my legs, that they'd gone from under me on the front steps: My stocking laddered and torn and my knees badly grazed.

Wearing trousers had allowed me to take my place on the pillion of my boyfriend's motorbike with rather more abandon than formerly. Unfortunately, my 'abandon' had been noted from behind net curtains in the basement of number 97. 'I always thought that Doreen was a lady until I saw her throw her leg over the back of that motorbike...I couldn't believe it!' said a shocked Mrs Green. Being just as 'shocked' then, at the younger generation, as I am at the 'goings on' of the younger generation!

In the March of 1951, my mother died. Her death was sudden and completely unexpected; although she had been unwell, with various symptoms, for several months: at which time our family Doctor had referred her to a local hospital. We had no idea of what was wrong or just how very ill Mum had been. At one time she walked out of the Royal London Outpatients on learning that medical students would be present during her examination...thus, rendering any investigation as a nonstarter.

It was not until a few days before her death that Mum had become bed-bound. A few weeks previously, she and Dad had gone to Southend for the day, where they'd had a photo taken by one of the beach photographers. When I accompanied Dad, who was in deep shock at the time, in order to obtain the usual Death Certificate and to give permission for a post mortem to take place; he kept producing the Southend photo of Mum and himself, almost as if to deny her very sudden death.

When Dr. Sachs had ordered her removal to hospital: Dad, Joan and I had been alarmed, to some extent but had concluded that it was all for the best. Having had her illness treated, Mum would soon be home again. 'Don't worry,' I said to Mum with all the cheerful optimism of youth, as I leant over her and kissed her on the cheek, before the ambulance men took her away. Maybe, it had been with a certain premonition that her reply had been: 'It was snowing too, when they took my mother away.' But I hadn't dwelt overly long on her words, choosing to ignore their implication.

During the following afternoon, a telegram had arrived from Hackney Hospital, requesting Dad's urgent presence. This had been delivered at his place of work in Morning Lane. As he was on his way by bus, Dad caught sight of Father Kelly, also speeding along by bicycle: to administer the Last Rites for my mother.

The reaction when someone close dies unexpectedly: especially a parent, can often be extremely complicated. A certain vague annoyance with the deceased, somewhere in the background, at having left so suddenly. Before one had the time to say sorry...to apologise for past thoughtlessness. But then, as they say: remorse is the most useless of emotions. Just the same, it was impossible for me not to have felt this emotion. I'd liked to have said;' sorry Mum, for being such a difficult child and later, a typical, selfish teenager. For not being more sympathetic when you were feeling unwell.' My sister; however, would have been spared this 'too late' reminiscing; for she'd often taken time off work to look after Mum when she had been poorly. One thing in particular had always puzzled me: thus, adding to my guilty feelings with regard to my mother's death. We loved Mum, who'd always been so caring. Great wrapper up. A compulsive sender of vests and warm clothing when we had been parted from her during the war; as though reaching out to us with tokens of her now, distant love, all those miles away in London. So why hadn't there been more visible grief when she died? Why hadn't we wept? 'It was the shock,' says my sister. It could of course, have had something to do with that four-year long separation. Or maybe unshed tears are temporarily stored in a lachrymosian reservoir. At one time in my life there had been an event, that of a personal nature: a betrayal, which had caused me such grief that a deluge had resulted. An almost unstoppable flow, over which, I had no control whatsoever. Even on my way to work, an outpouring which threatened to erupt and overwhelm me during that particular period. Sometimes, I would wake up in the middle of the night, to find tears streaming down my face. Eventually; of course, the reservoir ran dry... as it was bound to. By a stretch of the imagination, it began possible for me to hope that mingled with that deluge, were the tears that I should have shed for my mother all those years ago.

My mother's death had been due to Tuberculosis of the Adrenal Glands. Years later, we learned that her brother, Jimmy, had also died of this disease. During the early fifties, there had been a general out-beak of Tuberculosis, but I can't help wondering, whether their deaths had something to do with the kindly farmer's wife in County Cashel all those years ago...unwittingly supplying the rovers with 'warm milk straight from the cow.

Of all the months in the year, November, coming as it does just prior to all the Christmas festivities; must surely be the worst in which to be 'dumped!' My boyfriend was about to embark on his National Service, to do his compulsory two-year stint. But, he said, he 'didn't want me to wait for him because he wasn't serious,'... so that was that! My first relationship had lasted for only ten months. Although we had a lot in common, it seemed he didn't feel 'that way' about me. My first rejection left me, if not exactly heartbroken: then very upset at the time. So selfishly wrapped up in my personal concerns that I'd given little thought to my father's feelings...his first sad Christmas as a widower.

One of my New Year Resolutions had been to 'snap out of it,'... to stop moping around. One Tuesday evening in mid-January: I caught a bus in Kingsland High Street, changed at Stamford Hill, ready to throw my miserable self into the dancing throng on the dance-floor of the Tottenham Royal. The trouble was; however, that long before the age of Disco, accessing the dance floor required having a partner. No doubt appearing to be as miserable as my inner-self at the time: nary a young man sought my company. I spent the whole evening as a wall-flower...a wilted one at that and returned home feeling quite dejected...but still determined to try again.

As a result of my second attempt, I not only managed to acquire a few dancing partners (possibly by my endeavouring to present a more overtly cheerful image) but got into conversation with another girl; who introduced me to her sister. The following week, via the sisters, I met Jean, who was to become one of my best friends at that time. All three worked in a North London shirt factory. Not rough girls at all but slightly less prissy than myself; which was all for the best, because, on the whole I was far too serious for my age. Things were much more fun now, besides which, all three girls were, like myself, keen ballroom dancers. We all wore the appropriate gear for dancing: stiff black taffeta flared skirt, white blouse and high-heeled black satin dancing shoes…which we changed into on arrival at our chosen venue.

We had a routine: Tottenham Royal on Tuesday evenings, Fridays Hornsey Town Hall or Bruce Grove, Saturday evenings we even went as far afield as The Royalty in Southgate. 'Where are you going?' my father would enquire, on observing his pleasure-seeking daughter about to rally forth for the second time that week. Dancing came the inevitable response. This was obviously too much to bear; 'spivs and layabouts. What man after a hard day's work wants to go dancing?' But my father's scathing comments with regard to the want of manliness and sheer idleness of my perspective dancing partners, simply fell on deaf ears because, I knew full well that his displeasure was due to my own woeful lack of domestic prowess. It annoyed him just as my mother's had done. However, having spent all day at work and at least an hour travelling home from Westminster by bus; I had no intention of devoting the rest of my day to doing the housework. Apart from shopping and cooking each day, it could wait until the weekend.

My sister would have made an excellent housekeeper for Dad, but having recently married, she was no longer around to keep things in order. A badly flawed deputy had to suffice.

When Saturday came around, there was a considerable list of housework to contend with: three flights of stairs with a dustpan and brush, a deal of wooden banisters to dust and polish, plus an assault on our large front sitting room, in order to make it presentable should any weekend visitors turn up. By the time I'd got to the front steps: their sweeping, no doubt, would have been of a somewhat perfunctory nature. The fact of the matter was that I simply hated housework. 'You're a muddler...a muddler,' Dad would almost shout with exasperation. 'There will be plenty of time for housework when I'm married,' my casual riposte.

Meanwhile, having my former bookish-self on hold: I went dancing, dating and enjoying my newly found social life. 'Seizing the moment,' as it were. Which was really just as well: because close at hand, lurking in the background was the 'fickle finger of fate,' slowly but surely steering me in a certain direction.

One of the most popular Hollywood Musicals during the early fifties was 'Singing in the Rain.' One Sunday afternoon, my new friend Jean and I went all the way over to Winchmore Hill Odeon in order to see it. Halfway through the film, and much to my surprise, my friend nudged me and handed over a tub of ice cream; meanwhile, silently indicating our benefactors: two young men seated immediately behind us in the Upper Circle. They left a short while afterwards, but, before doing so, had whispered a few words to my friend. It appeared that the ice cream was by the way of an introduction. They wished to make an assignation: we were to meet them outside when the film was over. Neither of us particularly keen to take up this offer: we decided to see the film round again, hoping that by then our benefactors would have taken the hint and departed. Not so; however, there they both were, waiting by the exit door as we emerged...our unknown dates. They had turned out to be R.A.F. types, on leave and in civvies. First of all, we went on a double date to the Empire Cinema in Leicester Square where 'Angels on Fire' was showing, (or was it 'Twelve 'O'clock High?'). Anyway, it was an R.A.F. film...what else? Paul held my hand throughout the film. So, he suddenly swooped his head down, I experienced a brief moment of alarm: half expecting some kind of amorous wrist kissing. Much to my relief, it was only to peer at his watch face in the darkness. He probably had a bus or train to catch, after seeing me home all the way to Dalston.

Our new acquaintances: Navigators, quite posh or posher than usual. Gentlemen it would seem. Paul wasn't at all bad looking. He was tall with dark curly hair. But...I couldn't help noticing: he appeared to be one of those gentlemen with 'great expectations.' Once he mentioned something about 'showing me the stars at Weston-Super-Mare one weekend. On first seeing me home, Paul had almost instinctively navigated, with some alacrity, down Mrs Green's basement steps towards the dark and secluded area. 'No, I don't live down there, I live upstairs,' I told him. At which he was obliged to resume ground level. Living upstairs would have its drawbacks for any gentleman with 'great expectations.' He would have to kiss me goodnight on the top step, softly illuminated by the glow of a nearby street lamp. Being an R.A.F. Navigator, Paul would have been accustomed to 'living life in the fast lane' and this obviously wasn't 'it'! We went out together a few times before his leave was up, and, as a matter of fact, Paul had managed to kiss me several times one evening: and in the dark. It was in the back row of the stalls in the Odeon Cinema, Turnpike Lane. At least it was something; for me too as it happened: he was a lovely kisser.

As far as kissing went: Paul's are included with those recalled as 'kisses sweeter than wine.' Since a kiss goodnight: the fee for being seen home by one's date, (via public transport in some instances), during the so called 'repressive fifties'. Even though one came across the occasional slobberer (yuk!). When compared with the present day 'rate of exchange': 'you never know what they're going to do,' a young lady of my acquaintance tells me...all I can say is 'I'm glad I'm not young anymore.'

Paul said that he would phone me at my place of work. He never did of course. Neither had I expected him to. More than likely he had a regular girlfriend near his R.A.F. base. As for my friend's R.A.F. type: I took a strong dislike to him almost at once. He was a real snob. Even mimicking Jean's Northern accent, as we were on our way up to London, when on our initial double-date. I'd have dumped him there and then. I imagine; however, that their relationship had been of even shorter duration than my own and his friend's Paul's. But even if Jean had found her date's ungentlemanly micky taking hurtful at the time, I doubt very much if she lost any sleep over it.

As often happens, when one branches off into a serious relationship and prior to marriage; I lost touch with my friend Jean. She was vivacious, pretty and fun to go out with. Just the friend I'd needed at the time: who managed to jerk me out of my over ladylike self, in order to enjoy, if only temporarily, a livelier way of life.

On viewing my holiday snapshots that autumn...observing his elder daughter snuggling up to a hunky young man, who had his arm around her waist. Each party in working gear: standing amidst a muddy looking field. My father had obviously been lost for words: 'hem, hem,' he said, 'most unconventional.'

I had just returned from a working holiday: my second that year. Those 1950's 'Give a hand on the land' voluntary enterprises, were ideal for those would be holiday makers who happened to be short of cash; needing a change of scenery and willing to do a spot of voluntary work in the open air. All was for free in return for some really hard graft. This entailed hoeing or harvesting potatoes, depending on the season. Accommodation: ex-army huts. Food: plentiful. Much needed after such honest toil in the fields. Most of the volunteers were young people: a mixed bunch of various nationalities also. Nurses, Law Students, Secretaries, Clerks and Tally Clerks, from the London Docks occasionally. Everyone friendly and helpful. One or two evenings a week, a coach was provided, should anyone wish to attend a local dance. A trip to the Palace in Swindon had been on the agenda during my Wiltshire vacation in the June of that year. Choc a bloc with American Soldiers on a Saturday evening. A local village dance hall had to suffice later in the year. Our Nissen Hut quarters had been situated just inside a section of the New forest in Hampshire. Beautiful surroundings in the late autumn, all the changing hues that go with the season: reds, rusts and deep yellows...what could be a more romantic background for a holiday romance.

'What's it like to be Belle of the Ball?' Gerry had enquired, with that slight hint of irony cum sarcasm, peculiar to the male Aussie; referring to the fact that I hadn't lacked dancing partners that evening. He being the current one. Gerry was from Adelaide: a tall, fair, Robert Redford type fellow '. Or 'a Fair Dinkum Digger,' as he chose to describe himself...one who'd recently been 'dumped by a Sheila back home.' So...we were both footloose and fancy free!

However, I was under no illusion about this holiday romance. When Gerry said on one occasion, 'I might take you home and marry you,' I took his statement with a pinch of salt. 'A late beginner' I may have been, but as it behoved every canny girl of the fifties, always well aware of certain wiles likely to be employed by the opposite sex in some instances. Not to mention the possible consequences of succumbing to them. Even so, by the end of my holiday fortnight, I was just a little in love and I knew that Gerry was too. We said our formal goodbyes on the steps of Waterloo Station, (this was the fifties). Our private ones after the last night dance the previous evening and in more secluded surroundings. 'Remember this tomorrow,' said the Fair Dinkum Digger, who was going on to another farming job somewhere in Wiltshire. He wrote to me from there and we corresponded once or twice, but that was it really. A sweet holiday romance, which I still like to recall now and then. Especially since it was the very last before I met my husband to be, a few months later.

'Look! That's where I said goodbye to my Australian boyfriend fifty years ago,' I've been known to remark to one or other of my grandchildren, as we emerge from the Jubilee Line escalator and step onto the main thoroughfare of Waterloo station...enroute to the South Bank. As if they care! The last thing on my mind then, as a twenty-two-year-old late starter, was marriage. Although my friend and colleague at work, having recently become a Mrs herself, was forever encouraging me to settle down... When it turned out that none of my little romances had proved to be going in that direction: she was obviously quite disappointed.

Unfortunately, when I actually came across someone who shared my interests: classical music, literature etc., I didn't find him at all attractive. He was one of those tentative or shy types, who tend to throw out hints...'did you know that the Promenade Concerts start this week?' a ploy I always found to be extremely irritating. Quite possibly, my lack of encouragement had been due to the disparity of our backgrounds. His house in the suburbs...mine rented rooms in East London. My class consciousness, sadly, uppermost it would seem.

Early in the November of that year...1952, I was invited to a Holiday Reunion Party. This was to take place at a private house; kindly made available by a lady who had been at the Volunteers Camp in Hampshire, some months previously. It was here of all places: a semi-detached in Ealing, where I was introduced to my husband to be. Not that I hadn't noticed him beforehand that evening: dark haired, tanned, good looking, newly home from his two-year stint as a National Serviceman in Malaya. Although he hadn't fitted the requirements of the 'soul-mate' I'd always had in mind: for we shared no interests whatsoever, that didn't matter...it was love at first sight. An instant of mutual recognition.

I had only known my boyfriend for a few weeks, during which time I was taken home and introduced to his family...when fate, would seem, to have made an earnest attempt to intervene. It was after my second visit there. A twenty-minute journey by underground, when what came to be known as the great smog: a combination of thick smoke from countless London chimney pots and its traditional damp fog, began it's decent. 'Don't bother to see me all the way home or you won't get back tonight,' I told my boyfriend, as he saw me onto the train from his local station. 'I'll be ok, I'll change at Mile End and get a bus from Bethnal Green.

It must have been well past midnight when I emerged from Bethnal Green Underground; only to find myself completely surrounded by a thick, grey, blanket of fog. There was nothing for it now but to walk home. All buses would have stopped running anyway.

So, was I scared? Even though the route home; a distance of about three miles, happened to be quite straightforward, despite the fog: Cambridge Heath Road, on into Mare Street itself, a turn left at the traffic lights into Graham Road, then home in about fifteen minutes. I must have been quaking inwardly all the way!

When a mans disembodied voice had bidden me 'goodnight darling,' just as I'd crossed over the road at the junction with Mare street. Although my heart must have missed a beat and my pace immediately quickened; I would have felt safe in the knowledge that 'seeking me out' in all that thick fog, would have been the equivalent of finding a needle in a haystack.

Over the course of several days, the smog has worsened and most buses in the City now obliged to proceed at a snail's pace and by following the guidance of a manually held beacon. My number 76 bus was no exception: it had taken me hours to get home one particular afternoon that November. But it was the toll on human life that had led to the introduction of smokeless fuel shortly after the smog event in 1952. People who'd been prone to chest complaints had been unable to withstand smoke and vaporous London fog. Fifty years on and there's yet another form of air pollution in cities: only this time it seems to be due to exhaust fumes. But that is by the way. Apart from the Big

Smog episode, there had been other setbacks in the course of our eighteen-month courtship. (How old fashioned that term seems now), and there were times when I had my doubts with regard to our compatibility. But prudence tends to take a back seat when being in love prevails. And love, after all, is what makes the world go round.

And go round it did. Rather speedily too.

My dancing days were over.

Love and Marriage

In a way, it was almost as sudden as had been my fourteen-year-old transition from school to the world of work, ten years previously. However, there had been no hesitation on my part; no hesitation with regards to entering the married state.

Way back in the fifties: such had been the accepted role for most young women. There was no aspirations relating to a prolonged career. However; it was the relative speed with which events took place, the extra shove into reality that fate had in store for me: which for better or worse, bought me down to earth with an unromantic bump.

My fiance and I had been saving up and had planned on getting married in a years time. I'd even taken an extra Saturday job with this in mind: intent on putting something aside from my weekly salary. Meanwhile there seemed to be ample time for daydreaming: for planning our future. A rented flat seemed worth considering. We wandered hand in hand, drawn at intervals to local furnisher shop window displays. Though how we'd ever afford such luxuries, I didn't know. We had agreed on having four children-a nice round number. But one thing was certain, even before that took place, as far as my intended was concerned, I would need to give up my job. 'No wife of his would have to go to work. Since the breadwinner tended to be a male perogative then: I had no argument with this. Anyway; it didn't matter, my fiance's wishes were to be granted somewhat sooner than either of us had anticipated. But, prior to this particular event, and during our courtship, things at home had been quite difficult.

The fact of the matter was, that my father and I didn't get on: which no doubt had been due to parallel egos. In fact, I'd often considered getting a flat of my own. This state of affairs had been going on ever since I'd become Dad's inefficient housekeeper, since my mothers death, in fact. In addition to his annoyance at my lack of domestic prowess and application, (though I did my best), Dad appeared to be overly suspicious of my intended. If the latter happened to be still on the premises at 10.30, a discreet knock on the frontroom door, before we were bidden goodnight. Plus, the thrusting of an alarm clock, made this only too obvious. If this blatant hint was ignored , and the suspect still on the premises half-an-hour later, there would come a series of thumps on the ceiling. When I recount this form of parental behaviour to one of my grandaughters, she finds it quite outrageous. I have to explain to her, that way back in the fifties, so called loose women or pre-marital hanky panky, was highly dangerous (as far as the female in question was concerned), if it resulted in pregnancy: especially as there was no social security. For unmarried mothers, it would mean disgrace for one's familly and (more than likely), adoption for the child. Quite enough by the way of consequence to have kept any self-respecting young girl of the fifties on the beaten track. As I'd remarked on my father's veiled explaination later for thumping on the ceiling: ' I'm well able to look after myself'...goodness knows there'd been enough insentive to do so!

Ever since the commencement of 1954, my father had been increasingly subject to servere stomach pains: an ulcer suspected and a bland diet made no difference. I would often see Dad kneeling down with his elbows on the seat of a fireside chair, in an effort to recieve some relief from the pain. He still insisted on going to work though. In the end, he collapsed after having suffering a servere rectal hemorrhage. Accepting his doctor's advice, he went into hospital for a blood transfusion. After which he looked very much better. Even so, Dad had refused to be blanket washed by the nurses: altogether proving a very difficult patient. He discharged himself and sent a telegram home: requesting his clothes be brought to the hospital. He was quite adamant. I just didn't know what to do for the best: which way to turn. Having spoken to the hospital consultant, I was well aware of how seriously ill Dad was. Cancer of the stomach the diagnosis. Three months to a year was all the time he had left.

At my fiancee's suggestion, we brought or wedding forward. I gave up my job. We got married by special licence and he moved in as my husband (after some haggling with father!)

Our wedding took place on a Friday...a family affair only: we had no money for a big wedding. A one tier wedding cake, the reception in my mother-in-law's frontroom and a three day honeymoon in Dorset. Uncle Albert gave me away because Dad was too ill to have undertaken the journey to St Thomas' Church. My sister looked after him until I arrived back home.

Like the fighter he was, my father bore his illness with courage and even humour. His reading glasses a sight to behold, having been held together with sticky tape and the odd blob of sealing wax. Whenever the Sickness Benefit Assessor paid a visit, these reconstructed spectacles would be prominently on display; always in the hope that their sad condition might evoke the offer of funding for new ones. Much to Dad's amusement: the ploy was unsuccessful!

My father was always sceptical about any form of so-called benefits...'My dear,' he would say, 'they give it to you with one hand and they take it away with the other: It's called statistics.' Dad went out and about as much as he could. He had many friends in the area. Ted was well known: in fact, the cafe in Valette Street, Morning Lane, was frequently referred to as Ted's Cafe. Sometimes, I took Dad over to visit Clissord Park, and accompanied him in the ambulance when he was due at the hospital for his check-up visits. On the whole though, Father was a very independent person.

Unfortunately, there was a natural antipathy between Dad and my new husband: which often created an atmosphere and left me 'piggy-in-the-middle.' I found the situation quite stressful at times. Not the ideal start to married life I'd originally envisaged: being ever anxious to please my husband, but, concerned for my fathers's welfare. However much he and I clashed at times, one thing I knew for sure: that he had always been a good and caring father to my sister and I. He deserved some respect and consideration: especially now.

The trouble was; of course, that each of the protagonists would have preferred my undivided attention. If I ocassionally went out for the day with my husband, namely on a Saturday, to watch him play cricket for his company's team. On our return, it would be to discover that all the readily prepared vegetables I'd left for Dad's mid-day meal, had been left uncooked. This caused me to feel guilty for not having been at home to serve his lunch personally. Though, at that point in time he'd been quite capable of doing this for himself, had he chosen to do so...and so it went on.

Later, there was to be yet another person requiring my attention. Ten months after my marriage in May 1955: most welcome, though unplanned, ('What a shame' Aunt Bett had exclaimed, on receiving news of the coming event), came the birth of my first child. A little girl.

I knew absolutely nothing about the care of babies beforehand. In fact, I'd never been really interested in them, and had considered the whole subject of new infants to be extremely boring. What was all the 'cooing' about anyway? Feeding, nappies etc, all alien territory as far as I'd been concerned. When my fiancee and I had been rosily planning to 'have four children' eventually, and when we were married: it had seemed almost like a distant fairy tale. A romantic dream. The brave music of a distant drum! But, the future had zoomed in with almost alarming speed, No time for dreaming now. Life was real, life was earnest, and I was a mother.

And, strange to relate, a quite good one. It was as though my little girl had bought me the magic gift, because caring for her seemed to come quite naturally. In spite of the odds against it, given my former indifference to babies: motherhood proved to be, in spite of all the trials and worries, one of the most rewarding aspects of married life.

Maybe our unplanned baby had been an act of providence. My father, though very ill by now, had been there at home to welcome his grandaughter, when we brought her home from hospital. He died four months later.

One bright morning in the late autumn of 1957, had there been any curious neighbours looking from an upstairs window, drawn there perhaps, from the sound of a starting motor engine; they may have just been in time to observe a small removal van now making it's departure from outside one of the nearby houses. One or two of the watchers may even have noticed the actual loading of the vehicle: though standing a little back from the observation posts: reluctant to appear too inquisitive by any other 'curtain peepers' in the vicinity.

Having nothing better to do, they'd been taking note of the items in transit: if there had been worn covers or broken springs.; in which case, they would have been very disappointed. There were no large pieces of furniture to be seen: these had been left by the departing tenants, to be retained or disposed of according to the house owner's wishes.

Those odds and ends of household goods now in transit include: a folding Fleetway table-top wringer (the very latest in mangles), a green budgerigar in a cage, a cot matress and dismantled cot and two medium fireside chairs. A young woman sits in one, a fair haired little girl upon the other. Placed sideways and next to the chairs, is a pram in which, tucked up asleep, lies a small baby.

As the van pulls away, the young woman reaches forward, as though intending to move aside the canvas flap, which screens she and her children from public gaze: maybe just to catch a glimpse of the home she's so reluctantly leaving now. But, the impulse is almost immediately overcome: the children need her attetion at the moment. The noise of the departing vehicle has disturbed the baby's slumber and the little girl has climbed down from her seat. The van is gathering speed now, travelling away from familiar surroundings, busy main roads and the quiet side-streets with their tall Victorian buildings. The travellers are going from east to further east. To a thirties built housing estate. This is where they are to live from now on.

Although the streets are wide, the neighbours pleasant...once she got to know them. Although the local parks have well kept flower beds and nice playgrounds for the children. At the back of her mind, she knows she will never really like this place, with its grid-like streets which sprawl ad infinitum, mile upon mile. One of the largest thiries built council estates in the world, she'd been told. Which makes no favourable impression at all. The place had been imposed upon her against her will and she doesn't like being made to do anything in this manner. But, she has to submit to her husband's wishes. He holds the power because she finacially depends on him. There are two small children, one only seven months old. None the less, it rankles.

In time, of course, preoccupation with family matters will push her under-lying resentment to one side. Just the same, it will never be completely forgotten. Merely suspended pro tem. Some three or four decades ahead, she will continue to recall the forced removal from her family home, way back in 1957. The story will be brought forth, replayed: rather akin to an 'old days' recollection to exchange.

From my husband's point of view, naturally, it was the right thing to do. His mother had recently died, so now we were to leave our present home in Greenwood Road, give up our newly decorated flat, to 'go down and look after the old man' in my husband's former home. No consultation with 'the wife'. The matter had been decided upon...and that was that. When I had attemptd to demur about leaving my old home, I soon discovered for the first time, that my husband's affable disposition concealed a formidable temper. On being 'crossed,' he made it quite clear that he would brook no argument in the matter.

All in all, my married life, at that point in time, was turning out to be full of unexpected, and slightly disillusioning surprises. But, after all, I had two lovely babies now and luckily, I tend to have an optimistic nature. I was sure things could only get better.

It goes without saying; of course, that there exists within every family framework a variety of certain 'situations.'

Nonetheless, it occurred to me, shortly after my unwilling departure from Hackney, that what had taken place, was almost a reflection of my mother's own experience, some twenty-four years previously. Probably, at the tail end of 1933, when we'd moved away from Kentish Town, in orer to take up residence in Uncle's house in Edmonton. She too had been the mother of two small children, and, like myself, would not have had any say in the matter of our uprooting. My father would have made a prior agreement with his brother in respect of our proposed accomodation.

This turned out to be a medium sized lounge hastily converted into a bed-sitting room and totally inadequate for a family of four. Maybe the move was to help his brother out with the mortgage: our rent, as well as the upstairs lodger's contribution. This was only conjecture on my part. Our move to Edmonton may have been for quite a different reason. However, there's no doubt that as far as my mother was concerned, the move was under duress.

Now and then, when Mum was in the process of dwelling on 'what might have been,' our 1933 shift from Kentish Town to Edmonton invariably saw the light of day. 'If we'd stayed in Kentish Town, you would have gone to church school at Haverstock Hill and had a good education'. Thus, her 'long-ago' obsolete resentment voiced yet again, as a matter of course, no doubt falling upon indifferent ears: just as my own would come to do, evemtually.

In no way; however, did my susequent lot compare with that which had been my mother's, all those years ago. True, that I now had my father-in-law to cook for and to see that his washing was done. But, I was the presiding female here: I wasn't obliged to share a cupboard sized kitchen with another, or be cooped up for several hours a day in a cramped bed-sitting room, with two small children. My mother never spoke much about her time in Uncle Albert's house, and no mention whatsoever of the explosive family row that occured just before our departure. I remember it well though: it scared me no end at the time.

To manipulate, rather than to paraphrase a well-known quotation: 'Some women are born to be competent housewives: others have it thrust upon them.'

Any female with a natural flair for domesticiy...a penchsnt for household chores, having entered the married state way back in the fifties or sixties, would have realised at once, that all her dreams had come true!

There were others; however, who experienced no surge of joy at being faced with a mountainous pile of ironing, following a trip to the launderette with the weekly wash. Or who delighted in having to keep the front doorstep reddened or whitened (depending on the venue.) At the same time, taking care to shine up the letterbox and door-knocker with Brasso. In addition, any lucky housewife in a 'Hooverless' household then, would have the advantage of ridding herself of any hidden aggression in the twice-weekly beating of household mats, by first draping them over the clothes line and attacking them with a carpet beater.

During the evenings, when the children were tucked-up safely in bed, any idle moment might be occupied by darning hubby's holey socks: especially the heels. (We'd been introduced to this skill whilst still at school.) Even after the blessing of nylon socks had arrived, there would still be the inevitable frayed collar to unpick and turn. No money for new working shirts: only one pay packet.

Thus, for those of an undomesticated disposition, it had been necessary to work at improving one's skills. After all, this had been our chosen career: marriage and motherhood...a commitment to the family, all in the name of love. A 'kept-woman,' in fact, whose other half was the provider and the 'hunter gatherer.' An ideal set-up for one's children: the lines clearly drawn. One of the most important duties of a 'forties' cum 'sixties' housewife, regardless of whether she happened to be a compulsive polisher or a mere flicker with a duster: was to have the breadwinner's evening meal ready to serve up immediately upon his arrival home from work. Many a true word spoken in jest...'The way to a mans heart is through his stomach.'

In July 1977: I petitioned my husband for divorce. So, following 1957, there would be another twenty years of marriage. Putting pen to paper in order to cover such a long and winding road of family and domestic life: that 'world within a world.' I tend to feel rather like a time -traveller, who, having journeyed at a steady pace down memory lane's familliar highway, now comes to a sudden halt. The time machine needs to be restarted...set in motion.

Those twenty years need to be accounted for: they cannot be glossed over lightly now. As a result of that marriage, ther are four children and eight grandchildren: so pressing a fast forward button is not to be considered.

It would seem that there were two disparate sections that went to make up the score of years following 1957. The first up to and including the sixties. The second being the discordant seventies. 'The best of times, the worst of times.' Or, comparable to a series of weather forcasts: it could be said that married life beginning with plenty of sunshine with occassional light showers, followed by unsettled weather with short periods of sunshine, then becoming stormy with outbreaks of thunder, resulting in heavy rain. Even an habitual wearer of rose-coloured glasses would have found them of no use whatsoever in the midst of the inclement weather. But a mere summary will not suffice: for that would be the 'cowards way out.'

That being so...where to begin? The swinging sixties of course. Needing to refresh my memory with regard to background events, rather than concentrate on domestic matters only, (which would be boring), I've resorted to the use of an encyclopedia. I'd quite forgotten, until then, just how very 'swinging' those notorious sixties had been.

Yuri Gagarin became the first man ever to go into space. One year later, a woman astronaut made the same journey. Also in the sixties, the first space walk by a Russian Cosmonaut. It wasn't long after that event, when the first moon landing took place: this time by an American team. Francis Chichester made his solo voyage around the world in The Gypsy Moth and The Cuban Crisis came and went. The war in Vietnam continued to rage and oil was dicovered in Alaska.

In the midst of all these 'enerprises of great pith and moment,' the famous Beatles emerged, as if dispatched by providence, in order to supply us with some light relief.

This impresssive backcloth in family matters, and in the day-to-day process of living our lives: have our own little dramas to deal with occassionally.

'Domestic war.' Stormy outbreaks were not unknown to me as a child...but they soon blew over. 'Sulks;' however, were completely new to me and I found them hard to contend with.

All behaviour tends to be 'learned behaviour,' and all my husbands family had been notorious 'sulkers.' This one not speaking to that for weeks: even months at a time, if there had been a serious disagreement. It seemed to have been a matter of pride when they were discussing the comparative lengths of their mutual silences. My own learned behaviour, of course, had been quite the opposite: a sudden flare-up of short duration only...then all friends again. Which is all very well, if one's opposite is of the same mind: otherwise extremely frustrating.

Though, in the fairly harmonious sixties, prolonged silences were the exception rather than the rule. Besides which, my husband being a contract worker, was often absent from home for several weeks at a time. Not that I could claim to be home alone by any means: for by the time 1960 had arrived, I was a mother to three under-fives. Then; of course, there was my father-in-law: a night watchman at a local factory, who slept most of the day. A rather morose old gentleman, it has to be said, but little trouble really.

Viewed from distance of some forty years, those first few years of the sixties might well be described as a kaleidoscope of family life: with partings and reunions of my husband and myself and the pleasure and anxieties of motherhood.

School holidays, when I always took care to stock up on the contents of the first aid box...just incase. Picnics in the local park, which then had a paddling pool. Games of cricket with the children in our back garden: when I usually managed to swipe the ball over next-door-but-one's garden. Plus, at least one visit to the cinema, if a Walt Disney film happened to be showing.

The sixties were the heyday of Watch with Mother. None other than: Andy Pandy, Bill and Ben and The Magic Roundabout. For the older children there was always Blue Peter. The presenters of which were thirty-ish of the aunt and uncle varierty...but an enterprising bunch just the same. They always had to hand useful tips on how to construct something useful out of simple materials such as: stiff cardboard, old boxes and odd lengths of string. Now and then, the presenters came up with more advanced ideas...ones that would need some assistance from an adult.

'Ah yes, I remeber it well.'

In order to make a simple wooden sledge, all the materials needed were: two matching lengths of wood and a few cross section, plus a hammer and nails...not forgetting a length of rope to steer it.

Late January 1963, although my home made sledge left alot to be desired by way of 'finishing,' (indeed, it was a crude piece of carpentry), it actually worked! The snow in our back garden was at least two feet deep, even more in places. The children had a great time and took it in turns to be pulled around by mother on one of her 'sudden ideas.'

Mother was having a good time too and had quite forgotten other matters...of a less pleasurable sort, it had to be said Nonetheless, they needed her attention. Duty called but was unheard.

Came the dawn...as soon as I awoke the next morning, I knew there was something wrong. I was experiencing severe abdominal pain. It had come on quite suddenly. The first thing to come to mind was appendicitis, but, there were certain symptoms that had been present since Christmas. In fact, I'd been wondering, now and then, if I might be pregnant...but I wasn't sure yet. Soon, the pain had become so excrutiating that I couldn't stand upright. My husband had already left for work and there was no way of contacting him now. In the event, I sent my seven-year-old next door, (this was before we'd aquired a phone), to ask for my neighbours assistance and advice. 'I think I have appendicitis,' I told her, groaning at the time. Oh...the state of my bedroom: it was indeed showing signs of neglect. I'd really been caught napping and it served me right. I was ashamed: what would father have said? I could almost hear him: 'You're a muddler...a muddler!'

'All appendicitis cases walk in,' said one of the ambulance men. I can't,' I said weakly, collapsing back on the bed, as I stood up. My next-door-neighbour turned up trumps-as good neighbours tend to do, and took charge of the children. Mother; meanwhile, wrapped in a warm blanket, stretchered past the curious sightseers, past the front gate and carted off to hospital.

My appendicitis turned out to be a ruptured fallopian tube. My weird post-Christmas symptoms had been due to an ectopic pregnancy. I was given two pints of blood and spent two weeks in hospital.

The month of January has always meant 'bad vibes' for me. I've been in hospital twice since my Janusry '63 episode...but only for minor ops on those occassion. The first day of January 1978 had seen the house flooded due to a burst pipe in the loft.

In mid-January only a couple of years ago, I managed to trip over a raised paving slab. Due to family circumstances, I needed to get away for a few hours in order to chill out a little. What better than a stroll in St James Park? Alighting at the tube station, I bought a cup of coffee and a sandwich. I set off through a side street and ended up in St. Thomas' Casualty Department! I'd been concentrating on holding my hot coffee, in such a way as not to get my fingers burnt...instead of paying due attention to the dodgy paving stones underfoot. In no time at all, I was face down on the pavement: my hot coffee and sandwich kaput My nose streaming with blood!

One advantage...when it comes to tripping-up in the Westminster area, is that of being helped to your feet and given every assistance by actual 'gentlemen.' How very kind they were. The last time I'd met that rare species was in 1954, when I last worked in Parliament Street.

First, they escorted me to a nearby office, so that I could sit down until an ambulance arrived. It perhaps would be over flippant to venture that such courtesy was almost worth the trip, (since I only ended up with two black eyes and a purple big toe,) when, in actual fact, I could have recieved a fractured skull also. After my initial assesment at St Thomas' Casualty, (even though there was the usual wait.) The usual intermittent appearance of a Sister in Charge to inform us 'waiters' that 'it won't be too long now.' Plus, the courteous young doctor who shook my hand and appologised for keeping me waiting. Made a very pleasant change...a little sugar on the pill perhaps? But welcome nonetheless.

When I finally got round to visiting my G.P. (in this case a locum), about two weeks had elapsed. She appeared unusually interested in my recent mishap; whereas, my own G.P. would have seen the funny side of my panda-like visage. I explained the circumstances which had caused my accident: also mentioning the location. Now, the lady doctor, emanating from foreign parts and only some five years younger than myself (at a guess), was obviously unaware of that which enables senior citizens to wander 'course', namely, the Freedom Pass. 'What were you doing in St James' Park?' (actually I never got there!) My expination prompted yet another query: 'By yourself?...do you often go up to London by yourself?' I could only guess at her diagnosis! 'Sometimes...or with one of my grandchildren.' Enough said. 'Well...you should have a stick. If you had had a stick you wouldn't have fallen over.' 'But I tripped over a paving stone,' she said. Goodness knows what was written in my medical case notes that day.

1963: January and its negative vibes: frolics in the snow on mother's home-made sledge, dereliction of household duties, etcetera, etcetera. As to what became of that piece of modern art? Memory fails me here. More than likely; however, it had come to share the fate of certain other 'ideas' and 'inspirations' that had erupted in the past: namely by falling apart due to lack of planning, (or in this case...nails!)

As the wife of a contract worker, one of my ambitions had always been to have something put by for 'a rainy day,' which due to my husbands trade, tended to arrive with little warning. I had a theory that the sum of £100 would be ideal...enough to see us through any temporary financial difficulties, and, until the next contract became available.

Wishful thinking of course! For as soon as cash had been set aside, one or other of our children would be in need of new shoes or a winter coat.

Again, the term kaleidoscope serves to describe our fluctulating family fortunes over the year...ever changing patterns which came and went accordingly. Now and then we were riding high. On one of these occassions we aquired a second-hand car and even went on holiday. At another time, and when my husband had been out of work for several weeks, we were obliged to return our rented television set...we couldn't afford the payments. And a threatening letter that came from the local rent office, once had me doing the rounds of the pawn shops in East Ham Highstreet. I needed three pounds, ten shillings, to make up our fortnight's rent money...or else! The only asset I had was my new watch, for which I was luckily enough to obtain the necessary sum...rather to the annoyance of my husband, who had bought the watch for my birthday. It couldn't be helped though...desperate times call for desperate measures.

A very welcome source of financial deliverance was the quarterly visit of the gas meter collector. Spotting him coming along the road was enought to raise the spirits. For anon, would come a rat-tat-tat on the door knocker. Before long, the welcome rattle of coins cascading onto the kitchen table. All the two-shilling coins that had been deposited in the slot meter under the stairs, during the previous twelve weeks. Only a small proportion of the magic heap was ours of course: the rebate. Sometimes as much as two or three pounds...a negligible sum today, but a welcome personal bonus for the housewife of my generation. Ours to do what we liked with. Not 'manner from Heaven,' of course, but just as appreciated, as if it were, by many a cash-strapped recipient.

Living within an area; which, at the time had many light industries: there often occurred the opportunity for mother's with school age children to obtain temporary part-time work. Advertisements in the local newspaper now and then read: 'no experience necessary...training given.' Hours varied but were usually set as 9am-1pm, 10am-2pm, or evening shift 5.30pm-9pm. Given that my youngest was only three years old when I first spotted these alluring offers in the local press, and my husband on hand to child mind (since he happened to be working locally at the time).

I immediately went for the evening shift; booked myself in and went to obtain the necessary stamp card. I was quite looking forward to earning a little spare cash, and, I have to add, a new 'experience': something other than housework (unpaid.)

'You haven't got an employment card,' said my husband, when I informed him of my enterprise; unaware of his wife's 'fate accompli'. The fact of the matter was, that he didn't really like the thought of his spouse working in a factory. He'd married an 'office girl.' But the office girl couldn't have cared two hoots: mother was her main occupation; this was only a side-line.

And so, began my brief phase of being a bottle capper, along with other mums who'd been otherwise employed before marriage and children. It was good to have a little chat whilst waiting for the next line of bottles to come by on the conveyor belt...sometimes having to chase a missed one before it reached the packing point.

'Did you remember to clean your teeth?' I'd once enquired of my youngest the next morning. 'Daddy said don't bodder, he said don't bodder,' she repeated, doing a double snitch on her Daddy in case I'd missed the first one.

'You smell of disinfectant,' my husband remarked once, after I'd arrived home from my evening shift. I would like to think that subsequent acceptance of contract work, (which meant the end of my career as a capper), had nothing to do with his aversion to Jeyes Fluid.

In due course I hired a typewriter and spent time polishing-up my former typing skills. But the minute I embarked on any temping jobs, one or the other of my brood would go down with either a heavy cold or a bout of tonsillitis. A no win situation. I would have to be patient.

When the children were a little older, I found I now had more time to indulge in some of my own interests: within the home of course. Reading took preference, especially when my husband was working away from home. My bed-time reading included the latest Margaret Drabble's novels; also, Penelope Mortimer's current writings.

Then there was 'Bon Jour Trieste: Francoise Sagan's first novel, I believe. Doris Lessing's first came upon the literary scene about that time and I read a couple of her books also. Then, for some reason or other, I decided to try something more challenging. Having accidentally come across Marcel Proust's first volume of 'Remembrance of Things Past' in my local library-that memoir of memoirs-I decided to start there and gradually read my way through the whole set. I can't really remember just how many volumes this would have entailed but the sad truth is that I never got beyond the first: in fact, the only episode I am to call to mind is the madeleines dipped in tea event. There was; however, a positive outcome. I found that the author's detailed meanderings had a soporific effect and went a long way towards curing my long-standing bouts of insomnia. In no time at all I found myself drifting off too sleep.

It has never occurred to me since, to give M. Proust another try because I know that the effect would probably be the same; no doubt, because I tend to lack prolonged concentration.

On the other hand; maybe it is down to the subject matter. One of my favourite books is Martin Chuzzlewit. I must have read it at least four times over the years! Dickens isn't always an easy read, but then it's his motley characters who hold the attention. I never tire of Sairey Gamp, the Pecksniffs, Mr. Sweedlepipe and Mrs. Todgers: all colourful folk the author manages to weave into what is quite a dark murder story.

Somewhere in the mid-sixties, the BBC ran educational programmes: one of those being 'Say it in Russian'. I sent off for all four Russian language books. My attempt to learn Russian, quite a source of amusement for the family. But I've remembered a few phrases. Eto televisor, krachnia ploshoidi, I uttered recently, during a Russian programme, when visiting one of my daughters. My ten-year-old grandson gave me a penetrating look; 'Stop showing off Nan' he remarked.

After I had become more proficient at my typing, I was more or less all ready to go, and registered at a local agency for work as a part-time clerk/typist. But, during the interview foolishly let slip that I had a knowledge of shorthand. As a result, I was despatched to a large shipping office in Leadenhall Street and within half an hour of my arrival there, was called upon to take dictation. Apart from the fact that the terms of reference were completely alien to me, I soon realised that my shorthand was far rustier than I'd thought possible. To sum matters up: I'd jumped in the deep-end and subsequently sunk without trace.

Having lost confidence, I decided to go for something simpler. A local department store was advertising for sales staff. This was quite ideal for me, the hours (part-time), allowed me to be home before the children returned home from school.

But my new employment was to be rather more temp than I'd bargained for; because within a few weeks of returning to work, I discovered that I was pregnant. My youngest child was seven years old. Cot and pram had been dispensed with and I was thirty-six. I viewed the coming event with mixed feelings, even though I'd been going through a weird broody phase fairly recently: peering into prams etc. My husband was delighted at the news and I was back in the nest once more. It was to be almost another five years before I managed to leave it occasionally; to make a tentative return to work yet again.

 Meanwhile, there were preparations to be made for the new arrival. Like the previous one, this was to be a home birth. The big bedroom would need re-decorating. Later, notice boards scanned for pram and cot: bargain hunting again, which I always enjoyed. In early February, the following year, our fourth child was born. An eight-and-a-half-pound baby boy. A little brother for my ten -year-old, who said that he'd prayed to God that he wouldn't have another awful sister. He was to be envied, our new baby. An eight-year gap with the youngest of his siblings meant that he would almost have the advantages of an only child. Besides which, he would always be little bruv.

In the run-up to the seventies, family life had followed its usual pattern of pleasures and anxieties, ups and downs; during which time, my husband was away for weeks on end, involved in contract work. Thus, the ongoing pattern of partings and reunions- a pattern not to be recommended. For, in the course of time, the threads of married life are apt to become loose: people grow apart. By the end of the sixties, clouds were gathering.

1970 might be described as a catalytic year. Certain events therein, were doubtless portents of the subsequent downward spiral of our marriage. For this was the year of the vacation horribilis!

An unexpected reminder of which, came through my letterbox quite recently, when a wad of junk mail landed with a thud on my front doormat. One very brightly coloured brochure stood out from the usual Indian and Chinese take-away leaflets. And, what caught my eye immediately, was the heading: 'PONTINS HOLIDAYS, bargain breaks for all the family'. Judging by the photographic illustrations of 'happy families' splashing about in a large swimming pool, you could see that they were all having a whale of a time. The list inside the folder gave a choice of venues and I couldn't help but glance down the list...Yes! There it was: even after all these years: Pontin's Holiday Camp, Brixham, Devon. How inviting it had appeared then...

It wasn't as though we didn't have a choice when it came to selecting our proposed first luxury venue. I hadn't been keen to travel all that way, even by car, and suggested Bournemouth instead. It was my husband who'd been insistent that we all take our luxury holiday in the West Country. Which only added to the irony of the situation which I found myself in a few months later...and it is not easy to set down certain details of our family holiday, without a certain amount of personal angst creeping into the narrative; when I am reminded, once again, of my holiday horribilis. I stress the 'my', though, because the children themselves had a great time, even if their Dad was unable to be there: having been obliged to withdraw at the last minute, due to an unexpected offer of work that he couldn't refuse.

After having dropped us off in Brixham, my husband returned to our now empty, and peaceful, house. I was to phone him each evening during the fortnight, to let him know how we all were.

Fathers in big cities, such as New York, according to the movies, send their families away at certain times of year, to escape the city heat; where, no doubt, they meet up with other temporarily fatherless folk. In this situation; however, I am virtually a single parent in charge of four children: the youngest three-years-old, the eldest fifteen. When I had at first refused to embark as solo parent on this holiday, my husband had told me: 'You can't let the children down'. Neither could I of course. So, there I was: the youngest no problem, he was only three years old, so I hired a pushchair for him. The others, though well behaved and fairly obedient, all wished to do their own thing now and then. Because they were out of sight, I tended to worry about them unduly. During the early evenings, I'd accompany the children to watch various form of entertainment taking place in the dance hall. My eldest wins the singing competition one evening: the prize which turns out to be six cans of Pepsi Cola; but we are all pleased for her. My ten-year-old daughter had been successful in the Donkey Derby during the fortnight. The children were enjoying themselves and the weather was fine. Much to be thankful for.

After nine 'o' clock each evening, the band starts up with music for mums and dads to dance to. This is when we leave. It is simply torture to have to sit there and listen to all that rhythm without being able to dance. But then, my dancing days were over: brief though they were.

My thirteen-year-old son had made a friend; another boy, with the same hobby: fishing. We overlook St Mary's Bay. Steps lead down to the beach and rocks below. One afternoon, my son and his friend seem to have been down in the Bay for a long time, and I begin to feel uneasy. With my other three, I go in search of them; but the beach is quite empty. We call my son's name without success and look around, but there is no sign of him.

The tide is coming in. As though to confirm the dreadful feeling of apprehension I'm beginning to experience: a small helicopter appears out of nowhere. It flies backwards and forwards, almost skimming the rolling waves: as though searching for something or someone in the sea. Just as my knees are on the point of giving way, my son and his friend emerge from behind a group of rocks further along the beach, where they've been digging for sand-eels!

Sometimes I wander down to the harbour: there seem to be several interesting side alleys and walkways in the vicinity. I'd really love to investigate further, but with a three-year-old in a pushchair; however, it's best to limit any exploration to the harbour's gift shops.

What happened next (for this is not the last of my holiday hor-ribilis traumas), also came to involve my elder son. Though this particular incident wouldn't have taken place had it not been for one of my 'sudden ideas'.

I decided to take the children over to Torquay for the day. The ferry ran quite frequently, and it would make a change from the holiday camp scenario.

The beach at Torquay is fairly deserted: probably because it's off season at this time of year. The two younger children begin to dig: they're going to make a sandcastle. My elder daughter goes in search of a ladies cloakroom. My thirteen-year-old has spotted some pedal boats for hire, so I gave him some money and tell him not to go too far out. Just as he begins to pedal off, a boy, who has obviously been lurking nearby, dashes into the sea and jumps beside him. A free-rider, who soon takes over the steering. In no time at all they are way out and almost up to the red flag boundary. The hire man assures me that the riders are alright, to no avail. 'Mum you look so funny running up and down the beach waving your arms', says my daughter, on her return. It appears that my frantic 'come in' gestures have had effect, and the pedal boat returns to base. The free-rider disem-barks hastily and runs off.

I can't remember much else about that particular day, except that I was more than glad when it was over. When my husband arrived to take us all home on the final Saturday morning, the first words he addressed to me were: 'did you enjoy yourself?' Quite unaware, of course, that his enquiry had been somewhat ill-timed.

During the previous evening, I'd spent over half an hour wander-ing about in the dark, almost in a state of panic, looking for my fifteen-year-old, who'd been given permission to attend a last night teenagers dance; on the understanding that she was to be back at the chalet by 11pm. She had failed to show up by 11.30. Even more worrying, was, the discovery that the dance hall venue was now closed and in complete darkness. The area itself deserted.

Shortly after I'd arrived back at our chalet, the culprit had turned up. It was past midnight!

With the recent walk about in pitch darkness still fresh in my memory, not to mention a couple of other episodes that had taken place during our holiday break, the response to my husbands' enquiry had been in the negative; accompanied by a soupcon of unparliamentary language. 'You're ungrateful,' had been his rejoinder.

Until we reached the outskirts of London, our journey home had been uneventful. But somewhere near Heathrow, our temperamental Ford Zephyr V6 began to play up: now juddering along in fits and starts along the busy motorway. Having at last managed to coax the car into a layby before it came to a complete halt. My husband went to look for a garage. As the repair would take some time, apparently, myself and the children were sent home in a hired cab.

The cab driver was very young. He and my fifteen-year-old chatted away about the current pop music scene, and our journey home was accompanied by a pop music tape played at full volume. By the time we arrived home I'd developed a splitting headache.

A few hours later, my husband returned home. He was not in the best of moods. What with the cost of the holiday plus those of repairs to our car, he must have been well out of pocket? But I have to say, that at that particular point in time, I couldn't quite find it within me to offer my heartfelt sympathy.

A most peculiar event took place during the early seventies: which no doubt added to the undercurrent of marital discord prevailing at the time. And, I have to admit, that this unfortunate incident had occurred due to my misplaced, 'any port in a storm' attempt to forestall any further domestic unrest: to preserve family harmony (which was well out of tune already to some extent). In retrospect; however, even allowing for the cir-

cumstances that had evoked this 'sudden impulse'; the whole
episode seems so utterly bizarre and ridiculous, that to tell it as
it was becomes a mite embarrassing, to say the least! Therefore,
an oblique presentation of what happened at the time springs
to mind, as a face-saving solution. Namely a hypothetical court
hearing.

(Circa 1977.)

Counsel for the Prosecution:

'Mrs S, a cross petition with regard to your divorce has been
submitted by your husband, on the grounds of unreasonable behaviour. Whereby, with malice afore-thought, you deliberately
set fire to an article of his personal clothing. What have you to
say?'

Defendent:

'It was an accident, and anyway, he wasn't wearing them at the
time.'

Judge to Counsel:

'What does the Defendent mean by 'them'.'

Counsel:

'Y-Fronts Your Honour.

Judge:

'What are Y-Fronts?'

Counsel:

'Gentleman's underpants, Your Honour.'

Judge:

'I see. Proceed.

Counsel for the Prosecution:

'So where were the said garment when you set it alight? May I enquire?'

Defendent:

'Under the grill.'

(Laughter in the public gallery.)

Usher:

'Silence in Court.'

Defendant:

'Anyway, I didn't set them alight, they caught fire after I put them under the grill to air. They were a bit damp and my husband was in a hurry to go out.'

Counsel for the Prosecution:

'A strange and reckless accusation on your part, you must admit?'

Defendent:

'But it was a brand new cooker, had only been delivered the day before.'

Counsel for the Prosecution:

How very convenient for you.'

Defendent:

'Yes, I thought so at the time, but I must have turned the grill to mark 6 instead of 1. I only went out of the kitchen for a couple of minutes, and when I came back, my husband was in the garden stamping out the flames. He was very angry!'

Counsel for the Prosecution:

I would suggest that you quite deliberately set fire to said garment, in order to prevent your husband from leaving the house.'

Defendent:

Muttering: 'He was always leaving the house.'

Counsel for the Defence:

'Your Honour, I would suggest that my client's unfortunate course of action was born out of sheer desperation.'

Counsel for the Prosecution:

(aside):
'Insanity more likely.'

Counsel for the Defendent:

(aside to client):
'Do you wish to plead insanity?'

Defendent:

'No.'

Counsel for the Defendent:

'Your Honour, I would suggest...'

Judge:

'I would suggest that you have been wasting the court's time... case dismissed.'

If the summer of 1970 had heralded the 'wearing thin'...the gradual weakening of the fabric of our marriage, by the end of 1976 it had completely fallen apart.

There were many factors that had played their part in this almost inevitable 'end-of-the-line' scenario. Suffice it to say; however, I have no intention of providing certain snippets of 'dirty washing' to hang on it: tempting though it may be of course. That old 'observation of the niceties' requires adhering to, especially where family are concerned: whatever one's personal feelings.

That said, I have allowed myself the luxury of cutting a little slack. A complete whitewash is not on my agenda. It's my memoir anyway. Not out of revenge, after all this time, but so as to paint an overall picture of my stormy seventies marriage: and what led to its conclusion.

In the autumn of 1971, my husband signed up for a contract that took him away to work on a supervisory job on the other side of the world. The contract: for one year only. Batchelor status (wife and family not included.) Leave after six months. At first, I had gone along with this arrangement and tried to make the best of things. I joined a choir, took up oil painting at evening classes and did some occasional voluntary work. On the home front, three teenagers and a four-year-old kept me fully occupied, so it couldn't be said that I was bored. Eventually; however, the strain began to tell; especially after there had been a couple of family emergencies when I'd been obliged to call the doctor in. One instance of severe croup, the other gastro-enteritis (my four-year-old this time). My husband, on the other hand, had arrived home after six months to a hero's welcome party, given by his sister! I felt that there was something amiss here: Mrs Nasty was about to emerge. 'He thinks he's Lawrence of Arabia,' I remarked to someone at the party: my allotted role as 'Mrs spoilsport' now a certainty.

So, slowly but surely, what had been an almost whimsical acceptance of my lonely married life, was turning into an ongoing resentment. I felt completely trapped in a situation that looked set to continue indefinitely. 'What was the point of being married?' I asked myself.

There came a day, shortly after my husband had departed, once again, for the land of the Pharaohs, when I sat down and gave written vent to my objections at being a doormat wife. Once I got going, there was no restraint, and the moving finger wrote on and on. A virtual diatribe, which, almost of its own accord, came to unearth a considerable quantity of long buried ammunition: eighteen years of certain wrongs and shortcomings when it came to my husband's record. Not least, my erstwhile vacation horribilis at Pontin's Holiday Camp in Brixham. The indictment, on its completion, as far as I'm able to recall, covered approximately seven or eight pages of full-cap notepaper. Even I, came to the conclusion, that my missive was a trifle lengthy: so, I removed a couple of pages of narrative and forwarded the remainder to somewhere in the Western Dessert (via Cairo.) On its perusal by the recipient, there's little doubt that my treatise would have been scattered angrily to the four winds, and who knows? Subsequently eaten by a hungry camel!

Sad to relate; however, the baring of my wifely soul had proved ineffective: the indictment fallen on deaf ears. On completion of his current contract, my husband was intent on signing up for yet another years work in Egypt: which he said would set us up financially. Furthermore, we might even think about running a pub. 'Perish the thought,' had been my unspoken response. I'd been quite adamant when my blessing had been sought with regard to being left a perpetual 'contract widow.' 'No way Jose', or words to that effect, whatever the outcome. The outcome soon became evident: my husband, now thwarted of his life-style-footloose and fancy free, had become the resentful party. This all change situation did little to improve what had already come to be a 'very shaky house of cards.'

Part Five

And Pastures New

1974-1976. And so…now are left the last years of all, which end the long, domestic history. Things deteriorated fairly rapidly; although there had been a couple of 'patching-up' attempts. But it was already too late. The damage had been done. It was quite obvious to me that family life no longer held any charm for my husband. Having spent a way of life more-or-less unencumbered by the rules and confines of a domestic set-up: he was the one who now felt entrapped in it. And it showed. Disagreements were followed by overly long silences: making the atmosphere almost unbearable at times. A state of impasse, which culminated in my husband's departure. This time for the West Indies on yet another long-term contract. I knew for certain, then, as far as I was concerned, my marriage was well and truly over, and shortly after I wrote to my husband requesting a divorce. To have suggested a mere separation, would have been farcical in the circumstances.

What is it The Bible says? 'Many waters cannot quench love, nor the floods drown it.' I would take issue here, (no blasphemy intended), for there comes a time when even the application of a 'bucket-full too many' has been known to do the trick. And even though, just at first, there may remain a few sparks of love glowing in the darkness: these too will die out of their own accord.

July 1977…The Queen's Silver Jubilee, also coincides with the return of my husband for his six-monthly home leave. During which time, I come to discover, that I now have definite grounds for divorce. An unexpectantly painful piece of information; but that which will provide the key that I required: the means of my release.

But here a final jump forward, just as the orchard pathway of my Norfolk childhood had made it necessary, then, to avoid the painful stinging nettles now: in order to avoid excavating that which is purely personal. In fact, all the inherent emotional factors that come into play when endeavouring to break free, to pull up the tap root: of a long-term marriage. So here an extra long leap...enabling me to proceed that time...to go over the bridge (just like Billy Goat Gruff), over the bridge and into 1978.

Eager though I'd been to put events behind me and embrace the New Year of 1978: that which took place during the early hours of New Year's Day had surely been enough to dampen my initial enthusiasm, in more ways than one, due to an unfortunate combination of circumstances. Three days of bitterly cold weather, including unusually sharp frosts. An end terrace house with a water tank in the roof area, cosily situated between north and east facing outer walls; there occurred an event which I'd have entered in my 1947 jobs ledger, during the winter of that year as: 'Burst Pipe in the Loft.'

Having stayed up late because of the impending New Year, we were all still downstairs at 1am, when the contents of our water tank began cascading through the house. On first observing the deluge, which had commenced as an almost coy trickle seeping through the ceiling: I became as rooted to the spot. It was one of my daughters who had sprung into action with an umbrella to shield herself from the downpour; having first found a torch, she disappeared upstairs in order to rescue the family bedding. A plumber, having been sent for almost immediately, had arrived fairly quickly. By then; however, the water-tank had disposed of its entire contents.

Every electric socket had been affected by the flooding that night, which meant the current required switching off until the house was dried out by special machinery. Due to overwhelming demand, since we weren't the only 'carpet squelchers' in the area, and, because he wasn't under the age of seven, my son and I were amongst the last in the queue.

Two weeks later, we were still living the simple life, although my two daughters had returned to their own bases by then. All the carpets had been ruined, my electric cooker, needless to say, was out-of-bounds, so I was trying to cook our meals on a portable Calor Gas contraption: which took ages. What at first had been challenging, was by now more than a little depressing. My elder daughter had been horrified at our plight when she came to visit and phoned the local council immediately; threatening to contact The News of the World if my son and I weren't dried out at once. Within a few hours, that miraculous drying machine had been employed...we were back to civilisation.

Given that the first dawning of 1978 had begun on such an unpropitious note, had I not learned that 2,000 or so of my local fellow citizens had also been victims of the recent icy circumstances; there may have been a slight tendency on my part, to wonder if the Gods had, perhaps, required me to undergo a test of sorts: by way of baptism (not of fire; thankfully, in which case I may not have survived in order to tell the tale.) The recent deluge of water from above: confirmation of my worthiness. Thus, having earned the right to go forward now, to fresh woods and pastures new.

Well, if that were so, it would appear that I'd been successful: for on the whole 1978 proved to be a golden year. I've employed the word almost, because up to the beginning of May: when my divorce was finalised, I had been more or less trying to get my act together. Having been married for over twenty years, becoming single again was almost like being cast adrift: a strange inexplicable sensation of both relief and vulnerability. I was no longer a 'Mrs' but a divorcee...

Innocent party or not, thirty years ago there had been a certain stigma that attached itself to this particular condition:

if you happened to be one of the fairer sex. In effect, I had metamorphized into (had my identity been set down in cold print): Blond Divorcee! The very mention of which, enough to conjure up a woman of doubtful morals... a threat to all decent married ladies in the immediate locality. Even several years later, and much to my secret amusement, if I happened to be at a social event together with some of my usual work colleagues, a few of whom had brought their other halves along. There was one 'Mrs' in particular, who, having seen me approaching their table, had automatically brought one of her hands to rest on tubby hubby's knee- 'he's mine keep off', it said.

What happened next must have been pure coincidence. Though the thought had occurred to me, at first, that it may be due to my Aries luck. For just as I was emerging from the rough patches of 1978 and post-divorce in the July of that year: providence had stepped forward in order to give me a helping hand. As a beneficiary of my late Uncle Albert's Estate, I had come into a small legacy: the sum of £4,000. It couldn't have come at a better time. I paid my solicitor's divorce fees, treated my three elder children and daughter-in-law, replaced my old kitchen table with a modern kitchen unit, purchased some badly needed new bed linen and booked a six-day Hans Anderson holiday in Denmark for my younger son and myself with Danish Seaways. I also put aside a couple of Five-Year Bonds for a rainy day. Much as I tend to take after my mother, somewhere in the background there is always my father: ready to step forward with the ever practical...'now look here my girl'. A time would come in the future when my Five-Year Bonds proved their worth.

Meanwhile, life was for living: things were for doing. Passports to obtain and a cabin to book. Even if my son hadn't felt a certain degree of excitement at the prospect of our first holiday abroad: the same could not be said of his mum.

Our destination was Odense, the birthplace of Hans Anderson, which involved Esberg by ship from Harwich, then a fairly long journey by coach. Due to a shortage of twin berthed cabins, my son and I had been allocated a three-berth and at no extra charge.

As my son slept, I sat by the porthole for hours looking out to sea. Even if it was pitch black out there, I didn't want to miss anything that might be going on. A passing vessel perhaps? However, despite my intense peering out to sea, there had been nothing else to see other than the static lights of the North Sea oil rigs in the distance. I would have to be satisfied with these. Feeling very tired, I sought my own berth and fell asleep almost immediately.

When I awoke the next morning, it was to discover that the ship was rolling. In the space of a few hours the sea had gone from smooth to rough. 'Don't ever ask me to go on another ship,' groans my poor dear son, who now lays sprawled face down on the rising and dipping floor of our cabin: having already been obliged to stagger back and forth to our en-suite facilities at regular intervals. I can only imagine his discomfort because so far, the ships rolling hasn't affected me at all. However, by the time we reach our embarkation point at Esberg, I'm beginning to feel just a little queasy myself: which soon wears off once dry land has been reached. The same cannot be said for my son who is still feeling too poorly to appreciate the coach party's stop for lunch and our subsequent visit to Legoland.

Thankfully, our voyage home, five days later, had been pleasantly smooth: even though the ship had been awash with an invasion of celebrating Swedish bikers. No doubt bound for some bikers rally in England. A noisy lot, but quite inoffensive on the whole. Just the same, there had been a slightly worrying episode, when my son and I had been seated in the Harwich train, prior to its departure to Liverpool Street Station. For on glancing briefly towards the door of our carriage, I became aware that I was being gazed at in a benevolent manner, by a large Swedish fellow; who then entered the carriage and handed me some kind of magazine: possibly a Swedish comic. A flattering gesture, perhaps. Nonetheless, I'd been truly thankful that there hadn't been any vacant seats available. Newly single, I would have had no real expertise on tap, in order to deal with the attentions of a rather inebriated Viking gentleman: especially one with a fuzzy beard!

Much as we'd enjoyed our visit to Odense and the various tourist trips, as far as my son was concerned, the most memorable had been all the gorgeous Danish food, No miniscule pots of marmalade and teeny plastic boxes of butter: but large platters of assorted breads, slabs of golden butter and generous dishes of fruity preserves.

Our evening meals, after the days sight-seeing, equally delectable. The guest's appreciation always acknowledged by the Hotel Proprietor with a half-bow together with a swift clicking of the heels. Such over-the-top military style body language had led to the conjecture, by almost everyone in the party, that our host was of German extraction. Maybe an army left-over from the 1940-1945 German occupation of Denmark? A very young ex-soldier who'd never returned to his homeland. Whatever he'd been formerly, one thing was for sure: in the year of 1978, Herr Click, Hotel Proprietor, inherited the title of 'Host Supreme'.

With regard to other aspects of my life then, once the Denmark adventure was over, it could be said that, in effect, I was still dithering about. Like Mr. Fagin in Lionel Bart's Oliver: reviewing the situation. As far as going back to work: which I intended to do in due course, at the moment there was no rush. I was in receipt of maintenance, sufficient to live on for both my son and myself. This had been the result of a court order, taking into consideration the circumstances and length of the marriage itself, and my ex-husband's earnings. Much to my relief, for in the first instance, I'd dreaded the thought of having to apply for Social Security. Anyway, income tax, should I be lucky enough to find a job, would come into the equation and my office skills were well out of date. As to meeting new people, those on my own wavelength, where to start? As a 'toe in the water' exercise, I joined a local, ladies only singles group. All were ex-wives like myself. About eight of us met once a week at the foundling members house, for a good natter. There were social outings too, from time to time. On the home front, there was plenty of diversions also.

In late September 1978, my first grandchild, a little girl, was born: Maria. I'd also acquired two ready-made grandsons, my daughter-in-law's children from her first marriage. I really enjoyed taking them out and about. I was in my element here, even if mummy had become nanny! But where was 'I', the real 'me'? I wondered sometimes.

At one time, during my marriage, after battling my way through Carl Jung's The Psychology of Types, which I'd discovered in my local town library, I was more than sure I'd come across the exact definitions relating to both my own and my husband's 'types'. There was no doubt about it. My husband was the outgoing, confident extrovert: pleasure loving, the life and soul of the party (which indeed he was). Myself, 'me', being the complete opposite, it would seem: introverted, sensitive, thoughtful etc. etc. The proverbial goody two-shoes, in fact. But, how on earth had I come to that ridiculous conclusion then? As a child I had always been a little show-off: adventurous, confident and outgoing. I was indeed sensitive, perhaps over sensitive, but unmistakably...an extrovert!

Years later, on thinking the matter over (probably when I should have been doing the housework), the reason for my apparently having undergone a change of personality over the years, became quite obvious. On the one hand, because my husband happened to be the archetypal extrovert, I'd more or less been eclipsed. On the other hand, having been fully immersed in the role of full-time wife and mother. The lot of most married women who'd made their debut in the fifties. Any identity had been smothered-quashed. My own light, as it were, if not extinguished exactly, currently hidden under a bushel. And taking a long while to re-ignite, now I'd been liberated several years down the line: but time would tell.

Meanwhile, having some spare time on my hands, in order to keep my mind alert, and suddenly prithee to a new idea: I set about learning German. The first exercise hadn't required more effort: der wasser es blau (the water is blue). Easy: German was going to be a doddle. Wrong of course. There was all that complicated gender grammar to contend with. But I did at least manage to get half-way through the text book, and any form of knowledge is never really wasted. Even if it amounts to a few hundred words of German, which one is never likely to use (apart from a bit of showing off now and then).

What I should have really have had a go at though was French. The following summer, my younger son and I went on a three-day trip to Paris, via Channel Crossing and guided coach tour: long before the event of a Channel Tunnel and thankfully before Disneyland had invaded the beautiful city.

This is our second day in Paris. There have been the usual guided visits by coach. Our pretty young courtier, obviously well-versed in all the city's fascinating history. Equally pleasant, our coach driver, a good-looking young man. 'A nice couple', I remember thinking. Later that afternoon, as my son and I made our ways toward The Seine, we spot the pair of them walking along hand in hand, quite obviously in love. Or in more surreal terms, an item. A fact which would come to have some bearing on a certain predicament a few of us tourists found ourselves in later that evening.

Meanwhile, our bateau makes its way slowly along The Seine. 'In that apartment,' our boat-trip guide informs us, sweeping his arms upwards towards the roof-top area of a tall old building, 'Voltaire once lived'. I'm thrilled to bits. Everything about Paris, those of we romantic, arty types, tends to be thrilling. A real lift to the spirit. My son, busily surveying the riverside scenery through his new binoculars, also seemed to find Paris very interesting, especially the Eiffel Tower. He's going to join some of our coach party who are going up, later this afternoon, and, intends to go right to the top, where he'll be able to use his binoculars (a present from his dad), to advantage. I have no intention, myself, of taking part in this kind of adventure. Over the passing years I have developed a fear of heights; which is strange really, considering how often I'd climbed trees as a child. Some weird psychological reason, I expect, which would be too tedious a task to try and unravel now.

Although my son is quite mature for his age, a sensible twelve-year-old, I'm not keen on his ascending the Eiffel Tower un-accompanied. I'm pleased when a middle-aged couple on our coach offer to keep an eye on him.

The Museum of Modern Art lies just across The Seine, and as I've been given to understand that the coach party won't be com-ing to earth for at least forty-five minutes, I decide to go and investigate. Walking across the river, I am conscious of a mo-mentary feeling of elation: this really is something I had never imagined doing! On reaching my destination, my plan receives something of a set-back. The museum is closed. I re-cross The Seine and make my way to The Eiffel Tower area. I seem to have been hanging around waiting for my son for quite some time now. Before long, I begin to experience that slight flicker of anxiety, which is no-doubt familiar to all 'waiters' of unpunc-tual kith and kin: mothers in particular. Imagination begins to chip in now, but before it can really get going, one half of the pair who've taken my son under their wing, is now approaching. But her husband is nowhere to be seen, neither is David. Slight fluttering's once more. It appears that both have gone up to the next level of the tower, but she had not wished to do so herself. Maybe this does not augur well for husband and wife: the latter having confided in me that this Paris weekend trip was a 'last chance' attempt to save their marriage. Before long, her other half comes into view! 'WHERE IS MY SON?' I'm consoled at once on learning that he's now in the safe company of young ladies, a group of fellow travellers on our coach. Like David, they wished to access the very top of the tower. So, that's a relief anyway.

Common sense should have told me that he was up there some-where. Unfortunately, it had taken a back seat and no lesson had been learnt from a similar incident that had taken place, and in another country, a year previously in Denmark, when on our Hans Anderson trip.

My son had gone aloft in Ribe's Lutheran Cathedral, leaving heights phobic mother below. Waiting for so long that I'd even been on the point of going up myself. Otherwise, two odd looking gentleman coming down (a few minutes ahead of my son, as it turned out), I'd enquired: 'have you seen a little boy?' 'Nein,nein', they replied. Why hadn't they seen him if he was up there? A vivid imagination can be hell at times-: murderers! What a relief when the little boy (in fact eleven -years-old and quite tall for his age), reached terra firma himself: only to re-ceive a scolding because we'd almost missed the coach!

Even allowing for The Eiffel Tower episode, the Paris experi-ence had been really wonderful. True that I haven't managed to visit Le Louvre as I'd intended, or Notre Dame (years later I was to remedy this.) However, there had been Le Monte Marte: from where we'd been able to look down over the myriad roof-tops of the city itself... Le Arche de Triumph and all the long tree-lined boulevards. We will be returning home tomorrow morning. Meanwhile, we are in for a special treat this evening, our courier has promised us.

And so here we are...marooned, right in the centre of where it's all happening: the nitty gritty of night and the city, the region of La Pigale and Le Follies Bergere. We are to be picked up by our coach in three quarters of an hours' time, it seems. Meanwhile, the couple drive off: having dumped their cargo, probably in order to partake of a romantic last meal or to 'be alone' for a while. Whatever the reason for our sudden abandonment, for certain of our party: those perhaps who've, until now, been see-ing Paris through a magic mist, this special experience has come as a bit of a 'shaker!' Can Can dancers and Toulouse Lautrec my foot! All around us blazing lights, huge screens with illustrated captions which leave us in no doubt what is on offer. 'Don't look David,' I advise my twelve-year-old son; whose rosy cheeks have become even rosier, as he endeavours to withdraw his embarrassed young visage 'tortoise-like' deep into the collar of his jacket. We are joined by two middle-aged ladies who seem to be equally 'at sea'. On attempting to enter a café of sorts for some respite, and possible refreshments, we are all handed an invitation card by a tout type doorman. Standing about in doorways and between parked cars: highly painted young ladies in miniskirts and knee length boots, step forward now and then in order to present their business cards to any passing gentlemen. I am absolutely furious at being dumped in the Red-Light District. 'I'm going to complain to the courier,' I say to the 'last chance' lady when we're safely back on the coach: 'my son is only twelve-years-old.' 'But hasn't he ever been to Soho?' she enquires. 'I haven't been there myself!' I reply, but in the end say nothing to the courier: not wishing to appear too ridiculous. I've quite obviously led far too sheltered a life.

On our return home, and when I come to relate the Paris night life episode to my other three (now grown-up) children, of course, they find the whole thing hilarious. 'We can picture you Mum,' says one of my daughters, 'Mary Whitehouse in the Red-Light District of Paris.' I'd been so nick-named because when they were younger, I'd been fairly strict about their television viewing. 'That's it!' I would say, if anything unsuitable for children was about to be shown near their bed-time. 'Up to bed, you're not watching that!' Thus, I had come to earn the title of Mary Whitehouse: a lady who had been a thorn in the side of television broadcasting authorities, in the late sixties and early seventies, as far as I can remember. Frequently complaining at the unsuitable and even indecent content of certain TV programmes. Odd as it may seem at this point in time, one of Mrs Whitehouse's regular protests had been to do with the use of bad-language on TV. Without doubt, Mrs W. was rather over censorious, sometimes however, I believe that she had a point.

And now, alas, The Age of Innocence is obsolete: kaput. We of the older generation, who, as children were allowed to be children, are saddened by its passing.

It could be said, for want of a better description, that the recent trips abroad with my son had been part and parcel of my personal 'Gap Year', during which, I was trying to readjust before 'getting my act together,' as it were. I needed to get back as soon as possible, since I didn't relish the idea of existing on court-order maintenance indefinitely: a prospect vaguely humiliating in some respects. What to do about it was a different matter. An ex-office girl approaching fifty, whose office skills were well out of date: if not extinct, is bound to lack confidence. Especially when confronted with the latest in application forms... the dreaded Curriculum Vitae. In other words, what had I been doing workwise for the last twenty-five years? Any perspective employer unlikely to be impressed by either of the following: 'not a lot really apart from bringing up four children,' or 'employment of a miscellaneous nature in order to fit in with my family.' Anyway, I registered with a local agency for temporary clerical work. Nothing was to come of this for a couple of months at least; which gave me time to reflect certain of my past temp assignments of a miscellaneous nature! Vis-à-vis: Bottle Capper, Assembly Line worker, Shop Assistant, Early Morning Cleaner (very short-lived), Clerk/Typist (but rarely), and last, but certainly not least, the rather un-nerving experience of being propositioned by a very flustered: not to say desperate, supervisor, immediately upon my arrival at work as Canteen Assistant one morning. 'Can you cook?' she had almost implored of me, meaning that 'the cook hadn't turned up for work and I need a stand-in able to produce a roast dinner for two dozen factory workers by one O'clock today.' Since cooking en-masse had been sprung on me so suddenly, there had only been my 'once more unto the breach' instincts to rely on: whatever the outcome. Although preparing batter for Yorkshire Pudding from a big sack of Batter Mix, was almost the equivalent of mixing cement for a spot of bricklaying (I couldn't help thinking at the time), here was nothing for it but to hope for the best!

Fortunately, by the time my efforts had been served-up, I was already off the premises! My shift as Canteen Assistant having ended, before any comment from the diners themselves could have reached my ears. But the cook turned up next morning anyway...TBTG (my shorthand for 'Thanks be to The Almighty.)

One of the first instances of just how much more relaxed the social inter-changes between the sexes had become: - 'Just look at those two,' I'd exclaimed...drawing my dancing partner's attention to a nearby couple: 'But they're dancing with hands on bums.' ' It is quite ok now', he'd responded. 'Well not on mine it isn't,' I said jokingly. Although I knew Michael wouldn't have taken such a liberty. I wasn't really his type anyway. He usually went out with those of a more sophisticated nature. There had come a time, a couple of years down the line, when Michael had suggested we might become 'friends', (in the modern sense of the word.) Attractive as I'd always found him to be, I'd gently declined the offer: knowing full well that I couldn't have coped with such a suave customer. Another potential ex-friend to be added to his list!

Nonetheless: how very heady it had been then. How on becoming a born-again singleton: I'd been considered attractive and worth chatting-up! When for so long I'd been taken for granted as a wife: my ex-husband's protracted absences; which, I suspected, he preferred to family life: had done nothing to enhance my self-esteem. So; yes indeed, such kind attentions had been flattering and welcome, but I had no wish to become involved in a new relationship. It had taken me a considerable time to recover from the aftermath of a broken marriage. Now I was free and intended to remain so. 'Life' for me then- had begun not at forty but fifty. I was now working full-time and earning my own living (albeit as a born-again Grade One Clerical Officer.) My 1980's diaries full of names, addresses and phone numbers of fellow concert and theatre goers: not to mention fellow party goers. What a time it was for we revellers…mature in years but young at heart: for this was the age of DISCO…no dancing partner required…no being a wallflower.

So here I am at yet another party. I've brought the requisite plate and bottle contribution, although I do not intend to drink myself, except for a couple of glasses of orange or lemonade. I tend to do a lot of dancing this evening, and once the Disco beat gets going, that will be enough intoxication for me: I'll be well and truly away!

The food spread looks good, all contributions from the assembled guests at Ronnie's party: cheese and pineapple on sticks, sausage rolls, sandwiches, cakes and homemade trifles. All the drinks are here in the kitchen: cans of beer, fizzy drinks, fruit juices and bottles of wine. It should be a good party: roll on the dancing, I think. But just then I have been cornered by a fellow party-goer: it's Ken. Seems as though I'm about to be chatted-up…BLAST! As an opening gambit, he suddenly remarks 'er… Haydn.' Meanwhile automatically focusing his gaze on the area of my cleavage (had I happened to have it on display!) 'Haydn,' he repeats, just in case I have mishear him. This chap knows that I enjoy Classical Music. A few of our crowd had have recently attended a concert at Walthamstow Assembly Hall. Now; however, is not the place: this is a party for goodness sake, and I have no intention of taking part in a discussion about Papa Haydn. For one thing, I am not exactly an appreciator of his symphonic works; due to the fact that they seem to go on, for what seems to me, a considerable length of time. Having a limited attention span, any symphony that extends four movements, instead of the usual three, has the same effect on me as my long ago attempt to plough through Proust's Remembrance of things past. It had me nodding off: as will Kenneth if he doesn't clear off soon: what a bore! 'Look here,' I would like to say to this aggravating little chap, 'I don't wish to discuss classical music, this is a party, I want to dance: so, get lost! Instead I say: 'excuse me, the music has just started,' and so it has. And (Lord be praised), it's the national anthem of all we born again singletons: Gloria Gaynor singing 'I will Survive! Irresistible! How compelling the beat and how scintillating the rhythm? Lyrics so very apt. Except, I don't really go along with 'I have all my love to give': after twenty -three years of Holy Matrimony, with its ups and downs, that particular commodity is in short supply just now: and most certainly not up for grabs. What love I have to give is of the kind reserved for my children and ever delightful grand-children!

Tonight; however, I am not Mum or Nan, but one of the small throng here on the make-shift dance floor and 'letting it all hang out!' with the other 'survivors.'

For a while I had been toying with the idea of hosting a social event myself. Not a party to begin with...a coffee evening per-haps. These small informal gatherings were always popular with everyone. So; in due course I advertised my proposed coffee evening in our monthly news sheet: having rashly ig-nored the warnings of my 'inner-voice' as to what effect a social gathering was likely to have on one particular member of household: namely he of the swirling tail and Basil Brush grin. A handsome fellow indeed was our black cross border collie, who was forever bent on escape to the wide-open spaces of our local park. This Houdini of the canine world had become our pet about seven years previously: mainly due to the persistent en-treaties of his then owner, who happened to be a near neigh-bour. 'Oh, go on, take him, he's lonely, the only puppy left now.' From my children, similar pleadings: 'Oh please can we have him Mum? He's lovely.' So, I'd given in, Bobby was ours now: though he would have been more at home somewhere on the borders of Wales, rounding up sheep. We did our best to give him a good home and take him for regular exercise, but it wasn't enough for Bobby. He never missed any chance to make a run for it, must any of his foolish carers happen to be caught off guard for a few moments. He always came back though did Bobby. Usually during the early hours of the morning, when he would give news of his return by such a loud volume of barking, that I would often stagger down the stairs half-asleep, in-order-to let him in before he woke the whole street. Sometimes; however. Bobby's request for re-admittance would prove a false alarm: he'd obviously had a change of heart! Instead of making his re-entry, when I'd hastily opened the front door to let him in; Bobby would give me one of his delightful Basil Brush grins, turn tail and run off again! 'Sure, tis worse than having a husband,' an Irish friend of mine had once remarked, on hearing of Bobby's capers. If there had been an A.S.B.O. for dogs then, Bobby, our dysfunctional but most beloved pet, would have been worthy of one. He lived to be eighteen, but even as an old chap, hankered after the wild and would craftily feign sleep in his basket under the stairs, until someone unwisely answered a knock on the door, without keeping an eye on him first: then he'd be off again. When this happened, particularly when he was older and easier to catch up with, I immediately set out to bring him back: mainly because I'd envisage runaway Bobby being the cause of a road accident. A fruitless exercise when he was in his prime and gone like a rocket across to the local park. In old age; however, our pet Houdini was much easier to re-trieve: his occasional breakouts were mere amblings, as far as the next turning. Once I'd caught up with him, Bobby offered no resistance at all: 'Well it's a fair cop Mrs...I'll come quietly,' his docile manner implied, as I clipped on his lead and escorted him home. Not so in his rebellious youth; needless-to-say, when re-capturing the escapee had been difficult: not to say impossible!

An instance of Bobby's shenanigans, I've cause to remember with more clarity than usual. A day when my younger son had gone to answer the door to his friends and failed to be en-guard thus allowing yet another dare-devil dash by the conniving Col-lie, apparently asleep in his basket under the stairs. Having taken his lead with me, I managed to catch-up with Bobby be-fore he'd had time to notice my arrival: make a run for it up the two flights of steps and so across the main road to the park. He'd been otherwise engaged, further flight put on hold, due to the attractions of a sweet looking little lady dog, demurely trotting along and in tow of an elderly, meek looking gentleman: quite obviously unaware of the fact that his pet was being stalked and about to be seduced by an amorous young Border Collie. When I attempted to grab Bobby by his collar, in order to prevent the impending seduction, he'd skilfully dodged out of reach and persisted in his original intentions. Whereupon, I'm almost ashamed to relate, I'd lost my cool and taken a random swipe at Bobby with the dog lead: a foolish reaction on my part. Due to Bobby having dodged out of the way, I'd missed my canine target and the leash was now neatly coiled around the ankles of the meek looking old gentleman. As I made my profuse and embarrassed apologies. Close by, I could see my elder daughter, who'd accompanied me and so witnessed the whole debacle, bent almost double in a fit of hysterics. Bobby; of course, had disappeared, now en-route to the park...

Yet there I was: in spite of Bobby's unconventional, not to say disruptive disposition, about to welcome several unsuspecting guests to a coffee evening. An event, which in normal circumstances, would turn out to be a pleasant gathering of friends. So, what could I do about Bobby? I decided that he would have to be temporarily banished, whether he liked it or not. A shame really: because he was a very friendly chap on-the-whole. I gave him a doggy sedative on the evening in question, plus a couple of his favourite doggy chews and shut him in the box room upstairs.

By clearing my small living room of all unnecessary furniture, I was able to accommodate fifteen club members. It was turning out to be a very pleasant evening: everyone chatting away between eats...sandwiches, cake etc. At least an hour and a half went by (the sedative had proved it's worth) before Bobby made his incarceration known. 'Oh, go on, let him down,' my friends implored me. 'Be it on your own heads,' I thought.

After dashing into the front room, Bobby had immediately

introduced himself by sniffing at the crouches of all my male guests. Very soon, little screams of alarm erupted as Bobby, intent on treating everyone alike, had begun sniffing around the hems of the ladies' skirts and dresses. At my efforts to calm him Bobby had simply flopped over onto his back, in a passive resistance ploy, with his four legs akimbo, disclosing to all and sundry his obvious male attributes, as I dragged him out by his collar: much to the amusement of my friends.

So! There it was! Any latent plans that I'd been cherishing with-regard-to hosting a party had been well and truly nipped in the bud. I would have to limit my own attempts to do my bit, with-regard-to club events, by organising theatre or concert outings. The mere thought of an actual party, the whole caboodle: music, dancing etc. together with an excitable Bobby making intermittent efforts to socialise: was just too ghastly to even contemplate.

The very first time I'd clapped eyes on 'a stranger across a crowded room', had been one enchanted evening' in November 1952. This event was to lead to marriage, and, in-the-course of time, four children. This love at first sight syndrome, had therefore, led me to conclude; especially when I happened to be in a cynical frame of mind: that it had been mother natures' special ploy to ensure an ongoing propagation of the human species. Quite a flawed conclusion on my part; because, as I came to discover, this odd phenomenon: this sudden chemistry, isn't confined to the young! In fact, it was some twenty-seven years down the line, when, yet another 'stranger' came into my sights, across a similar 'crowded room.'

The sudden mutual awareness, although exciting in a way, threw me completely off balance; even if I'd been able to assume a certain cool indifference (an icy-personae is always helpful on such occasions). Had my stranger been the confident, pursuing type, I'm afraid it's more likely that the 'ice' would have come under the threat of melting. Fortunately, he was the shy type who required meeting half-way, which as far as I was concerned, simply wasn't going to happen. The fact of the matter was, that my fellow divorcee and I had really nothing in common at all.

The attraction was purely physical. I'd been down that road before and my own common sense told me not to venture there again. Just the same, it was a hard fight against instinct. A background of soft lights and sweet music at the occasional party event didn't help either. Bewitched, bothered and very bewildered was I.

Feeling the need to confide in someone, I consulted my elder daughter, hoping that she would be able to advise me in the matter. Should I stick to own common sense, or abandon it and take a chance? To cut a long story short: I drew a blank. For some reason as far as my grown-up children were concerned, any indication that Mum might be interested in a member of the opposite sex, was enough to induce barely concealed amusement: my current problem was no exception. 'I thought I saw a footstep in the cat litter', had been my confidents only comment.

After all, it was really up to me: this was nobody else's problem but my own. I needed to snap out of it! As soon as possible too. What a waste of time over a chap. I'd decided, for various reasons, not to get involved with anyway...mind over matter again!

My cold-shoulder or seeming indifference toward the gentleman: who for months had caused me such inward angst, had obviously not fooled him, due to the vibes that had been around since our first meeting. And during a recent club party, in-the-course of making polite conversation with him: there had been that certain 'gleam' in the eye. A gleam that was enough to put me on my guard: a signal in fact! Although the proverbial 'love light' in his eyes should have given me cause for pleasure: it had the opposite effect. Scared me to death! I panicked, coward that I was, and made for the hills...or in order to be precise: The Alps.

The following week I went to my local travel agents and booked myself a week's holiday with Blue Sky's Tours: Bachelors

Abroad. A mixed singles, middle-aged group in this instance. We were going to Austria by air: to Munich, then by coach to St Anton in Austria. This would be my first air-flight.

'Let me know if you meet anyone,' the girl in the Travel Agent's had called after me as I left with my holiday brochure. It would have seemed rather odd, I suppose, if I'd tried to explain that I'd already met someone here at home and had booked this trip in order to put some distance between us: to avoid the possibility of ignoring common sense and getting involved with him. I needed a diversion and hopefully this trip to The Alps would give me something else to think about. The reason I'd chose a singles group in the first place, for my St Anton break, was to avoid being the odd one out in a party of couples: which can be embarrassing to say the least! The last thing on my mind was meeting someone. I wished to be foot loose and fancy free for the foreseeable future. Not too difficult given my mature years and inherent wariness!

When our plane landed at Munich Airport, at first it had been slightly alarming to observed so many armed police around. All passengers had been required to pass through a special detector barrier, prior to be manually frisked. These precautions having been put in hand after the recent outbreak of terrorist activities in parts of Europe. The Beider Meinhof Gang being very much in the news at that point in time.

Even when our coach set off for St. Anton, all along the roadside which led from the airport armed police were very much in evidence. It was odd to have seen so many guns at the ready. But that was in the early eighties; of course. Two decades on, similar armed vigilance would come to be quite common-place at most of the main airports in England.

Apart from that unexpected armed welcome at Munich Airport, the only thing of note that I'm able to recall with regard to our journey to St. Anton itself, concerns my ongoing awareness of just how close the wheels of our conveyance to the edge of that very steep mountain road. The sort of adventure I'd not been familiar with until then. It was quite a long drop down there in the valley below.

Odd really how one's phobias come to sneak in almost unnoticed over the years: my vertigo came on quite suddenly when I was in my early thirties. With my three-year-old in her pushchair, I was in the process of crossing a local main motorway, via a fairly high road bridge. Before I was half-way across, my legs had all but turned to jelly. That feeling of vulnerability, of being at the mercy of all the oncoming traffic-though obviously beyond its reach, had been enough to effect a hasty retreat, making it necessary to walk a considerable distance, in order to find myself a 'terra firma' pedestrian crossing.

Even on my first (and last) air flight, I'd been unable to match the enthusiasm of my fellow holiday makers. 'Oh, look at those Alps,'...not if I could help it, not from several thousand feet! Meanwhile, I passed my air time by trying to imagine I was on a number 11 bus; or for that matter any form of conveyance whose wheels were actually touching the ground.

There were six bachelors in our group: four ladies and to gentleman. Two of the ladies were school teachers from Birmingham: Rosemary and Ann. Christine, a very pleasant young lady, who hailed from North London, and myself, made up the four. The two 'forty-something' gentlemen were amiable enough, but we saw little of them, apart from at meal times. One of them, an 'odd-bod' vicars son from somewhere in the Midlands, the other a run-of-the-mill grey-haired chap, who took off on his own every day.

Our hotel was very comfortable: almost luxurious, and the food was good. When it came to service; though: that was a different matter. It was almost as if certain members of staff resented having to wait on us. If we had been ill-mannered, noisy or pretentious even, there may well have been reason enough for their barely concealed hostility.

This off-hand attitude; of course, is said to be a peculiarity of the British, where 'service with a smile' tend to be the exception rather than the rule. We unfortunate tourists; however, had been unaware, until now, that this trait had apparently become International and was now flourishing in The Austrian Alps.

On reporting about five-minutes late for lunch one day, such had been the obvious displeasure of the Head Waitress, that we were half expecting to receive a 'slap on the wrist' and given 'one hundred lines' as punishment.

Perhaps this overt unwillingness to serve we British tourists had been in some way due to the fact that, in the not too distance past, Austria had been part and parcel of Hitler's Third Reich. During the war years, this part of the world, bordering on neutral Switzerland, would have been awash with German border guards. On the look-out for escapees: who would have been shot on sight. But now the vanquished were having to serve the victors (to whom the spoils): so, tough! Could we have some more chips please?

By the end of the week; however, the positive aspects of our St. Anton holiday far outweighed the negative. To begin with, there had been the almighty Arlberg: a spectacular backcloth, so massive and awe-inspiring was it, that I suddenly became aware of my own insignificance in the scheme of things. The irrelevance of my petty personal concerns. Being only human, my mood of self- abasement was short-lived and in no time at all 'ego' had reasserted itself. I couldn't wait to explore my surroundings and looked forward, eagerly, to visiting whatever local tourist trips that Freddie, our courier, had arranged for us.

'Call me Freddie,' our handsome Italian courier has said. But surely now this tanned, good-looking fellow, with his dark curls, deep blue eyes and lovely smile, wasn't a Fred! More likely his real name was something akin to Fredricchio: that sounded Italian enough!

One morning, as I'd been descending the hotel stairs, and on my way out to join the coach party, Freddie, who'd been waiting for us all in the hotel lobby, looked up and gave me a lovely smile. How had I come to merit such an honour? A gift from God no-less! And no more either because gorgeous Freddie was for 'looking' only. He would have been snapped-up years ago. Waiting patiently at home on the other side of The Italian Alps, there was bound to be a beautiful wife and several bambinos.

Because soft drinks and mineral water was so expensive in St, Anton, the cheapest way to quench one's thirst in the local Bier Keller (we were sure they'd turned the heat up on purpose), was by ordering ein grossen bier: which of necessity came in ein grossen tankard. Most un-lady-like, but a requisite accompaniment during the evening's entertainment, consisting for the most part of drinking songs. 'Om pah-Om pah' we sang: thrusting grossen tankards left and right in time to the music.

There were other musical high-jinks available in the immediate vicinity, as we discovered one evening on one of our strolls about town: not loudly, but persistently, from a below-steps venue, came the beat of Disco music...

'Oh, but we can't go in there.' Protests one of my holiday companions. 'Yes, we can,' I insist. 'Look, there's Larry, he's got grey hair...we haven't, if he's allowed in, then so are we'.

Although this Disco venue is fairly small, the place isn't crowded, so there's plenty of room on the dance floor and the funky Disco music is great. So, this is where our allusive would be lothario has been hanging out. He seems surprised to see us! The beat soon becomes irresistible. Before long I'm on the dance floor: hooray for disco. After a while Rosemary and Ann join in the dancing. During the interval Larry says, in an encouraging tone of voice: 'that was very good.' Quite possibly, he is under the impression, that my own, rather abandoned style of dancing, is for his benefit! But of course, it's all due to the music itself that I'm on a high and going with the beat. No doubt, that when it comes to therapy, dancing is one of life's most enjoyable cures. In my own case, a form of unwinding a release of my complex inhibitions perhaps? In fact, we're all having a good time this evening, even without the help of ein grossen bier!

After breakfast one morning, my room-mate Christine tells me that she intends to go on a guided mountain walk. The very day before, I'd been persuaded to join her on a ski chair-lift trip: rather against my better judgement. But she was such a pleasant and friendly girl, that I didn't want to be a spoil-sport. So, up we went, 'just look at the view. Isn't it beautiful?' exclaims my companion, as we dangle in mid-air, moving at a snail's-pace upwards and towards the first ski-station. I allow myself a brief sideways squint and try not to think about the drop beneath. Even though securely barred in, I feel slightly dizzy. In the event, we alight at the first ski-station and make our descent by foot down the mountain. A generous concession on my friend's part, which, allows me to view our beautiful surroundings from a less terrifying vantage point. As for climbing: definitely not! Too past my prime to begin now.

By 10am the next morning, my fellow bachelors had gone their various ways. What to do? I checked the local time-tables at the railway station and caught the next train to Innsbruck...

Strolling along the main thoroughfare, after leaving Innsbruck Station, what had caught my eye almost at once, were certain little side-streets: vaguely familiar cobbled-stoned alleyways set between tall quaint looking houses. Then it occurred to me, as to where I'd come across this unusual scenario before, not as substance; however, but as illustrations: sketches in a book of Grimms Fairy Tales. This may have been quite some time ago, when I was a child, or, more likely, as I'd been reading to my own children one of the less gruesome folk tales of the Austrian born brothers Grimm (which hadn't really been written with children in, mind anyway.) Unfortunately, I've quite forgotten the gist of the tale in quest, but not the illustration, where the alleyway isn't empty (as I perceived it now), almost about to disappear into the distance, is the figure of a boy in flight. Where was he running to? How interesting it would have been, had I the courage, just to wander up and around one of these winding narrow streets and find out where it led to...

But common sense prevailed. Not such a good idea to wander too far off the beaten track on one's lonesome: when in strange surroundings. And, I soon came to realise that being a sole female when on foreign soil, may involve certain constraints. Just enough to take a little gilt of the gingerbread.

Sight-seeing and walking around for any length of time, unaccompanied or not, is bound to induce hunger eventually. Another draw-back here. At home I would have no hesitation in entering an eating place alone. But not here in Innsbruck, where every dining establishment seemed to be full of families or couples. Driven by hunger, I bought myself a bag of cooked Vienna sausages from a delicatessen and consumed them on route: and very nice they were too. When it comes to adventure (by present day standards), such an epicurean, and faintly surreal little episode, however pleasant to recall, would surely only merit three, judging on a scale of one to ten: but never mind.

Later I went for a cup of coffee at the station café. BASEL it said in very large letters on the front of my homeward train. I prayed that it would be stopping at St. Anton on the way, otherwise I might end up in Switzerland. Which would have entailed rather more adventure than I'd really had in mind. However, when the train gradually slowed down and came to a final halt, a few stations down the line, mush to my relief, I could see St. Anton written, large and welcoming. My vague qualms had been quite unnecessary: I'd been delivered safely back to base.

Tonight, Friday, our last night farewell get-together. Not at our hotel though. Instead we've been transported to an inn further up the mountain to take part in the usual programme of farewell do's: music, dancing and silly party games. 'Go on Doreen,' one of my holiday friends urges me, 'ask Freddie to dance.' She seems quite surprised when I decline the dare; no doubt assuming, that because of my erstwhile confident foray into the local Disco, I was game for anything. The fact of the matter was; however, that apart from being almost old enough to have been Freddie's mother: never in a thousand years would I have approached our handsome courier and invited him to dance with me. To my old-fashioned way of thinking, such would have shown a lack of propriety: a want of taste.

That being said; however, somewhat later that evening, there had occurred a few moments, when (due to a couple of glasses of wine earlier on), my inherent sense of propriety, as we were seated in our home going taxi, had taken a back seat. 'Step on the gas kid,' I remarked in a sad imitation of Humphrey Bogart. Whether to call my bluff or taking me at my word: that's exactly what the driver did. In fact, he tore down and around the winding road at such speed, that he may as well have re-joined at the start: 'Hang on in there, we're in for a bumpy ride!' Which would have served me right, I suppose. My flight to The Alps had turned out to be a lovely holiday: one of the most enjoyable I've ever experienced in fact. And the reason why I love to dredge it up now and again? There had been plenty in the way of diversion: more than I could have hoped for. Having gone away to forget, by the time I'd returned one might say that I'd forgotten 'what' or 'whom'. Things were back in perspective.

'How old were you then Nan?' asks my fifteen-year-old grandaughter, as I'm in the process of regaling her with a couple of episodes relating to my social life back in the early eighties. I tell her about the time I went on a canal boating holiday in 1983, with three other club members. Raking out a couple of snapshots to show her a younger Nan, seated atop the roof of a blue narrowboat. I have a pink cardigan draped around my shoulders and appear slightly windswept. The weather had been unusually chilly for early May that year. Our river route had taken us from St. Neots to Cambridge via Ely: with much to see in the way of river wildlife. A very pleasant to recall cruising holiday on the waterways: though not entirely without it's occasional moments of tension. A crew consisting of one male and three females (unrelated), living within such a confined space for almost a week, is not destined to run completely smoothly. 'Enough material there for a Harold Pinter play.' I remember

thinking post vacation. As the old North Country saying goes:'
'There's nowt so queer as folk. (myself included.)

When I go on to recall the times when my friends and I were
dancing at The Café de Paris, although she doesn't make any
comment, I'm able to gather from the expression of slight surprise on her pretty face, that my grandaughter finds the idea of
her Nan going dancing when so old, very odd indeed. As well
she might...because when a couple of my club acquaintances
had suggested a Saturday night out at the cafe de Paris in Leicester Square: even my own credulity had been a little strained.
Surely, we middle-aged survivors would seem completely out
of place in such a sophisticated environment! Which would no
doubt be full of younger people I wasn't keen on the idea at all?
In the event, I went along and had a great time.

My assumption with regard to the probable youthfulness of the
café de Paris clientele had been entirely wrong. 'Cosmopolitan
and of indeterminate age' would just about serve to portray
the Saturday night crowd who frequented the dance floor there;
way back in the swinging eighties. Although, one of the drawbacks resulting from this serendipity situation, meant pot-luck
when it came to dancing partners. But, had my ill luck occurred twice during the same evening, I'd never gain have set
foot on the polished floor of The Café de Paris. Though Disco
predominated throughout the evening on a Saturday night, the
odd session of Ballroom took place from time-to-time. During
which, true to tradition, it was a matter of luck whether or not
one came to be left standing along wallflowers of indeterminate
age.

It was during one of these Ballroom sessions that I'd drawn my
first duff ticket: in the shape of a bear-hugger extraordinaire!
My worst experience, ever, of being bear-hugged, throughout
what I'd envisaged as a slow, gliding fox-trot, which happened
to be one of my old favourites. However, as there was obviously
no escape from my partner's clutches: I suffered it with forti-
tude. It was all I could do in the circumstances. To have loudly

uttered 'unhand me you villain,' might well have resulted in a dance-floor fracas: especially if my foreign looking hugger didn't understand English!

I was finally released as the last romantic chord died away. 'I knew he was going to be like that,' remarked my friend when I re-joined her: and, I couldn't help noticing with a certain underlying tone of satisfaction.

Runner-up to Cafe de Paris bear-hugger, mercifully, on another evening, was cracking-dancer, who surfaced one Saturday night after the band had broken into Latin American rhythm (which I absolutely loved): Rhumba, Samba, Tango or Cha Cha Cha always evoked an immediate response. I just had to dance to it! When I spotted this dapper-looking, grey-haired and slightly built gentleman coming towards me: I knew he'd turn out to be a cracking dancer. He even looked like a dancer: I could tell that by his upright bearing and theatrical looking striped waistcoat. An expert! I was dying to go.

The Cha Cha Cha, though basically simple, requires precise footwork and a sense of rhythm. To my utterly cracking dancer, obviously lacking either skill, began doing the Okey-Cokey instead! Being on the outer-edge of the dance floor we had a captive audience too...and so we continued right to the end, myself doing the Cha Cha Cha, my partner the Okey-Cokey. 'Thank you,' the dapper charlatan said, making a half-bow, at the conclusion of our Fred Astaire and Ginger Rogers routine, 'we'll have to do that again some time,' (my silent rejoinder far too obvious to set down in writing.) But what was he, when not masquerading as a dancer I wondered: butler, doorman, actor? The later seemed to fit the bill: for he had certainly fooled me to begin with. Or perhaps he was just a polite 'nutter.' Whatever else, he was a smooth operator.

But not the first I'd come across during those year of the swinging eighties, or the last either! 'There's a lot of them about,' as a confidant of mine had remarked sagely, referring to the accused, who happened to be within earshot.

There was one of 'em' in particular whom we'll call A for the sake of anonymity. Now A was not unknown to me then, but as a fellow club member only…another divorcee and one of our theatre going group. A was charming and sophisticated (as most of 'em' usually are), and never unattached for any length of time. Understandable really, since the lady members of our club far outnumbered the men. The latter obviously spoilt for choice (should one choose to be chosen that is.)

One evening, having been on a group to our local theatre, I had happened to be one of the throng making its way slowly towards the exit, after the plays conclusion. A had kindly offered to give me a lift to the station and was now walking beside me in the foyer. Glancing down at me-he was a tall fellow- he announced suddenly, and a little coyly I thought, 'all the lights are out in my flat.' What response he was hoping for was hard for me to fathom. Was this a 'will you walk into my parlour, said the spider to the fly' situation? Or was he in need of a coin for the electricity meter? Suspecting the former (I could have been wrong of course.) I feigned naivety and uttered a lack-lustre 'are they?' in reply: and as a result, was safely dropped-off at the station without any en-route stop off for possible larks in the dark, for which I was much too out of practice to have indulged in at such short notice.

Considering the fact that I actually happened to find A quite attractive (though highly dangerous), perhaps it was a bit two-faced of me at the time to have thought him a dead ringer for Alfred J. Prufrock.

Even before the London Eye made its debut there, on The South Bank of The Thames had been one of the most 'with-it' venues in London: especially in regard to our singles club events. During the eighties (as some of my diaries serve to remind me), plays at The National included: Animal Farm and Moliere's The Miser. A great production of Guys and Dolls is also noted in my 1984 diary. Slightly further afield, a few of us went to a matinee performance, at the Young Vic, of the Plough and the Stars: the first time I'd seen theatre in the round.

During the mid-eighties-as far as I'm able to remember- there had been two rather spectacular exhibitions on The South Bank: one at the Hayward Gallery, the other at The Royal Festival Hall (not simultaneously though.) Rodin's works in their entirety at the Hayward, an unmissable experience. Three-dimensional wizardry of another kind on display at The Festival Hall: Gerald Scarfe's daring cartoon effigies, both irreverent and vastly amusing. Deliciously insulting to politicians and royalty alike, occupied most of the available floor space on the ground floor. This exhibition was very popular, needless-to-say! Michael Foot, the Labour politician, often maligned in the popular press for both his left-wing politics and casual way of dressing: he had even worn his duffle-coat when attending the Remembrance Day ceremony at The Cenotaph that year. He had been reduced to a tiny forlorn looking effigy in a glass case, complete with horn-rimmed spectacles and the inevitable duffle-coat: who now stood gazing back at his passing audience as though to evoke sympathy for his current predicament? Margaret Thatcher-the Tory Prime Minister then- if anything seemed regardless of us all. She hadn't been referred to as The Ice Maiden for nothing. And the moment had somehow been transmogrified into a large white refrigerator on wheels, hell-bent on speeding across the floor. The intent being obvious by dint of the sharpness of the nose, flying hair and maniacal gleam in the eye. Clearly it wasn't she, but we, who needed the sympathy, obviously. The lady was certainly not for turning.

This rather daring and unflattering depiction of our then Prime Minister, was as nothing when compared with that of young Prince Andrew, whose night-clubbing jaunts with a series of girlfriends had been well noted and photographed by the tabloid press

Towering above all the other exhibits, and given pride of place by the main entrance, there stood a young Goliath, in shorts, half squatting with hands on knees and sporting a wide lascivious grin: with a lolling tongue of red carpet, which extended several yards across the floor of the display area. Subtle it was not! Obviously, there must have been other note-worthy, three dimensional effigies, which went to make up the exhibition. At this point in time; however, these three (as mentioned), are the only ones that I'm able to recall. Once seen never forgotten!

Had it not been for the lack of air-conditioning (which has lately been remembered), in the London Coliseum during the mid-eighties...the privilege of seeing Nureyev dancing Petrushka, together with a choice selection of his famous ballet solos...would have been equally unforgettable. The upper circle had not been a wise choice of seats for my friend and I: especially on a hot summer's evening. With the balcony above and the lower circle below us: it became the equivalent of sitting in a hot air sandwich! Making it almost impossible to sustain the volume of applause both expected and deserved by the artiste: every time he responded to yet another curtain call. In fact, we'd been quite relieved when they'd come to a conclusion. I believe that this had been one of Nureyev's last performances in this country. Rather a shame that we hadn't been able to enjoy it to the full: due to heat exhaustion.

How I both admire and envy writers of fiction. Those gifted with the ability and imagination to simply invent people: endow each of them with a particular personality and involve them in whatever situation or relationship he or she happens to think fit. 'Who hither and thither moves and mates; and, in some cases, slays.'

Furthermore, since these fictitious people happen to be entirely at their creators mercy, the whistle can be blown on them without any fear of repercussion. There will be no hurt-feelings to consider at having their private lives disclosed, together with certain weaknesses of the character or instances of infidelity. Once the writer's imagination gets going, there will be no limit to just how obnoxious any of them may turn out to be. Even if based on real-life acquaintances: people, or an individual whom the author had come across at one-time-or-another, there will be no law suit in the offering: as there undoubtedly would, should an unwary memoir writer overstep the mark.

True; of course, that even the writer of fiction is bound to experience the proverbial writers block, from time-to-time: the flow of the written word, temporarily on hold. Having got going again; however, there will be no need for actual caution or discretion. Page after page may now be completed: full steam ahead. Living proof of the author's hard work and expertise.

Not so for the ungifted or would-be writer though. The urge to write may have been always there, so that bits and pieces have come to be written: sometimes just on impulse. Scribblings-some of them lengthy, which have been either torn-up in frustration, cast aside and forgotten. In fact, the only sustained volume of writing, per-se, achievable by a mere scribbler: may turn out to be a memoir. A personal one of course: relating to the past, a touch of history and people one has known in the fairly-distant past. Should they now be long-gone: then the writer has a fair amount of carte blanche. Otherwise it involves more-or-less writing with the brakes on!

And; having come to a halt, yet again, the non-fiction scribbler knows only too well, due to past experience, that it may be quite some time until they are able to proceed. In fact; it may take several days: a week even, before getting back on track. The whole enterprise so-to-speak, having gone completely off the boil due to a temporary lack of steam.

Meanwhile, tempus fugits at an alarming rate, and there, waiting in the wings, almost accusingly, a thick-ish heap of A4 typing paper: a pristine pile crying out for immediate attention. The very sight of which, may be the flick of the whip needed by the procrastinator: the scribbler back on track.

But once back on track: slowly does it, no full speed ahead at this juncture. Even though a wealth of literary fuel may be to hand: there are certain no-go areas to take into account. However, potentially amusing various recollections involving ones immediate family-or indeed certain incidents at one's former place of work, an observation of the niceties is required. A trifle frustrating in the latter case, since I worked in an 'Holby City' environment for almost fifteen years: recollections of which providing enough material for a couple of chapters at least. This leaves only a limited amount of permissible recollections when it concerns my contemporaries.

This is when I become aware of what might have been. Due to the fact that hopefully my memoir will cover at least three score years and ten (It dates as far back as 1933), had I the gift of creative writing per-se: the whole content of my memoir could have been spiced-up with a coupe of extra dubious characters; together with fictional accounts of childhood poverty and adult cruelty. (Such fraught-like recollections sell like hot cakes at the present time.) I might have produced an actual novel...I could have been a contender! ¬ (vis-à-vis Marlon Brando: frustrated boxer 'On the Waterfront' circa 1955.) ...I made a point of going to see this film when it was showing at the Dalston Picture House. A matinee performance which I popped in to see on my way home from Sainsbury's in Kingsland Road; complete with my bag of shopping and some six-months pregnant with my first child then: a last-chance visit to the pictures. In fact; I did once belong to a creative writing group, but sad to relate, my participation had turned out to be for a limited period only; having come to, what might be described as an unfortunate conclusion, and before I'd had time to acquire much in the way of creative writing savvy. 'Call me Stan,' our sixty something tutor had invited his new mature type students. Stan was a sturdily built gentleman, a great communicator who also liked to regale us with the odd episode concerning his past life abroad. We were obviously in need of brushing-up our vocabulary. 'You'll learn at least two thousand new words,' he assured us.

Our tutor, by definition, happened to be, what one might call a real extravert, (I should know: being one myself!) One of the inherent faults of nearly all of such ilk: is the inability to remain silent for any length of time when in the company of others. He or she always eager to get their two-penn'orth in: to strut their stuff as it were...mea culpa, mea culpa! When I was in my early twenties, there was a joke card doing the rounds. Once, when at a party, I happened to be in earnest conversation with a friend, a white card was suddenly thrust into my hand by Johnny (a pal of my fiancée's then). In large black capital it said: WHY DON'T YOU SHUT-UP AND LET SOMEONE ELSE HAVE A GO? Why not indeed? Many a quiet type; no doubt, has often longed to say as much, (but only thinks it.) A shut-up card would be ideal in such circumstances.

Trouble is bound to arise when two outgoing types happen to be more-or-less in the same arena. I was definitely the miscreant here: 'Call me Stan' happened to be the class tutor after all. It was my own inability as a mere student to shut-up, that came to evoke his ire eventually. But such is my enthusiasm for literature, that any opportunity to converse on the subject is apt to get-me-going. I should have joined a literary discussion group; of course. Unfortunately, I wandered into the wrong camp

During the first week, probably as an opener on descriptive narrative, our tutor began reading a particular example: a scenic passage par-excellence for our delectation; which alluded to the passage of a boat as it leaves Tilbury and sails out into the English Channel. I recognised it at once: the opening lines of Conrad's 'The Heart of Darkness.' Having found the book so enjoyable to read-for the second time- quite recently: I couldn't help but mention it. When Stan sought to introduce the class to some poetry by the black American writer Maya Angelou: guess what? I'd read a couple of her books and knew all about her turbulent background. Thus; enthusiasm was my downfall. If only I'd been able to supress it. Like the proverbial fog in the library: I'd reddit...reddit!

Finally, Stan came to make his displeasure known in no uncertain way. When the short stories, (those submitted by the class), came to be read aloud one Monday morning, there was only one that had been left unread: and that was mine! 'I'm afraid that I haven't had time to read yours yet,' our teacher informed me when the class session had ended. 'That's ok, it doesn't worry me,' I had replied, with all the nonchalance I was able to muster at the receipt of my put-down.

During the morning session, there had been a class discussion on the interpretation of dreams. On my attempt to join the debate, I had received from my tutor, as he looked in my direction: such a glance of pure loathing, (the only way I can describe it), that it shook me to the core. There was no doubt about it: Stan absolutely hated my guts. I'd got the message, well and truly, and went home that lunchtime 'sick-to-my-stummick,' as the saying goes: and never went back.

On reflection, the whole situation put me in mind of some of the classroom scenes in the old black and white Will Hay comedy films. In which, the teacher (Will Hay), is constantly being upstaged by a bespectacled, know-it-all youth (Charles Hawtry.) In the film, Will Hay possessed the ultimate deterrent in the shape of a cane. In my own case; though: all it had required was a certain look. In order to try and obtain some back-ground data relating to the eighties: I paid a visit to my local library. Having spent an hour leafing through a thick folder of old eighties newspaper cuttings; I came to realise that I'd forgotten just how turbulent that decade had been. Both on the home front: and internationally.

These; of course, were 'the Thatcher years': the heyday of the Conservative party. In fact, I'd spent many a moment involved in heated discussions (often in someone's kitchen), holding the fort for the Labour Party: though heavily outnumbered by my right-wing friends. Odd, really, how these political flare-ups actually took place as part and parcel of the Singles Club social scene. There were no winners; of course, and fortunately no ill feelings afterwards.

When the Falklands War was in progress, the sinking of The

Belgrano resulted in much controversy. Prior to this, there had been the Greenham Common riots: when 20,000 women had clasped hands in a vast circle of protest, all around the American air-base: the proposed siting of 96 American cruise missiles. If it had been at all possible, I'd have joined them: an admission which didn't go down too well with some of my colleagues at work. Most of whom, seemed to have reached the same conclusion as that of the Tabloid Press: namely, that all these protesting women should have been at home looking after their families...apart from which: 'most of them were probably lesbians anyway!' The Miner's Strike took over the headlines in 1984. Much T.V. footage of the clashes between the police and striking miners. Apartheid was in full swing in South Africa, and the protesters were in constant vigil outside South Africa House. My own, rather pathetic protest, in common with other members of the public, was to boycott certain items of food which had been imported from South Africa: a feeble gesture in the face of such injustice.

In the mid-eighties, newspaper headlines were no-less startling than today's of course- as the saying goes: 'history repeats itself. I can't think why I had taken a trip to my local library to bring such an obvious fact to mind. I think it was Hegel who maintained that history resembles a pendulum swinging backwards and forwards through time, or words to that effect.

One of the opening gambits of the local Jehovah Witness, who has now been doing-the-rounds on our estate for at least a quarter-of-a-century, is: 'don't you think the world has become a worse place?' This being the preamble necessary for quotes from the Book of Revelations. Which; in effect, amount to the end is nigh and if we don't all pull our socks up and duly repent, Hell is undoubtedly where were bound, (except for the Jehovah's it would seem.) When I was a child, Hellfire sermons were quite the norm: except the brand was different.

The last time I'd failed to recognise the merciless, loud, bailiffs hammering on my door, (after all, it could have been the police), on being confronted with the hammerer himself, I knew what to expect: even after a gap of several years. What ensued; however, which I've come to excuse as a form of outlet in the way of conversation: having spent a week without anyone to talk to, (except the cat...who could only manage a yawn in response.) Before he could get started, I'd launched into a ready-made counter attack. 'No, as far as I was concerned, the world had always been the same, and I didn't believe in Hell anyway...what about the poor people in Darur? Surely after all that suffering, they weren't bound for Hell too?' I also threw in a mention of the letters of St. Paul to the Corinthians: namely the one on charity. Also, the life of St. Thomas Aquinas, (which I'd recently read)...not that I seemed to be getting any feedback. Apart from the fact that the recipient of this unstoppable flow of meaningless rhetoric, appeared as if mesmerised. He would have been hard put to get a word in edgeways. Poor, poor man! What a nutter had opened the door to him! By way of recompense, I bought a couple of his Watchtower pamphlets: in the circumstances, it seemed the only decent thing to do.

On a much brighter note: Halley's comet entered the earth's atmosphere. The last time it had done so had been in 1910. So, it was well worth watching out for its brief streak across the sky on one of its 76 yearly visits. The next one not due until 2062! Enough inducement to seize the moment!

In the autumn of 1987, yet another phenomena of Mother Nature occurred: only this time, it took everyone by surprise. An extremely powerful hurricane swept its way across the British Isles one night: tearing off rooves and shattering windows, uprooting trees and causing the kind of havoc usually associated with other parts of the world. Britain, as a whole, doesn't do hurricanes or tornados!

Strange to relate; though, in spite of all those blustering, and mighty gusts of wind which must have moaned at the walls of our house, even rattled the window panes at some point: both my son and I slept through the whole cacophony. It was only on hearing the first early morning news bulletin on the radio, that I discovered the reason for our lack of electricity! Power cables had been torn down as well as the trees! Further evidence of the night's random devastation became evident when I happened to be passing through a local side-road on my way to work: a sad and rather awesome sight. A large sycamore tree, having been wrenched up by its very roots, now lay stretched right across the road: almost like a slaughtered giant.

Although the overnight hurricane, obviously due to one of those rare freaks of nature that are apt to strike our islands shores from time-to-time: and this might be described as an act of God. The popular press, having more or less conducted a form of inquest with regard to the recent event, had, (on reading between the lines), come to the conclusion, that the country's unpreparedness had been due to the unfortunate weatherman's failure to warn us all! Otherwise we'd have had time batten down the hatches! That was the gist of it anyway.

All this took place way back in 1987. As far as I can remember, there was only one television weatherman frequenting our screens: namely poor Mr Fish. The unfortunate forecaster at whose feet lay all the blame, (as per the red top press anyway!)

How times have changed. Such is the competition now between T.V. channels that there are weathermen and weathergirls galore popping up at intervals during the daytime and evening, in order to notify us, in detail, of the weather in store: short-range, long-range, Celsius and Fahrenheit. Technology has moved on so rapidly during the last two decades, that no rogue hurricane would have the slightest chance of sneaking in suddenly, to take us all by surprise. The latest high-tech device of a rolling map of the British Isles, complete with colourful graphics of a sophisticated nature, swirling patterns indicating: wind velocity, high-pressure, low-pressure and anything suspicious which might be approaching from the Atlantic.

Just in case certain of us have failed to grasp the message, having been a mite overwhelmed by all that high-tech paraphernalia on our screens; standing to one side of the display: is the pre-senter. Often an earnest looking young man, who uses sweeping arm gestures, in order to emphasise the salient points: rather like a musical conductor who's mislaid his baton. 'Trust me,' his earnest gaze entreats: 'you know it's true.'

Consequently, when a slip-up occurs, and the forecasters get it wrong, despite all the modern equipment at their disposal: I would hazard a guess that the all-round reaction of we old nit-picking, irascible types, is that of quiet satisfaction. These modern chaps are not infallible after all, (which doesn't sur-prise us anyway.)

Last year was a case-in-point. The forecast had been for a heavy fall of snow in the South. After so many mild Januaries and win-ters in general: it certainly made one sit up a little; especially since the heavy snowfall was to include the London area. Just to be on the safeside: I made sure of purchasing my food-stuffs before the snowy weekend arrived. True, that there had been a very bitter North-East wind during the Friday night. I awoke the next morning, (and the morning after), expecting to see snow covered roof-tops. Not a snow flake in sight: or for that matter, the whole winter!

Having experienced Arctic winters in the countryside as a child, and as a teenager in post-war London: when the 1947 fuel shortage led to fuel-rationing, power to be cut-off at intervals during the daytime, both at home and in the workplace: which for me meant chilblains on my fingers and trying to type with my gloves on. For my sister, trips to the Graham Road Coal yard with Dad, in order to collect the odd bucket of coal: it being too slippery underfoot for the Coalman and his horse to make the usual delivery. Yet, having known those extremes, those icy winters of long-ago; there sometimes occurs a mis-placed nos-talgia for their return: for 'a few little white feathers now filling the air'. (One of our old school songs.)

Misplaced nostalgia it certainly is. For the older one gets (no matter how young-at heart)! losing one's balance on a slippery pavement, brings with it the likelihood of a fractured knee or hip. However pretty the landscape after a fall of snow, there's a marked reluctance to venture outside, unless absolutely necessary. Shopping has to be done sooner or later: regardless of prevailing icy conditions. Which means treading very carefully and hoping for the best!

The last time there'd been a heavy fall of snow, some five or six years ago now; feeling anxious about braving the slippery pavements but needing to get in some food: unless I wanted to end up like Old Mother Hubbard, it occurred to me that there might be a simple solution. A safety-first idea! A copy of the prototype itself, which I'd read about in a current newspaper article, but had been unable to find on display anywhere: even in Marks and Spencer! Namely: padded knickers! A Cause Celebre indeed for nervous pensioners. These clever undergarments, padded around the hip area, guaranteed to protect the wearer's vulnerable hips, should they come in contact with a concrete pavement. Lacking the article itself, I hit upon the idea of a copy. Material galore to hand- the remains of an old duvet in the box room upstairs. For ladies of a certain age, the wearing of tights under trousers in cold weather is in order to keep the legs warm. In this instance; however, they provided secure anchorage for my home-made hip and knee protectors. With my padding in place and feeling smugly invincible, I set off for the shops.

As invariably happens in the wake of sudden ideas, there turned out to be a fly-in-the-ointment. On this occasion in the shape of a local bus, which had just rounded the corner and pulled in at the bus stop...just as I was passing by. Acting on impulse and abandoning my original plan, I boarded the bus: I would go into town instead. Due to the knee movements which had been necessary to mount the platform of the vehicle, and in turn the lower gangway itself, then finding a seat and sitting down (knees again), my tights had shifted position, as had my insulation padding: now working its way slowly towards my ankles. By the time I had alighted at the first bus stop in town: to all intents and purposes I'd suddenly become victim of a certain fat-leg complaint known as Elephantitis.

Crossing the main road in order to access the shopping mall, I realised that yet more of my insulation had shifted position. Acutely aware of my bulky hip-line, I offered up a silent prayer that I wouldn't accidently come across someone I knew: my sudden increase in weight might need some explaining! Once in the mall, I made for the ladies cloakroom and removed my surplus inches. After which, I went about my usual shopping chores. Should another need for extra insulation crop up in the future, all I need to remember when setting forth into the snow is avoid public transport-keep on walking!

Having, in the mist of my reflections, managed to accelerate at a faster rate than I'd originally intended. Instead of remaining on course, a certain amount of back-tracking is necessary to mention the concluding year of the eighties. Spring 1989, when as if from out of nowhere, the smoothest operator I'd ever come across, made his debut.

By the end of the eighties, various of my Singles Club friends had paired up. Some couples had married, and as far as I know, went on to live happily ever after: having found their ideal at last. Or, maybe they had merely taken a chance, rather than face the prospect of remaining single.

Taking a chance was not on my agenda; however. As for remaining in the single state, that wasn't a problem for me either. Due to my ex-husbands frequent absences from home in the course of his employment; for quite long stretches of our marriage, it was a way of life I'd grown quite accustomed to. As for finding a soul-mate: I had no illusions about that either by now. It obviously wasn't meant to be.

BUT...as the old saying goes: stuff happens, whether one desires it or not! There's no real antidote against this out-of-the-blue complaint; which is apt to strike when the victim is least expecting it. Rather like getting the flu, falling in love produced the same effect: being swept of one's feet. The difference being;

however, that being struck by Cupid's arrow is apt to induce a state of temporary insanity: which in retrospect, may cause the victim to admit 'I must have been mad!'

Having suffered the same complaint twice within the space of seven years or so, i.e. the pangs of despised love, I can only assume that in each instance, it was due to old Cupid having a bit-of-a-laugh at my expense. The first Mr Wrong, (whom I'd spotted across a crowded room), was a heavy drinker-such a trait is easily discernible at parties-in which case, I'd managed to take evasive action. The cure for love involving my trip to Austria.

As for the second Mr Wrong: who happened to be one of those class A smooth operators, conversant with all the tricks of the trade concerning the game of love, that was an entirely different matter. Not so much a 'Brief Encounter' but rather a frequent crossing of paths. Thus, rendering escape out of the question. 'But nothing happened did it?' asks one of my granddaughters: obviously disappointed that I've nothing forbidden to reveal.

Well, in real terms: no, I didn't. There was no affair to speak of. For although love was in the air: that's where it stayed. Despite the attention paying manoeuvres of a certain gentleman with an eye for the ladies, whose gaze had wandered in my direction: unsuspecting lady with fair hair and minus a wedding ring. Though, luckily for her with an inbuilt instinct for self-preservation. Which in the end, proved to have been well justified? My game playing admirer was a married man! As far as I was concerned: game over and out.

When it comes to stuff happening: mutual attraction, chemistry, falling in love; being only too well aware of the intensity and vulnerability of my own nature, with regards to affairs of the heart. I had been obliged to summon that boring old common sense to my rescue...via a piece of self-advice. If you can't stand the heat get out of the kitchen. So, that's what I did. Not that I got off scot free during that rather odd non-affair episode. Even the struggle of mind over matter, of head over heart, is not

DOREEN STEADMAN

without its own moments of anguish.

Part Six

What Goes Around

When I was yet one of those oh so busy people, commuting betwixt home and work each day, there may have been the odd occasion when I may have been heard to make the slighting observation: 'you should have heard those old dears on the bus this morning, talking about their illnesses and operations.' Well, that was then, as the saying goes: 'what goes around comes around.' In what had seemed to be no time at all, I became one of those old dears myself. Thus, learning by experience that certain illnesses and operations tend to go with the territory when past ones prime. As does the tendency to include such experiences when comparing notes with ones contemporaries occasionally. Along with the weather and various matters relating to one's family. Those of a positive nature, naturally. In fact, any inconsequential chitchat that serves as a means of communication when travelling on a local bus. It renders the journey less tedious and takes one's mind of the immediate surroundings. Depending on the time of day, this may involve: three chariot style push-chairs, a couple of box-like shopping trollies, together with several standing passengers and the background wailing of a disgruntled infant.

But that is by the way. For not only would I come to make occasional mention of my erstwhile operation, en route to the local town shopping centre, but find myself writing about it also: though hopefully not Ad Nauseum. Possible; of course, to employ a fast forward tactic. A meagre paragraph perhaps, when including this particular episode in my memoir. There has come a time; however, when having had to adhere to that ever present and frustrating observation of the niceties. There's no alternative but to make use of whatever memoir material is available. Every little helps as it is.

I should have seen it coming; of course. I should have taken note of all the early warning signals, but I had been far too busy then, what with family matters and working in the National Health service.

On having been accused, now and then, of looking at the world through rose coloured spectacles, my automatic (if silent), riposte has always been: 'well it's better than seeing it as through a glass darkly.' Which to my way of thinking, it certainly is... otherwise, how could we possibly bare it?

But, in all fairness, I have to admit that in some instances, the charge as given, seems to have been justified. Especially with regard to my post retirement bouts of wax lyrical: when recalling my fifteen years as an employee of the National Health service.

Proof, if ever there was, that distance lends enchantment, lies in various of my eighties and early nineties diaries. Until glancing through them, I'd quite forgotten just how very stressful things had been in the N.H.S. then, not only for myself but for my colleagues. And, I daresay, that stress is still the keyword within that institution. But, when it was in the process of being overhauled originally, namely at the behest of Margaret Thatcher, who'd set things rolling with a vengeance. There were increased workloads and targets to reach: with all the clerical staff being monitored. Everything speeded up, regardless that quantity is no fair exchange for quality. Setting foot on the premises each morning, was almost the equivalent of mounting a treadmill. Though; hitherto, my work had been both challenging and satisfying: it had now become a daily slog.

My diaries for this period abound with the entries 'hectic' or 'very stressful today' and 'worked until 6.45 this evening.' Then, as the pressure increased, many of us worked through our tea and lunchbreaks. On one occasion, one of my colleagues had found it necessary to forgo her Bank Holiday, just to keep pace with her work-load.

Just to add to the fun, we were informed that our department was soon to be closed: as was most of the present hospital. All staff to be transferred to the new hospital in order to comply with the recent shake-up. We were to be virtually dismissed and would need to re-apply for our own jobs! But, subject to successful interview, we'd finish up in our original jobs...otherwise reshuffled: even dispensed with!

This last, had been the unfortunate lot of our regular hospital cleaners: local ladies who'd taken a pride in their work, always, now obliged to seek other employment. All cleaning had been put out to contract; the hours thus altered; no doubt the pay and conditions also. 'They'll do the same to you one day,' the cleaners had warned us then. And so, they had: but we hadn't seen it coming.

Quite a sad day for me, when the colleagues and friends I'd worked with for years, went over to the new hospital. The end of an era in some ways. The ground floor offices all empty. No-one behind the main reception desk. The wards upstairs empty too. A ghost hospital in fact: destined eventually to be removed from the landscape.

Meanwhile; I had decided not to re-apply for my old job, but to put in for a current part-time vacancy in one of the remaining hospital departments. Twenty hours a week would suit me down to the ground: full-time work was getting to much for me. By the weekends, I'd been feeling too tired even to enjoy the visits of my grandchildren. Ridiculous for someone of my age I thought: after all I was no spring chicken, this was 1993, two more years to go until my retirement. Working at the new hospital would involve a two-bus journey each way; as well as working my socks off. Enough was enough.

Even if my new job application as receptionist fell through, I was prepared to do part-time work of any sort: filling shelves at a super-market if necessary. Full-time of any description was out. I needed to slow down.

Usually when I take a chance, (as is my wont), I tend to come unstuck. On this occasion luck was on my side. Also, the fact that I'd always kept my typing skills up-to-date, plus a bit of shorthand: which stood me in good stead. A bit late in the day; perhaps, but better late than never.

Although a change of pace is what I'd been looking for, I have to admit, that for a couple of months at least; I found the whole process of standing behind a reception desk, even for a few hours a day- when I'd been used to being 'on the hoof, as it were- quite difficult to adjust to. I was now reigned in, when every instinct urged me to get moving: to work against the clock, as I'd been accustomed to for so many years.

The positive outcome of the changeover, as far as my private life had been concerned: was immediate. I was no-longer too tired to go out for the odd social event and, even more importantly, I could now look forward to visits from my grandchildren: three boys, two girls, plus extras. But all equal when it came to birthdays, Christmas and trips up to town occasionally.

Recorded in my early nineties diaries, so many comings and goings of my various offspring. Flights to and from the family nest: always a temporary haven in a crisis. But no matter how welcoming a loving parent may be during such emergencies, there is apt to come a time when living by oneself is beginning to look like a far off, unattainable dream. It may have been during such a moment of contemplation, when I'd been wistful enough to make the somewhat truculent entry in my diary: house overrun! Probably, also the weekend that I took myself off to Canterbury...which turned out to be over-run with visiting students. I also ended up with a streaming cold.

In 1994, the year prior to my retirement, I seem to be involved rather keenly, in organic gardening, which from this point in time appears to be not only enthusiastic, but slightly manic. A hard-back journal, given over entirely to: crop-rotation, crop-yields, spraying etc. Complete with diagrams and notes.

<u>Losses this year</u>, reads one entry: Lupins attacked by weevils.

<u>Sunflowers:</u> only three left...attacked by slugs.

<u>Morning Glories</u>: extinct!

Fortunately, flowers were only a side-line. On the vegetable front, results were more rewarding. At one time I grew: runner beans, broccoli and courgettes, as well as potatoes and tomatoes. Time; however, has rather dampened my zeal for organic gardening, or for that matter, any type of gardening that requires constant application. Apart from which, poor results from runner beans, (the only vegetable I've attempted to grow during the last few years), suggests that the soil itself, as well as the gardener, has seen better days and gone 'off-song.'

Quite possibly, what the soil lacks, has been sapped by the wild cherry tree, which stands about forty foot high. It's branches extending to cover the width of my garden and part of next doors. It has been in situ, just beyond the boundary fence at the end of my garden, for as long as I can remember. Not the original; however, for the parent tree was felled by the Railway Authorities quite some time ago. Due to their lack of thoroughness in cleaning away the remaining brushwood, Mother Nature's healing powers have done the trick: reincarnation with a vengeance. In the spring, the cherry blossom is a sight to behold.

Several summers ago, alternative bouts of hot weather and heavy rainfall had resulted in a bumper crop of wild cherries: quite small but edible when ripe, masses of them on the lower branches alone. Natures wonderful bounty for the taking. Altogether, I managed to gather several pounds of fruit, leaving successive flocks of marauding starlings to clear the upper branches. The tree stripped of cherries and the roof of next door's summer-house strewn with a profusion of discarded cherry-stones. Not the only pip-disposal venue close to home: as I came to discover in due course, and when in the proceed of repainting my kitchen walls. High up on the inner wall, there is a small square chimney vent with a hinged door- now obsolete, once something to do with the old wash boiler: essential for the family wash, long before the advent of launderette and washing machines. Mounting the step-ladder in-order to clean around the upper wall area, on coming level with the chimney vent, I opened it. There, on the narrow chimney ledge in front of me: an unexpected sight. Namely, a small amount of what appeared to be dry cat food granules. My first thought: 'how had they got there?' My second: 'Samuel Whiskers! Who else?' A swift association of ideas followed. I had a rat in the chimney: not the one in a green waist coat who wanted to turn Tom Kitten into a roly-poly pudding, but a real rat, who emerged at night, scampered down the kitchen wall, raided Tigger's feeding bowl and scarpered up the chimney, via the work-top and gas cooker with his loot. It was right there in front of me. On closer inspection, the hoard in question turned out to be a small pile of discarded cherry pips, courtesy it would seem of a litter conscious starling who'd passed next door's summer house and dropped them down my chimney instead.

On the subject of pips; when I'd hit upon the idea of turning nature's bounty into home-made jam, I hadn't taken into consideration the diminutive size of the cherries, or for that matter, the scant ratio of fruit to stone (or pip.) Consequently, the ratio of pip to jam was slightly disproportionate. At a rough guess: sixty to a jar. Not exactly the home-made produce to be given as a goodwill gesture. Such an abundance of pips presenting a potential hazard to any unluckily recipient wearing dentures or with fragile teeth. The last time I avail myself of nature's bounty with such alacrity. Wild fruit is meant for wild life, like starlings and other feathered species, certainly not for impetuous jam makers of the human variety.

1995- Wednesday 19th April: retirement day. My diary reads 'finished working for the N.H.S., not sorry. So! Was it goodbye to all that...after fifteen years of service?' Well, not entirely: fate had decreed otherwise. In fact, I was to be involved with the National Health Service for at least another five years. Only this time, on the other side of the fence.

In November 1994, I'd suffered yet another bout of laryngitis. Rather than letting it take its course this time, I paid a visit to my G.P. in order to obtain some antibiotics. Almost immediately she'd enquired: 'how long have you had that lump?' If my long-standing goitre had been the lump referred to, the answer would been 'for the last twenty-seven years, ever since the birth of my younger son.' But her eager eye had noticed the extra nodule I'd self-diagnosed as a cyst: just like the neighbour of mine had several years ago. It hadn't occurred to me at all, that my 'guess' might be at fault: I might be about to encounter the big C!

Then; of course, the long drawn out process of actually getting to see a consultant: after all, I was one of many in the queue. Still not that concerned though, busy at work, picking up ones grandsons from school each day. No doubt about it, family a definite asset at such times: it helps to dilute the matter in hand until the point of arrival.

The first step involved having a scan. No idea until then that I now had another phobia to add to my list. Not until the large piece of equipment zoomed in over my neck area: 'Geroff, geroff!' I wanted to shout. Instead of which, I shut my eyes, ignored my quickened heartbeat and repeated to myself all I could remember of 'The Lady of Shalot.' That darn scanner seemed to be looming over me forever. Though if I'd given voice to my discomfort; been brave enough to mention my inner qualms, the radiologist might well have said: 'You ain't seen nothing yet.' He would have been right there: I hadn't.

It's not the consultant that I get to see at the Endocrine Clinic, when I attend for my scan, but his Senior House Officer. My case notes on the desk are open and I can spot at once, the familiar yellow results form, having been long-acquainted with such symbols of good or bad news. 'Is it malignant?' I enquire, diving in at the deep-end. 'Oh no, nothing like that,' the S.H.O. assures me. Phew...what a relief! My lump must be a cyst after all.

But a few weeks later, while still at work in reception, I receive a phone call from the new hospital. It appears that the consultant, himself, now wishes to see me. 'He's an expert on thyroids,' my contact informs me. I begin to feel decidedly uneasy now.

Although he doesn't actually pronounce a verdict, the consultant suggests further investigation...and I can't help saying: 'but I was told that it wasn't malignant,' At this, he looks me straight in the eye: ' we don't know what these cold nodules are until there's been a biopsy,' a slight pause here, as though he's giving me time to digest this information briskly: 'so when can you come in?' and no messing about! his tone implies. Even now, I attempt to postpone the coming event: 'not immediately, we're very busy at work just now.' Which was quite true. I've always maintained that working for the N.H.S., in whatever capacity, for a number-of-years, induces a sense of duty almost comparable to that of having taken Holy Orders: of not wishing to let the side down. Being a part of the N.H.S. status quo himself, though on a considerably higher level: my consultant seems to understand my hesitation. In the event, we agree on a few weeks' time: which gives me a little breathing space. Time to get my act together.

To sugar the pill a little, I treat myself to some new night-clothes: two pairs of pyjamas and a dressing gown, also some scented soap and a nice sponge bag. I'd intended to get these before my next holiday in June anyway. One of my best laid schemes, which looked as though it might be doing a little algae! I tried not to think about it.

Late January, my T.C.I. (to come in), notice had arrived. The day before I'm due to be admitted, I try and make sure that all my desk work and typing is up-to-date. Can't help feeling guilty on learning that I'll need to be off work for six-weeks in order to recover from a thyroid biopsy: a process, which of necessity, involves having one's throat cut! So really it can't be helped.

D-Day arrives: up at 6.30. Cab already ordered for 8.30. I arrive at the hospital by 8.45a.m. But it seems that I won't be going to theatre until early afternoon.

Hospitals, being second nature to me in some ways: I feel quite at home. Even if somewhat apprehensive about my forthcoming op and a little disturbed to find myself in a mixed-ward for the first time. A section which contains six beds. Two of which are occupied by members of the opposite sex. One of whom, a very sick gentleman. The other, middle aged, foreign-looking, emaciated. When the duty nurse attempts to administer his medication, he swears at her and spits it back in her face. During the course of the day, he breaks into sudden fits of giggles and laughter: as though enjoying some secret joke. No way of knowing whether or not he's on a high due to his medication (possibly morphine.) Perhaps he's mentally ill? Wherever the patient is at these moments of hilarity, he's obviously having a good time.

Feeling slightly sorry for myself later that afternoon and post biopsy. Nothing worse when coming round from the anaesthetic during visiting hours. So many visitors on the ward now: including children...noisy. 'Like being on Paddington Station,' I've noted in my diary. Next day; however, I'm feeling back to normal and able to sit in a chair beside my bed. Appetite no problem either. Hospital food or not: the sheer luxury of being waited on for a change.

During the night, he died, poor Norman: the very sick gentleman in the bed next to mine. He'd been calling for his wife for a while, then, complete silence. I guessed at once what had happened. Shortly afterwards, the night nurses, having made the discovery that Norman was no-more, drew the curtains around his bed.

It doesn't take much savvy to be aware of the fact, that Norman is now swiftly being prepared for his removal to the hospital mortuary. But the nurses speak to him during the process: offering platitudes as though he hadn't departed this world forever. A trick-of-the-trade no doubt, regularly employed to reassure any eavesdropping insomniac, that all is well in the next bed.

The next day, after being discharged, I phone for a cab and went home. A little traumatised, I have to admit but otherwise feeling quite well. So very glad to be back in my own surroundings: to savour the bliss of sleeping in my own bed once more.

Six weeks later, I was back at work behind the reception desk: still ignorant of my biopsy result. Somehow assuming that if there'd been anything amiss, I would have been contacted by now. But, it's usually only on the film screen that the patient is accorded such a facility. In real life, it means waiting one's turn. My turn came soon enough when I came to attend the Endocrine Clinic once more. Even though I'd half expected bad news, the diagnosis...thyroid cancer...gave me a bit of a jolt at first. The realisation that the Big C had cast it's dreaded shadow in my direction took some getting used to. 'Surely not'! I thought because apart from my upper respiratory bouts, I'd been feeling quite well. In my ignorance, the signs: the virus factor, had been of little significance to me. The portents had been in vain.

On attending the combined clinic in order to be briefed by both my own consultant and an Oncologist from the Royal London, I learned that I had two options: radiotherapy or complete removal of my thyroid gland...which would necessitate being on Thyroxine tablets for the rest of my life. The latter seemed the most effective way to deal with the matter in hand: so, I chose that. Up until now, I'd preferred to go my independent way. On this occasion; however, I was more than glad to have had the supporting company of one of my daughters. It was a great help at that particular point in time.

Having learnt that I would probably need some form of follow-up treatment following my forthcoming operation, I wrote to the Holiday Fellowship Organisation and cancelled the walking holiday that I'd booked several months previously. Having been on a couple of weekend walking breaks in the Scarborough area, this time I had intended to try the Lake District. I was really looking forward to my week in Derwentwater, but it wasn't meant to be. And thus, it was, that my faithful old walking boots, having at various times supported my ankles over the rugged terrain of the North York moors on one weekend the previous year, across the lower inclines of the Conway Valley, were now put on hold. Relegated to the top-shelf of my bedroom cupboard until further notice.

But I needn't have been in such a rush to get things in order after all. Due to unforeseen hold-ups within the N.H.S. system, my T.C.I. date had been cancelled at short notice. It was not until the beginning of May 1995 that I found myself being trolleyed along in the direction of the operating theatre. 'Here she is,' exclaims my consultant (expert on thyroids). As his first on the list that day patient makes her entry. No escape now: 'Di-Morphine,' I hear him say to the anaesthetist…then oblivion.

'Can I take this off now?' I ask the anaesthetist when he makes his check-up visit to my bedside during the afternoon: feeling stifled by the oxygen mask. 'How do you feel?' he enquires. 'Very sorry for myself!' I mumble through my mouthpiece: which has to stay in place for a time, in order to diffuse any remaining Di-Morphine. 'It can hang about in the system for days,' a nurse informs me, when I happen to mention the rather odd sensation in my head the following day. However, these are only fleeting and disappear completely in due course. But, by then, I've had my breakfast and in a more cheerful frame-of-mind. Even hospital type porridge is like manna-from-Heaven after nil-by-mouth for almost 24 hours. The next morning I'm discharged and allowed home.

'I can't think why you were so worried about it,' remarks my Oncologist, a few weeks later, having disclosed the details of my follow-up treatment. Quite unaware of his patient's flights of fancy, on being told that it will involve swallowing a radio-active iodine capsule, and incarceration in a specially constructed chamber for almost a week!

No wonder my Oncologist had found it difficult to understand my reluctance to undergo this form of treatment. For in some ways, it appears to be far less intrusive or debilitating than most. My fears had turned out to be groundless since the only side-effects that I had experienced on becoming radioactive was that of feeling rather tired. Another pleasant surprise had been the discovery that my room wasn't windowless after all. And, since it was at the far end of a ground floor ward, the window itself was practically facing the public house opposite. Several evenings a week, my solitary confinement was livened up by the sound of a heavy rock band. I also had a telephone in my room, and a television set. Furthermore: the food was lovely.

But it was those regular body scans that proved to be my main problem: or rather my reaction to them. Having at one time been the proverbial Phlebotomist's nightmare...a potential fainter after too much needle probing...I was now the scanner's scourge. On one occasion, having been talked through the forty-five-minute procedure, by a very kind young radiographer. No matter how rational I tried to be about my body scans: how determined to stick-it-out. As I lay feeling trapped between the formidable looking scanning device above me, and the stretcher below: the result was inevitable. Palpitations at the time and weird after effects the following day. When out shopping, I had sometimes felt on the point of collapse: my legs about to give-way for no apparent reason. Eventually, I decided to confide, rather shame-facedly, in my ever-helpful G.P. Problem now solved. Henceforth one Diazepan tablet to be taken twenty minutes prior to scanning. Result? calm and acquiescent patient, almost ready to drop-off during the whole procedure. (To sleep that is, not the stretcher!)

December 1996: the birth of my fourth grandson in St Mary's Hospital Paddington. Who, just like his elder brother and various cousins, destined, when of suitable age, to be escorted hither and thither up to London, in order to visit all the usual attractions and events on offer occasionally?

'Do you remember when we joined in the dancing at the Festival Hall?' I asked my number four grandson recently. 'Yes,' he replied, 'I wanted to cry!' Oh dear, an adventurous Granny may be one thing, I suppose, bur one with rhythm also…quite another.

1997 was the year in which I became involved in a spot of voluntary work. This amounted to a few sessions a week hearing young readers at a local primary school and, turned out to be not only quite enjoyable, but entertaining also on occasion.

Remembrance Day 1997: six-year-olds line up eagerly, waiting to drop their coins into a collecting-tin on the teacher's desk, each receiving a poppy in return. 'Do you know what the war was about?' I enquire of the little girl now returning to her seat. 'Yes Miss,' she replies promptly, 'It was the Saxons.'

On another afternoon, during which I've been helping slightly older readers, I am accompanying a seven-year-old along the school corridor in order to select a stage higher book (all the good readers seem to be girls), she holds my hand as we walk along: a friendly little soul. 'Shall we skip along?' she asks me. 'Better not,' I answer, 'It might look as if we were dancing.' 'No, it wouldn't,' she reassures me, 'you're too old to dance.' Not rudely, though: just stating a fact as seen through the eyes of a seven-year-old.

So, 1997 appears to have been a very busy year, when all things considered. A hotchpotch of gardening, babysitting, trips up to London with older grandchildren, several body scans and one episode of radioactive iodine treatment…even the odd social event including a Nigel Kennedy concert at the Barbican. A lucky last-minute seat for £7 only. Limited viewing being no detriment to the listener of the music.

The year, also, of Lady Diana's tragic death in Paris. I've marked it down in my 97' diary as being on the last day of August. I heard of the accident via late night television news-reels throughout the previous evening.

The following is an old piece of scribbling circa 1997:

Monday: my afternoon for helping out in Mrs. Graham's class. This turns out to be a creativity session. I share a small table with three seven-year-olds, and we are busy cutting out flower petals from squares of coloured felt when, my opposite number: a boy child with angelic countenance, suddenly enquires of me, 'why are you so old?' To which, I manage to reply, quite coolly, 'I've been around a long time.' Nothing daunted; however, angelic boy child continues, 'why do people have sex?'... at which I feign deafness (what else?) and ask the other children 'who needs more flower petals.' The following day, I come to learn, that this precocious child, happens to be one of those recently suspended for several days, having deliberately set-off the school fire alarm.

Meanwhile, the background din in the classroom has gradually increased: almost to deafening point. In order to induce a less chaotic atmosphere, the teacher takes out a large tambourine and rattles it vigorously for a few moments. This seems to me such a weird form of modern-day discipline, that I'm taken off-guard and automatically say to my three desk mates: 'If I were a teacher, I'd give you all a whack with it,' The thought of which caused them to titter briefly before they resume chattering on between themselves and comparing notes on the subject of their computer games.

All quiet now, for its nearly home-time. A slight disturbance suddenly occurs at a nearby group of tables, whose occupants, obviously now bored with their colouring-in activities, are making little jabs at each other with their colouring-in pencils.

November 1998: My final treatment of Radioactive Iodine is about to take place. Such a spacious room here in St. Bart's, and so pleasant a vista, without that, I might well have been one of those weekend away breaks. Only one drawback...having been off my Thyroxine for a period of seven weeks, as advised, I now tip the scales at well over twelve stone...

Not long after my final treatment had taken place, there had occurred a certain bizarre confrontation between myself and a small boy. One of those cheeky chappies whom we maternal types are apt to regard with a certain degree of fond benevolence. There are; of course, exceptions to every rule. I came across him one afternoon when I was at my most vulnerable and struggling my heavy way, step by step, up the stairway of my local railway station. For although I'd been back on my tablets for several weeks, I was still more or less in slow gear: finding it necessary to use the handrail for support. Having paused for breath on the very last stair, I had almost jumped out of my skin when cheeky chappie, having crept up behind me, shouted BOO very loudly in my ear. When my heartbeat had settled down a little, I called after him 'you ignorant little pig,' at which his face lit-up: no doubt expecting me to give chase...as if!

Once I has calmed down though, I couldn't help but see the funny side of the situation. What was more tempting to a small boy bent on mischief, than the rear view of a fat lady puffing her way up a flight of stairs? And what an inspiration to myself, to set about losing my surplus, even though temporary, weight?

1991...Saturday 8th May. Diary entry reads: 'went to pick up tickets for Oklahoma. This was when I found myself tagging along with a small army of protest marchers (re: the proposed first Iraq war), whose rallying point was by Embankment Station. However, having almost reached Hyde Park, I did a swift about-turn and made for the Lyceum. How, would I have explained to my friend that I'd gone walkabout instead of collecting our theatre tickets? Duty having been done, I had lunch at the Crypt in St. Martin's, then went home.

Mid December 1999: summoned to St. Bart's. My Oncologist wishes to give me the news himself... my last scan was completely clear. I'm discharged (apart from check-ups), just in time for the new millennium...

Were I to have set down in writing my immediate reaction on learning that I was finally in-the-clear, it may have read: 'I was overjoyed,' too effusive perhaps? More appropriate response would have been: 'much to my relief.' In any event, I made a point of thanking my Oncologist, to begin with. The following Sunday, of going to Mass in order to give thanks: which seemed only fitting in the circumstances, after all, I had much to be grateful for.

Nothing more likely to deflate the ego and to bring an A.W.O.L. Catholic scurrying back to base, however lapsed, is the prospect of impending mortality. In fact, I had been going to Mass, occasionally, ever since 1996. Initially, this had been at my local R.C. church were the service was being conducted by an exceedingly charismatic young priest. Such his Modus Operandi, and so frequent the chuckles of his (mainly geriatric) parishioners, that it wouldn't have surprised me in the least, had he concluded his sermon by turning a cartwheel on the alter steps.

Having found this form of worship not only unfamiliar, but rather distasteful, I travelled further afield and began attending Mass at Westminster Cathedral: fifty minutes on the District Line and a short walk from Victoria Station. My sister and I had been confirmed as Roman Catholics there in 1944. Having been, at the time, a secretly stroppy and unenthusiastic candidate for Confirmation. At my young sponsor's enquiry afterwards, 'how do you feel now?' (she being a truly devout Catholic), I'd answered ungraciously, 'just the same.' None-the-less, upon my re-entry, after all those lapsed years, I had found the experience unexpectedly moving. Almost the sensation of returning home at last. But: the old order changeth, as it's bound to of course; though much more than I'd been prepared for. No more Latin Mass, little music and strange hymns. It was almost like returning home after a prolonged absence, only to find the entire contents have been removed and replaced with new, strange, difficult to adjust to.

Everything, but everything, comes to be taken for granted eventually. No matter how relieved one may have been at the point of rescue or deliverance from evil, (of any kind.) In the height of 1944, as one of those droning Doodle-bugs, lurking overhead as we lay on our shelter bunks, had suddenly cut-out before plunging to earth, hands over ears, I'd prayed: 'please God don't let it be on us.' A few seconds after a loud explosion somewhere else, but not on us. Whether I'd offered up a prayer of thanks as I got ready to go to work next morning; or simply taken Mum, Dad's, my own and my sister's survival for granted, I can't remember: the latter more than likely.

Although, I still go to Mass occasionally, or make a point of going to Westminster Cathedral, if I happen to be in the vicinity, sometimes just to sit there quietly within its peaceful precincts, I remain, to all intents and purposes, a lapsed Catholic, though still clinging on by my fingernails, still hanging around outside. Still it's the only religion (as a Cradle Catholic), that I know. The trouble is; of course, that I don't happen to possess a blind faith, that which is the prerequisite of the Catholic Church. Reason tells me, that being a Catholic is not the only 'stairway to paradise.' (always supposing there is such a place.) Anyway, what about Richard Dawkins? Who assures us that there is no God, 'we might just as well be worshipping a teapot floating in space? So, enjoy yourself,' he tells us all. Actually, I rather thought that this is exactly what almost everyone's been doing...for a long time now! Not, perhaps, to the point of decadence, far too strong a word. Slightly over liberal when it comes to boundaries. (As seen from the perspective of an elder relic of the so-called sexually repressed generation.)

Darwinism and all that jazz? Questions, questions, but no real answers. Except from the born again's, of course. But 'The Bible says, The Bible says,' is all you get out of them... They're not budging, it's not up for debate: which I suppose is what is meant by blind faith. How simple life would be for some of us, had we been encumbered by that which caused the elephant's child it's nose, not only tweaked but constantly lengthened: the mixed blessing of satiable curiously. Why, for example, has Dawkins gone to the trouble of plastering his 'No God' message all over numerous London buses? To advertise his book of course! A down to earth friend of mine assures me. Thus, putting paid immediately to the complex, deep analysis I'd hitherto had in mind.

But, with regard to faith, or matters of religion, I'm surely not the only waverer who finds the experience of being targeted and preached-at by the already saved, both tedious and rather irritating. On the other hand, it could well be argued that when it comes to proselytising per say, there's little to choose between the proverbial Bible-thumper and the Literary buff. The former bent on quoting from the scriptures, and the latter well on cue with bits of lit at the slightest opportunity.

Having succumbed, quite frequently, to this form of literary garnish myself, and having left a trail of it behind me: the only excuse I have available for this addiction to bits-of-lit, is that of a lowly scribbler's ongoing need for occasional back-up. After all, even writers of great renown have been tempted by this delectable side-dish now and then. William Hazlitt, for example, makes ample use of various poetic quotes all throughout the essays. Which in effect, allows me the excuse (or effrontery) to do the same.

'Now, mind how you go dear,' says the well-meaning shop assistant, to the elderly lady in front of me at the Co-op check-out. During our short chat by the frozen food cabinet a little earlier, (about the war as usual,) it turns out that when of similar age to the check-out girl, this 'little old lady' had driven a number 11 bus throughout the London Blitz.

'Don't forget to mention me, will you?' says a passing acquaintance, as we both mount the steps of our local station. We'd got chatting just before embarking about ten minutes earlier, during which time...as per usual...we ended up talking about our Second World War evacuee experiences. I make mention, also about my seemingly unending effort to get my memoir completed. It seems that this ex-evacuee had departed from this very station in September 1939, together with other local evacuees en-route to London. Then, by another train to Somerset. Her first billet was at the home of a Lady Fraser: where she even had her own maid. A brief glimpse of paradise. Before long, she and her sister had been billeted on a remote farm in the Mendip Hills: where the farmer was both elderly and blind.

Every morning, she and her sister were awoken at 5 a.m., given a warm drink of milk laced with whisky, to keep out the cold, while carrying out their allotted task of milking the farmer's cows. 'I was up to my ankles in cow-muck,' the evacuee tells me. Although she seems to bear no bitterness with regard to, what could be considered at the present time, such a traumatic experience. All hands to the pump in wartime, has somehow toughened we old folk up and contributed to our longevity, (so that we can send the younger generation into yet another trance, as we dredge up our war-time memories.)

'Avoid repetition,' was one of the rules that I set myself before launching into my memoir...referring to the cliché etc., which has entailed a fair amount of re-writing, unfortunately. When it comes to repetition, apart from the written word that is, one of the more worrying aspects of growing older, especially when one lives alone, is the realisation that, even in the midst of a conversation, be it with an acquaintance or family member, that one is merely churning out more of the same...possibly due to a lack of stimulus.

Possible cue for a couple of snippets from the 'Seven Ages of Man?' Perhaps not! Far too depressing: instead, refer to diaries.

2000: Much of a muchness in Millennium year, apparently. Much involved with grandchildren: trips up to Town, the toy museum at Bethnal Green and Victoria Park. In the September of that year a special visit, at long last, to see my old school friend in Norfolk. She drives my sister and I through Necton village. The old corner Post Office is still there! And, much to my surprise, still in situ, though rather the worse for wear, the same red telephone box I'd dashed into almost sixty-years previously: having seen one of our returning air-craft coming down in flames, though some distance away, with child-like naivety assuming I should let someone know about it.

Surprised to note, that I was still into veggie growing then: bumper crops of runner beans and tomatoes! The year, also, that I joined a choir, took up water colours and made the discovery that, even though I can draw reasonably well: I'm no good at painting. Yet another downer that year. My ill-omened foray into the world of creative writing: detail of which is old history.

2001: Highlight of which is the birth of my fifth grandson. I last saw him when he was toddler. He and his little sister now live in the Far East: both safe from the attentions of a slightly adventurous granny.

2002: October 10th: My third grand-daughter is born (aforementioned little sister.)

Apart from the odd concert, the mixture as before that year. Except that my gardening enthusiasm appears to be on the wane.

2003: February the 15th: Protest march. Having growing tired of trying to restrain myself from throwing things at my television, as Tony Blair, again, puts forward his excuses for going to war in Iraq. With those infamous weasel words: 'weapons of destruction.' Equipped with flask and sandwiches, I travel via the District Line, up to the Embankment Station. Alighting there, I join the steady stream of peaceful protesters, who are making their way up Villiers Street towards the Strand. But, as the crowd thickens, I am beginning to feel slightly uneasy. More and more people are pouring into Trafalgar Square. I have also noted, poised in situ at the junction with Whitehall: a double row of mounted police. It is at this point, that I decide to make a strategic and cowardly retreat. The possibility of being hemmed-in or even charged at by horses, quite enough to envoke the obvious. The fact of the matter being that: 'I'm simply too old for this lark.' Apart from which, Charing Cross Station is conveniently to hand: making my means of getaway far too tempting to resist. An over-ground train to London Bridge, and thence home via the Jubilee lines.

Not that my tentative gesture, pathetic though it had been: not that of the million anti-war protesters made any difference to the outcome. I found it almost impossible to watch the subsequent television newsreels. I just could not help thinking of all those innocent Iraqi children, and the awful terror which they must have experienced during the cruel, relentless bombard-ment. What I'd known in the way of air-raids on London during the Blitz of 1944, as nothing, compared to this.

Since this narrative is beginning to sound rather like one of those excruciating 'round-robins,' skipping various entries and employing a fast-forward tactic would seem to be appropriate: even an act of mercy.

2004: 20th February: My diary entry reads: 'went to Kentish Town...28 Queens Crescent missing. Old block demolished 1974, according to local resident.'

So, is this the very cue I've been waiting for? The gap-in-the-hedge whereby, I may now escape at last. Relinquish a task which I set myself over five-years ago now. Stopping and start-ing along the way, as time and circumstances allowed. A task becoming burdensome now, and I wish to be rid of it at the earli-est opportunity.

On reflection: two great escapes within a twelvemonth? Per-haps not. Merely time to take-a-breather before the final run...

Procrastination: being as it undoubtedly is, the thief of all time. It goes without saying, that to over indulge in it when one is past the three score years and ten mark, is little short of folly. So never mind that urge to stand and stare, instead there are some of us who need pointing in the other direction...stiffen the sinews (well, those that aren't stiff already), summon up the blood...and get cracking A.S.A.P.

Nonetheless, when diversion is but a stone's throw from my kitchen window on some mornings, it is very hard to resist. Clearly visible, and just under the buddlia tree, squawking, jost-ling and splashing around in the bird jacuzzi (an inverted barrel lid), are a flock of young starlings. Darting in and out between the raucous invaders a feisty, or two, determined to enjoy a dip themselves, and obviously nothing daunted by the big-boys, having a peck at them from time-to-time. The yobs of the bird world are starlings: regardless of their amusing antics.

Such moments of contemplation; however, usually have their price. If I had stuck to washing up the breakfast things and to carrying out the routine household chores instead of idling by my kitchen window, I would now have be obliged to add yet more potential tasks to my jobs list. I wouldn't have noticed that the grass needed strimming quite urgently and that my poor woman's patio, (a few paving stones and lots of gravel), was currently awash with dandelions: which; however bright and cheerful to behold, need turfing out before they run-to-seed.

No wonder the upper-classes employ gardeners and domestic helps. I don't blame them. How lovely it must be just to do the things you enjoy: writing, painting or drawing, a little gardening perhaps or simply taking-off somewhere when the mood takes one, without first having to do the housework. It's inescapable, though. There, niggling at the back of my mind, while I'm typing away at my memoir: is my outstanding job list.

Several years ago, now, I believe it was in the seventies, I came across a very amusing paperback. It was written by an American comedienne, as far as I am able to remember, her name was Phyllis Diller. The book was entitled: 'The Occasional House-keeper': giving name to the lackadaisical type housekeepers with whom the author obviously had some empathy. Not an admirer of those meticulous domestic routine paragons, but the kind of casual or laid-back homemaker, who is often caught napping by unexpected visitors; unless she's been lucky enough to have given notice, however short, of their impending arrival. Enabling her to fly into a guilty flurry of domestic activity, such as dusting an old tin of peas at the back of the kitchen cupboard. And for ladies of such occasional ilk, the author kindly offered a few snippets of sound advice:

1) Never move to a district where the windows are sparkling and the washing on the line is extra white. 2) If you've always a pile of left-over ironing, which nobody seems to have missed, get rid of it.

What an excellent piece of advice! I well remember the utter boredom of shirt ironing: two fronts, one back, two sleeves, plus collar and cuffs; multiplied by five sometimes, if there were any leftovers from the previous ironing session. But that was in 'the olden days'; of course, well before one's other-halves were prepared to iron their own shirts.

When it comes to dashing away with the smoothing iron, there are still those, especially of my own generation, who seem to get a kick out of it. Giving one proud detail of: sheets, pillow-cases, tablecloths and even tea-towels, which they've recently smoothed with loving care. Well...good luck to them! I've other fish to fry; however. If I ever get to finish this memoir, (the end is in sight) ...there are books I want to read, places I intend to visit, (day trips only...cat to consider.) So many possibilities come to mind that, should it happen to be a bright sunny morning, and I've managed to actually get a good night's sleep: I can hardly wait to get going.

First on my list: via the Northern Line to the Pentonville Road area, just to see if Arnold Bennet's original Riceyman Steps are anywhere in the vicinity of Riceyman House, (which is shown on the A to Z map.)

At the present moment; though, it's all in the mind. Reason being I have unfinished business to attend to. The long over-due and final eviction of that long-staying elephant in the room: still hanging around when I'd been sure of its imminent depart-ure, some five-months ago. In other words, I need to complete my memoir.

When I began this painstaking trip down memory lane, I had no idea that it would take such a length of time to complete or turn out to be such a hard task master. Neither; of course, could I have foreseen the numerous occasions when other matters: usually relating to kith and kin, would require my immedi-ate attention. Times when the luxury of writing, when idling over the past needed to be set aside...yet again. And whilst still in plaintive mood here, make mention of my initial disap-pointment on discovering, that despite all my hard work, I've comparatively little paper-work to show for it. A situation; in fact, which might be described as an own goal. The result of impetuous bouts of literary cleansing along the way: the ripping-up of what the writer considered to be irrelevant rubbish. However, given that personal memoirs tend, on-the-whole, to be covert ego-trips, the writer needs; perhaps, to leave behind them footprints in the sands of time. In my own case there's really nothing for it but to simply just settle for less: footprints? Pages? To employ the popular jargon...whatever!

Apart from family matters over the last few years, relating to my stop/start writing efforts; when it comes to special needs, another party comes into the equation. The nominee I have in mind; however, has neither the facility to defend himself, or for that matter, the inclination. Most of his time being otherwise occupied in a manner as befits a cat: snacking and snoozing.

When a certain long-haired ginger cat, now known as trigger, turned up on my doorstep one day: homeless, hungry and devoid of fur on quite a large area of his back. I took him in. What else could I have done?

In order to have my new lodger checked out at the vet's, I bought one of those cage-like animal carriers and lugged him there via two buses. When, I had recovered from the £68 vet's bill, I hauled trigger home again, via two more buses. I've used the terms lugged and hauled quite deliberately. It was a very hot summers day and Tigger happens to be a fairly large pussycat. Almost eight years have elapsed since he happened to stray in my direction: no doubt sensing that a cat lover was available. A bit of a soft touch perhaps: even though she didn't want to replace her late, lamented, dear little tabby cat.

Rumour had it, at the time, that the large bald patches on Tigger's back were due to having been attacked by a fox. In actual fact, his missing fur had been due to cat dermatitis: in other words, Tigger suffers from allergies. Consequently, there have been regular visits to the vet's, both for check-ups and treatment. But lately, thank goodness, there haven't been so many instances when I've found myself waiting on tenterhooks for the mini-cab to arrive before bundling a struggling Tigger into his carrier. Reluctant to confine him to its limited space until the very last moment.

A very risky business; however, for on hearing the mini-cab driver's motor horn, informing me of his arrival; the patient, by now sensing that something is up, is more than ready to do a runner.

Although due to aging, said patient has been prone to other complaints, which on occasion have even involved emergency runs to the vet's. I will, out of consideration for the reader, forgo to mention the actual details. Illnesses and operations having already featured largely in part six of this memoir...enough is enough. Anyway, at the moment, Tigger is doing fine: snacking and snoozing to his heart's content, his coat in beautiful condition. So now would seem a golden opportunity to actually do a runner myself: disappear through the gap in the hedge while I still have the chance. Even though, still toying with the idea of concluding with a few more paragraphs. Comments relating to various aspects of contemporary life, especially with regard to dumbing down of just about everything conceivable. I've decided to bow out on an upbeat note instead. And who wouldn't on such a lovely spring day? No rose-coloured specs' required. Observing from my window clear, blue skies with snowy white puffs of cotton wool clouds. And there, at the fence's edge: that loveliest of trees, triumphant yet again, bearing a mass of glorious white blossom...

Epilogue

Since the word 'epilogue' had no actual meaning for me until recently; having been requested, quite suddenly, to produce one by my sponsor: who'd been to some trouble to help me publish a personal memoir. (Over seventy-five years of history: pre-war, life on a farm in Norfolk for four years during the second-world-war, post war memories of doodle-bug raids, even a V-2 German high-in-the-sky, which blew our windows in and killed several young and old readers in our local library, (not known at the time of course.)

Since the title of my memoir is: 'Five Woodbines for Dad'- an old soldier of upright standing, who'd been gassed by the enemy during the 1914-18 war. Buried for a time, together with his horse: after being shelled. Had been an outrider with the Royal Horse Artillery: which had left him completely deaf in one ear, (walk on the other side he would say.) A no-nonsense old soldier, who'd never mentioned any hardship, (we learned of these through his sister: our Aunt Bett.)

So, those five woodbines (fags), were well deserved were they not?

Once a geek...always a geek: old habits die hard, of course. However obvious, it has to be said. What? Well... that dawdling around or 'shilly-shallying, (or is it dilly-dallying?) for one of advanced years, might be a trifle risky...or is it risqué? Perhaps it's wise to rev-up? So here goes...

I must say; though, that finding myself in completely new surrounding: so suddenly, is, if anything, a little odd. Is it to do with being a fire sign? An Aries?

That one night- not long after returning from a month's stay in hospital, due to an attack of Sepsis- I, rather foolishly, placed a sheet to air on a rod (or cane), at what seemed several feet away from my two-bar electric heater.

Oblivious to the catastrophe smouldering away in the front room: I happily potted around in the kitchen. But all of sudden...the blaring forth of all my fire-alarms- seemingly waking all my neighbours- and those wicked sheets a mass of flames! Quick thinking on my part? Trying to extinguish the blazing sheet by hitting it with a wet tea-towel, to no avail surprisingly!

Next: the arrival of fire engines and an audience of local neighbours-more or less, if not enjoying the spectacle: just looking on. As the flames engulfed my front room downstairs. Thankfully, a neighbour called through my letterbox for me to get out.

The aftermath of which? A blackened, smoked damaged house: dirty and sooty. A lifetimes possessions destroyed: all due to a stupid err of judgement.

My son did not relish receiving a phone call from his ex-wife saying: 'do you know your mums house is on fire?'

My daughter to the rescue, as always, taking me home with her and sorting everything out with the council.

The result of which? A lovely, sheltered ground floor flat in Barking. T'was time to move on I concur!

No cherry trees around at my new home though.

Sparsely furnished at first due to only a very few of my personal belongings being saved from the remains of the carnage. It is now a cosy new home. Do I miss my house, my home of 60 years? Not at bit! After all, there's no going back 'home'. When all is said and done, I didn't want to come to that area all those years ago did I? In the back of a removal van. Two infants, the younger one only seven months old. A cot, a pram, a clothes wringer, two small armchairs and a budgie in a cage. I like it here in the centre of town: carers to attend to my medication three-times-a-day. A few yards from a main road where there are cheerful constantly passing red-busses.

Very frustrating though-I'm used to being independent you see. I've just turned 89- 'no you haven't!' says The Self, 'I'm only about fifty! I'll just pop across to the shops.' 'Count your blessings!' says reality, 'who do you think you are? Be thankful that your scribbling might be published after all-due to the help and kindness of another. And a daughter, too, living nearby; who works full-time herself: but keeps my fridge full of eatables.

I've always been an insomniac but now I'm able to flop-out for a couple of hours, now and then; with a nice cup of tea at hand.

Since my numbed old fingers continue to hit the wrong keys of my old manual typewriter, I've decided to print the rest of the epilogue instead: my writing not too good (blame the cataracts.) So, printing might be best.

Anyway: 'life is real' life is earnest.' What else? Not a lot really!

'Avoid repetition,' has always been one of my self-mottos when trying to put together a story. That; however, is almost impossible- but I'll try hard not to recall the olden days.

Back to the present then.

At the moment I'm confined to barracks: in other words, housebound. But, whether or not I like this is irrelevant. To quote from some past reading matter: 'The spirit is willing, but the flesh is weak.' It goes without saying (or writing), of course; that old age isn't the sole cause of bodily weakness-or oddness of any kind in fact.

Of my geeky recollections, one of the most basic sayings that spring to mind is: (sorry Will Shakespeare), Aunt Emmy's Yorkshire observation regarding the human race: 'There's nowt so queer as folk.'

How cheerful and optimistic that quote: Houseman's, loveliest of trees the cherry is-wearing white for Eastertide.' How long ago I used it for the conclusion of my memoir: 'Five Woodbines for Dad,' thus to offer my saga for publication? Some years ago, now.

To an upbeat note indeed? I'm not quite sure why I didn't really.

They're have been other family concerns, of course, like all families.

Plus, my bus accident (another adventure), that jerky driver who sent me reeling and left me lop-sided and with three legs instead of two. Maybe my cherry tree turned out to be a trifle tempting to submit at the time.

Please forgive my rambling one and all. I must take the advice of a joke card handed to me by one of my late ex-husbands friends: 'Why don't you shut up and let someone else have a go!' it said. Why not indeed?

Here endeth this fire sign's epilogue.

About The Author

Doreen Steadman.

Doreen is happily living in sheltered housing in Barking, East London.
She is 90 years young.

Printed in Great Britain
by Amazon

77571682R00138